Thirty Years of Islamic Banking

Also by Munawar Iqbal and Philip Molyneux

BANKING AND FINANCIAL SYSTEMS IN THE ARAB WORLD

Thirty Years of Islamic Banking

History, Performance and Prospects

Munawar Iqbal
Chief, Islamic Banking and Finance Division
Islamic Research and Training Institute
Islamic Development Bank, Jeddah

and

Philip Molyneux
Professor of Banking and Finance
University of Wales, Bangor

palgrave
macmillan

First published 2005 by
PALGRAVE MACMILLAN
Houndmills, Basingstoke, Hampshire RG21 6XS and
175 Fifth Avenue, New York, N.Y. 10010
Companies and representatives throughout the world

PALGRAVE MACMILLAN is the global academic imprint of the Palgrave Macmillan division of St. Martin's Press, LLC and of Palgrave Macmillan Ltd. Macmillan® is a registered trademark in the United States, United Kingdom and other countries. Palgrave is a registered trademark in the European Union and other countries.

ISBN 1–4039–4325–7

This book is printed on paper suitable for recycling and made from fully managed and sustained forest sources.

A catalogue record for this book is available from the British Library.

Library of Congress Cataloging-in-Publication Data
Iqbal, Munawar.
Thirty years of Islamic banking : history, performance, and prospects / Munawar Iqbal & Philip Molyneux.
p. cm.
Includes bibliographical references and index.
ISBN 1–4039–4325–7 (cloth)
1. Banks and banking—Islamic countries. 2. Banks and banking—Religious aspects—Islam. I. Molyneux, Philip. II. Title.
HG3368.A6I64 2004
332.1'0917'67—dc22 2004054894

10 9 8 7 6 5 4 3 2
14 13 12 11 10 09 08 07 06

Printed and bound in Great Britain by
Antony Rowe Ltd, Chippenham and Eastbourne

Contents

List of Tables and Boxes

Tables

Boxes

Preface

Thirty years ago Islamic banking was considered wishful thinking. However, serious research work over recent decades has shown that Islamic banking is not only feasible and viable, it is an efficient and productive way of financial intermediation. The industry that started on a modest scale in the early 1970s has shown tremendous growth over the last 30 years. It is one of the fastest growing industries, having posted double-digit annual growth rates for almost 30 years. What started as a small rural banking experiment in the remote villages of Egypt has now reached a level where many mega-international banks are offering Islamic banking products. The practice of Islamic banking has now spread to all corners of the globe. The size of the industry that amounted to a few hundred thousands of dollars in 1975 had reached hundreds of billions of dollars by 2004. While it is the preferred way of banking for one-fifth of humanity, it offers a wider choice of financial products to all. A complete Islamic financial system is still in its early stages of development, but various elements of the system and institutions are fast coming into existence. These include full Islamic commercial and investment banks, Islamic banking windows in conventional banks (including some prominent international ones), Islamic investment funds, Islamic insurance companies, infrastructure support institutions, and research and development institutions.

This text aims to provide an objective and professional assessment of Islamic banking over this period. It explains what Islamic banking is, how it differs from conventional banking as a model of financial intermediation, and why it started and where it is going. Who are the main players at present and who will it attract in future? What are its strengths and weaknesses? How does it compare with conventional banking in performance? Are Islamic banks efficient? Will they be able to compete in globalized financial markets? What are their prospects and potential? These and similar issues are studied using both theoretical and empirical tools.

We hope that this text provides an extensive coverage of the industry throughout its history. In this sense, it is expected to be the most comprehensive text ever written on Islamic banking. We have tried to provide the most authentic information ourselves or guide the reader to other relevant sources of information. In order to help non-Arabic speaking readers, a glossary of Arabic terms has also been provided.

MUNAWAR IQBAL
PHILIP MOLYNEUX

Glossary of Arabic Terms

aḥādīth	Plural of *ḥadīth*. For meaning, see below.
aḥkām	Plural of *ḥukm*. For meaning, see below.
al-muḍārib udārib	A financial arrangement whereby someone receives funds from someone else on a profit-sharing basis and then extends these funds to a third person (s) also on profit-sharing basis.
al-Qur'ān (also written *as Qur'ān only)*	The Holy Book of Muslims, consisting of the revelations made by God to the Prophet Muhammad (peace be upon him). The Qur'ān lays down the fundamentals of the Islamic faith, including beliefs and all aspects of the Islamic way of life.
bayʿ	Stands for sale. It is often used as a prefix in referring to different sales-based modes of Islamic finance, such as *murābaḥah, istiṣnāʿ*, and *salam*.
bayʿ al-mu'ajjal (also written as *bayʿ mu'ajjal* only)	Sale on credit (i.e., a sale in which goods are delivered immediately but payment is deferred).
bayʿ al-murābaḥah (also written as *bayʿ murābaḥah* or simply *murābaḥah*)	Sale at a specified profit margin. The term, however, is now used to refer to a sale agreement whereby the seller purchases the goods desired by the buyer and sells them at an agreed marked-up price, the payment being settled within an agreed time frame, either by instalments or in a lump sum. The seller bears the risk for the goods until they have been delivered to the buyer.
bayʿ al-musāwamah (also written as *bayʿ musāwamah* only)	Sale on competitive prices. As compared to *murābaḥah,* this is the usual practice of sale in which parties freely bargain without specifying the cost price to the seller or the profit margin.
bayʿ al-salam (also written as *bayʿ salam* only)	A sale in which payment is made in advance by the buyer and the delivery of the goods is deferred by the seller.
bayʿ al-ṣarf	Currency exchange.

fatāwā	Religious verdicts by *fuqahā'*. It is plural of *fatwā*. Some times *fatwās* is also used as the plural form.
fiqh	Refers to the whole corpus of Islamic jurisprudence. In contrast with conventional law, *fiqh* covers all aspects of life, religious, political, social, commercial or economic. The whole corpus of *fiqh* is based primarily on interpretations of the Qur'ān and the Sunnah and secondarily on *ijmāʿ* (consensus) and *ijtihād* (individual judgement). While the Qur'ān and the Sunnah are immutable, *fiqhī* verdicts may change due to changing circumstances.
fiqhī	Relating to fiqh.
fuqahā'	Plural of *faqīh* meaning jurist, who gives rulings on various juristic issues in the light of the Qur'ān and the Sunnah.
gharar	Literally, it means deception, danger, risk and uncertainty. Technically it means exposing oneself to excessive risk and danger in a business transaction as a result of uncertainty about the price, the quality and the quantity of the counter-value, the date of delivery, the ability of either the buyer or the seller to fulfil his commitment, or ambiguity in the terms of the deal; thereby, exposing either of the two parties to unnecessary risks.
gharar fāḥish	A considerable degree of *gharar*, one which renders the contract invalid.
gharar yasīr	A small degree of *gharar*. This is tolerable because it may be unavoidable.
ḥadīth	Sayings, deeds and endorsements of the Prophet Muhammad (peace be upon him) narrated by his Companions.
ḥalāl	Things or activities permitted by the *Sharīʿah*.
Ḥanafī	A school of Islamic jurisprudence named after Imam Abū Ḥanīfa.
Ḥanbalī	A school of Islamic jurisprudence named after Imam Ahmed bin Ḥanbal.
ḥawālah or *ḥawālah al-dayn*	Islamic rules governing transfer (sale) of debt.
ḥukm	*Sharīʿah* ruling having general applicability.
ʿIbādāt	Duties of man due to God.
Ibāhah	Permissibility from a *Sharīʿah* point of view.
Ijārah	Leasing. Sale of usufruct of an asset. The lessor retains the ownership of the asset with all the rights and the responsibilities that go with ownership.

Ijtihād	In technical terms, it refers to the endeavour of a jurist to derive a rule or reach a judgement based on evidence found in the Islamic sources of law, predominantly, the Qur'ān and the Sunnah.
ʿillah	Reason/characteristic behind a *Sharīʿah* ruling such that if a particular reason/characteristic is found in other instances, the same ruling will apply.
Istisnāʿ	Refers to a contract whereby a manufacturer (contractor) agrees to produce (build) and deliver a well-described good (or premise) at a given price on a given date in the future. As against *salam*, in *istīsnāʿ* the price need not be paid in advance. It may be paid in instalments in step with the preferences of the parties or partly at the front end and the balance later on as agreed.
Juʿālah	Performing a given task against a prescribed fee in a given period.
Khiyār-al-ʿayb	Option available to a buyer to return the purchased item if he finds any defect in it which was not explicitly mentioned at the time of the sale.
maysir	Literally, it refers to an ancient Arabian game of chance with arrows used for stakes of slaughtered animals. Technically, gambling or any game of chance.
māl	Asset. Property.
Mālikī	A school of Islamic jurisprudence named after Imam Mālik
muʿāmalāt	Relationships/contracts among human beings as against *ʿibādāt* which define relationship between God and His creatures.
muḍārabah	A contract between two parties, capital owner(s) or financiers (called *rabb al-māl*) and an investment manager (called *muḍārib*). Profit is distributed between the two parties in accordance with the ratio upon which they agree at the time of the contract. Financial loss is borne only by the financier(s). The entrepreneur's loss lies in not getting any reward for his services.
muḍārib	An investment manager in a *muḍārabah* contract.
murābaḥah	Sale at a specified profit margin. The term, however, is now used to refer to a sale agreement whereby the seller (bank) purchases the goods desired by the buyer and sells them at an agreed marked-up price, the payment being settled within an agreed time-frame, either in instalments or in a lumpsum. The seller (bank) bears the risk for the goods until they have been delivered to the buyer.
musāqah	A contact in which the owner of a garden agrees to share its produce with someone in an agreed proportion

	in return for the latter's services in irrigating and looking after the garden.
mushārakah	Partnership. A *mushārakah* contract is similar to a *muḍārabah* contract, the difference being that in the former both the partners participate in the management and the provision of capital, and share in the profit and loss. Profits are distributed between the partners in accordance with the ratios initially set, whereas loss is distributed in proportion to each one's share in the capital.
mushārakat	Legal partnership or joint venture. A bank provides
nmushārakat madanī	Civil partnership. As practised in Iran, it refers to a project-specific partnership for short and medium terms. It involves mixing of capital from a bank with the capital from a client (or clients) for the performance of a specific job on a joint-ownership basis.
muzāraʿah	Crop-sharing contract. Two or more parties contribute land, seed, fertilizer, water, etc., and share the crop in agreed proportions.
qarḍ or qarḍ al-ḥasan or *qarḍ al-ḥasanah*	A loan extended without interest or any other compensation from the borrower. The lender expects a reward only from God.
qurūḍ	Plural of *qarḍ*.
rabb al-māl	Capital owner (financier) in a *muḍārabah* contract.
ribā	Literally, it means increase or addition or growth. Technically it refers to the 'premium' that must be paid by the borrower to the lender along with the principal amount as a condition for the loan or an extension in its maturity. Interest as commonly known today is regarded by a predominant majority of *fuqahā'* to be equivalent to *ribā*.
ribā al-faḍl	*Ribā* pertaining to trade contracts. Alternatively called *ribā al-buyuʿ*. It refers to an exchange of different quantities (but different qualities) of the same commodity. For example, exchanging one kilogram of dates (of one quality) with two kilograms of dates (of a different quality) in a barter exchange. Such exchange in some commodities defined in *Sharīʿah* is not allowed. Different schools of *fiqh* apply this prohibition to different commodities.
ribā al-nasā'	*Ribā* pertaining to loan contracts. Alternatively called *ribā al-nasī' ah* or *ribā al-qurūḍ*
salaf	The short form of *bayʿ al-salaf.*
salam	The short form of *bayʿ al salam.*
ṣarf	Islamic rules governing currency exchange.
Shāfiʿī	A school of Islamic jurisprudence named after Imam Shāfiʿī.

Sharīʿah	Refers to the corpus of Islamic law based on Divine guidance as given by the Qur'ān and the Sunnah and embodies all aspects of the Islamic faith, including beliefs and practices.
shirākah	Partnership. Technically, it is equivalent to *mushārakah.*
shirkat-ul-ʿaqd	Contractual partnership.
shirkat-ul-milk	Partnership in ownership.
suftaja	An instrument for transferring money.
ṣukūk	Plural of *'sakk'* which refers to a financial paper showing entitlement of the holder to the amount of money shown on it. The English word 'cheque' has been derived from it. Technically, *ṣukūk* are financial instruments entitling their holders to some financial claims.
Sunnah	The Sunnah is the second most important source of the Islamic faith after the Qur'ān and refers to the Prophet's (peace be upon him) example as indicated by his practice of the faith. The only way to know the Sunnah is through the collection of *aḥādīth,* which consist of reports about the sayings, deeds and endorsements of the Prophet (peace be upon him).
Sūrah	A chapter of Al-Qur'ān.
takāful	An alternative for the contemporary insurance contract. A group of persons agree to share certain risk (for example, damage by fire) by collecting a specified sum from each. In case of loss to anyone of the group, the loss is met from the collected funds.
ʿūqūd al-amānah	Fiduciary contracts.
wakālah	Contract of agency. In this contract, one person appoints someone else to perform a certain task on his behalf, usually against a fixed fee.
wakīl	Agent.
zulm	Unfair, unjust, unduly encroaching upon the rights of others.

List of Abbreviations

AAOIFI	Accounting and Auditing Organization for Islamic Financial Institutions
BBMB	Bank Bumiputra Malaysia Berhad
BBMBK	Bank Bumiputra Malaysia Berhad Kewangan
BGC	Binladin Group of Companies
BIB	Bahrain Islamic Bank
BIMB	Bank Islam Malaysia Berhad
BKBN	Al-Baraka Islamic Investment Bank
BKTF	Al-Baraka Turkish Finance House
BMA	Bahrain Monetary Agency
BMMB	Bank Muamalat Malaysia Berhad
BNM	Bank Negara Malaysia
BOCB	Bank of Commerce (Malaysia) Berhad
BOT	Build, Operate and Transfer
DIB	Dubai Islamic Bank
FATF	Financial Action Task Force
FIBB	Faysal Islamic Bank Bahrain
FIBE	Faisal Islamic Bank Egypt
GCC	Gulf Cooperation Council
GCIBFI	General Council for Islamic Banks and Financial Institutions
IBBG	Islamic Bank Bangladesh
IBIS	Islamic Banking Information System
ICD	Islamic Corporation for the Development of the Private Sector
ICIEC	Islamic Corporation for Insurance of Investment and Export Credit
ID	Islamic Dinārs
IDB	Islamic Development Bank
IFSB	Islamic Financial Services Board
IIFM	International Islamic Financial Market
IIRA	International Islamic Rating Agency
IMF	International Monetary Fund
JIB	Jordan Islamic Bank
KFH	Kuwait Finance House

LIBOR	London Inter Bank Offered Rate
MoF	Ministry of Finance
OIC	Organization of the Islamic Conference
PIRI	Prudential Information and Regulations for Islamic Banks
PLS	profit and loss sharing
QIB	Qatar Islamic Bank
SFSC	Sudan Financial Services Company
SPTF	Skim Perbankan Tanpa Faedah (Interest-free Banking Scheme)
SPV	special purpose vehicle
UAE	United Arab Emirates
VRS	variable returns to scale
ZZT	Zam Zam Towers

About the Authors

Munawar Iqbal is Chief of Research in Islamic Banking and Finance at the Islamic Research and Training Institute of the Islamic Development Bank, Jeddah, Saudi Arabia (the largest Islamic financial institution in the world with an authorized capital of US dollars 20.5 billion). Professor Iqbal has also served as Economic Adviser to Al-Rajhi Banking and Investment Corporation, Saudi Arabia (the largest Islamic commercial bank in the world). Earlier, he served as the Director, International Institute of Islamic Economics, Islamic University, Islamabad, Pakistan. He has taught at the International Islamic University, Islamabad, McMaster University, Canada, and Simon Fraser University, Canada. He has published/edited more than ten books and published more than thirty papers in the field of Islamic Banking and Finance. Recent publications include *Islamic Banking and Finance: New Perspectives on Profit-Sharing Risk* (Edward Elgar, 2002) and *Islamic Banking and Finance: Current Developments in Theory and Practice* (The Islamic Foundation, UK, 2001). He was the founding Editor of the *Review of Islamic Economics*, the Professional Journal of the International Association for Islamic Economics, and also founding Editor (and continues to date) of the *Islamic Economic Studies*, the professional journal of the Islamic Development Bank. He has lectured extensively in the field of Islamic Banking and Finance throughout the world.

Philip Molyneux is Professor in Banking and Finance and Director of the Institute of European Finance at the University of Wales, Bangor. He also has a chair at Erasmus University, Rotterdam, Netherlands. His main area of research is on the economics of the banking and financial services industry and he has published widely in this area including recent publications in the *Journal of Banking and Finance* and *Journal of Money, Credit and Banking*. Recent texts include: *Efficiency in European Banking* (Wiley 1998), *Private Banking* (Euromoney) and the latest, *European Banking: Efficiency, Growth & Technology* (Wiley, 2001). Professor Molyneux has acted as a consultant to New York Federal Reserve Bank, World Bank, European Commission, UK Treasury, Citibank Private Bank, Bermuda Commercial Bank, McKinsey's and various other international banks and consulting firms. In November 2001 he was the Visiting Bertill Daniellson Research Fellow at the Stockholm School of Economics and University of Gothenburg. Professor Molyneux has recently been appointed as one of eight expert financial sector advisers to the European Union's Economic and Monetary Affairs Committee that implements financial services regulations for the European Community.

1
Introduction

Islamic banking started on a modest scale in the early 1970s and has shown tremendous growth over the last 30 years. What started as a small rural banking experiment in the remote villages of Egypt has now reached a level where many mega-international banks are offering Islamic banking products. The practice of Islamic banking now spreads from East to West, all the way from Indonesia and Malaysia towards Europe and the Americas. The size of the industry that amounted to a few hundred thousands of dollars in 1975 had reached hundreds of billions of dollars by 2004.

Thirty years ago Islamic banking was considered wishful thinking. However, serious research work over the past two-and-a-half decades has shown that Islamic banking is not only feasible and viable, but is an efficient and productive way of financial intermediation. A number of Islamic banks have also been established during this period in heterogeneous social and economic milieus. The successful operation of these institutions and experiences in Iran, Sudan, Malaysia and Bahrain are sufficient to show that Islamic banking offers an alternative method of commercial banking. The fact that many conventional banks, including some major multinational Western banks, have also started using Islamic banking techniques is further proof of the viability of Islamic banking. Islamic banks have succeeded in mobilizing large amounts of funds. While the estimates about the exact magnitude of the Islamic banking market vary, it can be safely assumed that it presently exceeds $150 billion and is poised for further growth.

Even though Islamic banks emerged in response to market needs of Muslim clients, they are not religious institutions. Like other banks, they are profit seeking institutions. However, they follow a different model of financial intermediation. The fascinating features of that model have attracted world-wide attention. While it is the preferred way of banking for one-fifth of humanity, it offers a wider choice of financial products to all. After more than quarter of a century of practice, it is time to evaluate this experience.

This text aims to provide an objective and professional assessment of Islamic banking during this time. It will explain the salient features of Islamic banking as another model of financial intermediation and compare it with the conventional banking model. It will also provide some comparisons between the two models in terms of their characteristics and performance. It will examine whether the Islamic banks are running efficiently and whether they will be able to compete in globalized financial markets. It will identify who are the main players in the Islamic financial industry at present and who will the industry attract in future. It will address the challenges that the Islamic banks are facing as well as their prospects and potential. These and similar issues will be studied using both theoretical and empirical tools.

Chapter 2 examines the theoretical foundations of Islamic banking. It discusses the Islamic rationale for the prohibition of interest, lists the key principles of the Islamic theory of financial contracts and outlines the alternative modes and instruments on which Islamic banking and other Islamic financial products are based.

Chapter 3 outlines the Islamic banking model as an alternative way of performing financial intermediation. It then goes on to explain how an Islamic bank works in practice and what are the salient features that distinguish Islamic banking from conventional banking. It finishes by describing some of the benefits that are expected to be derived from the practice of Islamic banking.

Chapter 4 gives the history and growth of Islamic banking. It explains how Islamic banks started on a modest scale and how they have developed into viable and efficient institutions. It underscores the fact that Islamic banking is now well established and recognized at an international level and highlights various manifestations of Islamic banking and finance in various parts of the globe. It provides key information about Islamic funds, Islamic insurance (*takāful*), and industry-support institutions. It presents empirical data on the expansion of Islamic banking and analyses the growth of key variables such as assets, deposits, revenue and investments by Islamic banks. It shows that the Islamic financial industry has been one of the fastest growing industries during the last 30 years and presents remarkable opportunities for further growth.

Chapter 5 evaluates the performance of Islamic banks based on a scientifically selected sample. It uses growth and ratio analyses to examine the performance of Islamic banks and compares it with a similarly selected sample of conventional banks. It shows that Islamic banks meet, and in many cases surpass, international standards on capital adequacy and liquidity. In most cases they have also outperformed their conventional counterparts in profitability.

Chapter 6 follows up the analysis of Chapter 5, but using more rigorous methods of evaluating efficiency of Islamic banks. It discusses relevant theoretical developments in the field of studying efficiency of banks and then provides a survey of several studies analysing the efficiency of Islamic banking in some countries of the Gulf Cooperation Council (GCC), other Middle Eastern countries, Turkey and Malaysia. It concludes that the empirical studies provide clear evidence that Islamic banks are at least as cost-efficient as conventional banks, and in many cases more so.

Chapters 7 and 8 respectively highlight the challenges currently faced by the Islamic financial industry and the prospects that it offers during the twenty-first century. These chapters draw attention to the fact that despite remarkable progress over recent decades, Islamic banking is still a nascent industry and has a long way to go before it can rival other well-developed models of financial intermediation. They discuss on the one hand the unresolved issues which may hinder further development of the industry and, on the other hand, highlight how resolution of these issues can provide bright prospects in the future for the industry. Chapter 9 provides a list of issues that need to be further researched in order to provide continued support to the practice of Islamic banking, and Chapter 10 provides a summary and the conclusions of the book.

2
Theoretical Foundations of Islamic Banking

Why Islamic banking: the rationale

Banks are the most important financial institutions in a modern economy. They perform some very important functions for society and in this process significantly influence the level of economic activity, the distribution of income and the level of prices in a country. Although initially the major function of banking was to mobilize savings and transfer them to entrepreneurs, over time they have come to perform a number of other functions as well. In addition to offering their services for safe custody of money and other valuables, they also offer current account facilities, easy transfers of money, letters of guarantee, payment of utility bills, and loans for consumer durables and investment. As a result of developments such as credit cards, automated teller machines (ATMs), repurchase accounts, and so on, it has become very easy to make payments through banks. Therefore, in a modern economy, a very large part of current incomes are deposited with the banking system. Due to the facilities mentioned above, people do not need to physically withdraw their money nearly as much as they used to. As will be discussed later, this phenomenon enables the banks to 'create' money on their own. This feature increases banks' influence over an economy. The functions that the banks perform are very important, and an Islamic economy cannot operate without these functions. Consequently, Islamic scholars have dealt with the theoretical foundations of banking activities with a view to finding alternatives.

The functions of financial systems are the same whether these relate to developed or less developed economies, or to Islamic or conventional economies. Similarly, the practical problems encountered in performing these functions are also common to all financial systems. Where paradigms diverge, this relates to precisely how the universal functions of banks are performed (the different modes of finance, for instance) but, more importantly, to the mechanisms by which universal problems are solved in practice. The latter relates largely to the type of contracts issued. It is in these two dimensions that the key differences between Islamic and conventional finance lie.

Four key roles are performed in a financial system. First, it provides financial intermediation services, channelling funds from ultimate savers to ultimate borrowers (and, in the process, removing budget constraints). Financial intermediation enhances the efficiency of the saving/investment process by eliminating the mismatches inherent in the needs of surplus and deficit units of an economy. Surplus units are often households who save relatively small amounts and deficit units are typically firms who require large amounts of cash. Financial intermediaries remove this size mismatch by collecting small savings and packaging these to make them suitable to the needs of users. In addition, the users of funds typically require finance for relatively long-term deployment, which cannot be met by individual suppliers of funds. This creates a mismatch in the maturity and liquidity preferences of individual savers and users of funds. The intermediaries resolve the conflict again by pooling the small deposits. Moreover, the risk preferences of small suppliers and large users of funds are also different. It is often considered that small savers are risk-averse and prefer safer placements, whereas the fund users deploy the funds in risky projects. As a consequence, the funds cannot be directly supplied. The role of the intermediary again becomes crucial. They can substantially reduce this risk through portfolio diversification. Furthermore, small savers cannot efficiently gather information about investment opportunities. Financial intermediaries are in a much better position to collect such information, which is crucial for making the investment successful.

Second, the system provides a wide range of other financial services not immediately related to financial intermediation: payment services, insurance, fund management, and so on. Third, it creates a broad array of assets and liabilities, each of which have different characteristics with respect to, for instance, liquidity, maturity, the type of return generated, and risk-sharing. The fourth central role of any financial system is the creation of incentives for an efficient allocation of resources within an economy, and the allocation of scarce financial and real resources between competing ends. These key roles of the financial system are not specific to conventional or Islamic-based systems; it is in how these roles are performed that differences arise. This can be illustrated by giving some examples.

The function of financial intermediation requires providing mechanisms for saving and borrowing so that agents in the economy can alleviate budget constraints. This involves creating a variety of financial assets and liabilities with different characteristics that appeal to different savers and borrowers. Conventional commercial banks provide financial intermediation services on the basis of rates of interest (charged and paid) on both the assets and the liabilities side. Since interest is prohibited in Islam, Islamic banks have developed several other modes through which savings are mobilized and passed on to entrepreneurs, none of which involves interest. Similarly, for performing the function of providing other financial services, such as payment services, insurance, fund management and so on, Islamic banks have developed alternative contracts which are compatible with the *Sharīʿah*.

The third and fourth common functions require the creation of a wide variety of instruments and incentives for an efficient allocation of scarce financial and real resources between competing ends. An efficient allocation of resources requires an accurate assessment and efficient pricing of risk. Somehow, the price of finance needs to include an allowance for the risks involved. Similarly, the rates of return to the suppliers of finance should also reflect the risks taken. Once again, in conventional systems a major route for this is through the rate of interest with risks of alternative projects or loans being reflected in different risk premia incorporated in the interest rates on different loans. Clearly, this route is not relevant in Islamic finance, which means that alternative mechanisms are needed. However, it must be noted here that the prohibition of interest in Islam does not mean that capital is not to be rewarded or that risk is not to be priced.

The role and functions of the financial systems outlined above are indeed highly useful and socially desirable. These functions are important whether the economy concerned is secular or Islamic. People need banking and financial services. However, conventional banks perform their borrowing and lending activities and most other functions on the basis of interest charges that give guaranteed returns if risks are priced accurately. In an Islamic economy, both the giving and taking of interest is prohibited. Now, since the banking and other financial services are needed but interest are prohibited, Islamic economies have to find alternative ways of performing the universal functions of financial systems. This challenge provides the rationale for Islamic banking. Islamic scholars have provided a number of alternative ways of providing necessary banking and financial services that will be studied in later chapters.

Principles of Islamic finance: the basis

In Islamic jurisprudence there are two kinds of *aḥkām* (rulings). The first kind, called *ʿibādāt* (worship), governs the relationship between man and God. The general principle in the case of *ʿibādāt* is that nothing is permitted unless covered by explicit or analogical permission by the Law Giver. In other words, an act is considered worship only if so ordained. The second kind of *aḥkām*, called *mu ʿamalāt* (mutual dealings), governs the relationship among mankind. In this case, the general principle is that of *ibāḥah* (permissibility): that is, everything is permitted unless clearly prohibited by God. We call this the 'Doctrine of Universal Permissibility'.

There are very few kinds of activity that are prohibited. The purposes of such prohibitions are to provide a level playing field to protect the interests of weaker parties, to ensure justice and fairness and in general to ensure mutual benefit for the parties as well as society at large, and to promote social harmony.

In addition to the Doctrine of Universal Permissibility, Islam permits the contracting parties to agree on any conditions as long as they do not violate any *Sharīʿah* ruling. There is a well-known authentic *ḥadīth* which states: 'All the conditions agreed upon by the Muslims are upheld, except a condition which allows what is prohibited or prohibits what is lawful' (Sunan Abū Dawood, 1981).

We call this the 'Golden Principle of Free Choice'. As may be seen, this principle gives a very wide scope for designing contracts. In the following paragraphs we discuss the few prohibitions that are most relevant for constructing financial contracts.

Prohibition of *ribā*

Islam prohibits all form of *ribā*, but what does this term encompass? The word *ribā* as a noun literally means an increase, and as a root, it means the process of increasing. *Ribā* has been understood throughout Muslim history as being equivalent to interest paid on a loan. The prohibition of *ribā* essentially implies that the fixing in advance of a positive return on a loan as a reward for waiting is not permitted by the *Sharīʿah*. It makes no difference whether the return is big or small, fixed or variable, an absolute amount to be paid in advance or on maturity, or a gift or service to be received as a condition for the loan. It also makes no difference whether the loan was taken for consumption or business purposes. In its basic meaning, *ribā* can be defined as 'anything (big or small), pecuniary or non-pecuniary, in excess of the principal in a loan that must be paid by the borrower to the lender along with the principal as a *condition*,[1] (stipulated or by custom), of the loan or for an extension in its maturity'.[2] Throughout history, there has been near consensus among Islamic jurists that bank interest is covered by this prohibition.

However, Islamic jurists have used the term *ribā* in three senses, one basic and two subsidiary. The kind of *ribā* described above is called *ribā al-qurūḍ* or *ribā al-nasā'*. It is also referred to as *ribā al-Qur'ān* as this is the kind of *ribā* which is clearly mentioned in the Qur'ān and is known today as interest on loans. Islam, however, wishes to eliminate not merely the exploitation that is intrinsic in the institution of interest, but also that which is inherent in all forms of dishonest and unjust exchanges in business transactions. Thus the term *ribā* has a more comprehensive meaning and is not merely restricted to loans. *Ribā* may even surreptitiously enter into sales transactions. Hence the two subsidiary meanings of *ribā* relate to such transactions and fall into the category of *ribā al-buyuʿ* (*ribā* on sales). The first of these is *ribā al-nasī'ah,* which stands for the increase in lieu of delay or postponement of payment of a due debt. It may be mentioned that the debt may have arisen because of a loan contract, in which case it will be covered by *ribā al-nasā'* mentioned above. On the other hand, the debt may arise from a sales contract in which the payment has been deferred. A third kind of debt may arise as a compensation for certain rights: examples of this include dower money due to a wife if not paid to her at the time of marriage, and blood money as a compensation for unintentional killing. A modern-day example would be payments due in libel cases. All these are covered by the term *ribā al-nasī'ah*. Once the amount has been determined, the debtor cannot be asked for any increase if the payment is delayed.

The second subsidiary meaning relates to *ribā al-faḍl*, which arises in barter exchange of commodities. In this context, *ribā al-faḍl* refers to the excess taken by one of the trading parties while trading in any of the six commodities mentioned in a well-known authentic *ḥadīth*, which says: 'Gold for gold, silver for silver, wheat for wheat, barley for barley, dates for dates and salt for salt, like for like, payment being made hand by hand. If anyone gives more or asks for more, he has dealt in *ribā*. The receiver and giver are equally guilty' (Ṣaḥiḥ Muslim).

The discussion of *ribā al-faḍl* has arisen from this *ḥadīth*, requiring that if gold, silver, wheat, barley, dates or salt are exchanged against themselves they should be exchanged spot and be equal and alike. Islamic jurists have over the centuries debated the question of whether *ribā al-faḍl* is confined only to these six items or whether it can be generalized to include other commodities and, if so, what should be the reasoning (*ʿillah*) used for this purpose.

Of the six commodities specified in the *ḥadīth*, two (gold and silver) unmistakably represent commodity money used at that time. One of the basic characteristics of gold and silver is that they are monetary commodities. As a matter of fact, each of the six commodities mentioned in the *ḥadīth* has been used as a medium of exchange at some time or the other, and hence it has been generally concluded that all commodities used as money enter the sweep of *ribā al-faḍl*. Furthermore, the requirement of spot payment in monetary transactions has implications for future sales of currencies. These are still in the process of discussion between the *fuqahā'*, economists and bankers.

The other four commodities specified in the *ḥadīth* represent staple food items. There is a difference of opinion with respect to the *ʿillah* for the prohibition in this case. One opinion argues that since all four commodities are sold by weight or measure (Ḥanafī, and Ḥanbalī), therefore all items which are so saleable are subject to *ribā al-faḍl*. A second opinion is that since all four items are edible, *ribā al-faḍl* is involved in all commodities which have the characteristic of edibility (Shāfiʿī and Ḥanbalī). A third opinion is that since these items are necessary for subsistence and are storable (without being spoilt), all items that sustain life and are storable are subject to *ribā al-faḍl* (Mālikī).[3]

It must be mentioned that economically speaking it would be irrational to exchange one kilogram of wheat for 1.5 kilograms of wheat in a spot exchange.

Therefore, some *fuqahā'* have pointed out that *ribā al-faḍl* has been prohibited because, if it was not prohibited, it could be used as a subterfuge for getting *ribā al-nasi'ah*. It is not always possible to determine the scale of difference in the quality of two brands of the same kind and hence what should be the ratio of exchange in case of direct hand-to-hand transfer. It was therefore proscribed to sell the commodity of one quality on the market for money and then buy the same commodity of different quality from the market. In this way the true value of each can be determined and there is no scope for exploitation of one party by the other due to lack of knowledge.

The scope of *ribā al-faḍl* is much wider in a barter economy than in modern-day market economies. One important application in modern times is the trade in currencies. Currency exchange in Islamic systems is governed by the rules of *bayʿ al-ṣarf*, which require that exchange of currencies must be hand-to-hand (that is, no future trading) and at current market exchange rates.

As mentioned in the definition of *ribā* given above, anything (big or small) stipulated in the contract of loan to be paid in addition to the principal is *ribā* (see Box 2.1). Such additional payment in modern terminology is known as interest. Thus *ribā* and interest are the same. The equivalence of *ribā* to interest has always been unanimously recognized in Muslim history by all schools of thought. In conformity with this consensus the Islamic Fiqh Academy of the Organization of the Islamic Conference (OIC) has recently issued a verdict[4] in its Resolution No. 10(10/2) upholding the historical consensus on the prohibition of interest. It has also invited governments of Muslim countries to encourage the establishment of financial institutions which operate in accordance with the principles of the *Sharīʿah* so that they may be able to respond to the needs of Muslims and save them from living in contravention of the demands of their faith.

Box 2.1 Definition of *ribā*

In its basic meaning, *ribā* can be defined as 'anything (big or small), pecuniary or non-pecuniary, in excess of the principal in a loan that must be paid by the borrower to the lender along with the principal as a *condition** (stipulated or by custom) of the loan or for an extension in its maturity'. According to a consensus of *fuqahā'* (Islamic jurists), it has the same meaning and import as the contemporary concept of interest.

* Thus any excess given by the debtor out of his own accord, and without the existence of a custom or habit that obliges him to give such excess, is not considered as *ribā*.

Reasons for prohibition

Even though there is no explicit statement in the Qur'ān and/or Sunnah giving the rationale of prohibiting *ribā*, Islamic scholars provide a number of reasons for its prohibition. Siddiqi (2004), for instance, singles out five such reasons: *ribā* is unfair; *ribā* corrupts society; *ribā* implies improper appropriation of other people's property; *ribā*'s ultimate effect is negative growth; *ribā* demeans and diminishes human personality.

Among the most important reasons that has been emphasized by most writers is that interest is prohibited because it is unfair (*ẓulm*). A contract based on interest involves injustice to one of the parties, sometimes to the lender and sometimes to the borrower. The *ribā* contract is unjust to the borrower because if somebody takes a loan and uses it in his business, he may earn a profit or he may end up with a loss. Now, in the case of loss, the person using that money (let us call him the entrepreneur) loses his labour. In addition to this loss, he has to pay interest and the capital to the lender. The lender, or the financier, in spite of the fact that the business has ended up making a loss, gets his money as well as his interest; therefore it is unjust. Now, let us see how sometimes interest contracts can be unjust to the lender. Many people do not realize that a *ribā* contract can be unjust to the lender and not always so to the borrower. In most of the underdeveloped countries perhaps it is more unjust to the lender. We will explain how. In most of the underdeveloped world, and even in many developed countries, most of the borrowers today are large companies. They pay, let us say, a 10 per cent or 15 per cent rate of interest on their loans. We know that if the rate of inflation is higher than that, then the real rate of interest becomes negative. The lenders, surplus units, are usually small savers like you and me. Banks collect the savings of all small savers and pass them on to the industrialists who may earn a rate of 50–100 per cent profit but pay back only 10–15 per cent in the rate of interest, which in a real sense is not even equivalent to the rate of inflation. Based on that rate of interest and of course minus the administrative expenses of the bank and their own margin, the banks pass on the difference to the lenders in the form of interest paid on deposits. This is why the banks give very small rates of return to small savers. In an inflationary environment the real rate of interest is even negative. Therefore, had these savings been invested on the basis of profit-sharing, then small savers would have obtained much better returns.

Interest also has many adverse consequences for the economy. It results in inefficient allocation of society's resources, and contributes to the instability of the system. In an interest-based system the major criteria for the distribution of credit is the credit-worthiness of the borrower. In a sharing system, the productivity of the project is more important. Therefore, the finances go to more productive projects. In this way, instead of resources going to low-return projects for borrowers with better credit-worthiness, bank lending is more likely to flow to high-return projects even if the credibility of the borrower is somewhat lower. Therefore, the system is more efficient in the allocation of resources. It is also more efficient because the return to the bank is now linked to the success of the project. In the interest-based system banks do not have to care as much about project evaluation since they obtain a return on their loans irrespective of the success of the project. Also, in Western banking, if security is provided then a return is guaranteed (or at least part guaranteed) even if the project is a disaster. While conventional banks, of course, make losses, the argument is that interest-based systems force borrowers to continue to repay loans even when their circumstances are ill-suited to making such repayments, ultimately exacerbating the problem and resulting in default. Interest-based banking systems therefore may accentuate downturns in the business cycle.

The ease of availability of credit on interest also creates inherent instability in the financial system. As Nobel laureate Maurice Allais (1993) rightly points out:

> The world economy as a whole rests today on gigantic pyramids of debts, buttressed one against another in a fragile equilibrium. Never in the past had such a colossal accumulation of promises to pay been witnessed. Undoubtedly, never will it be so difficult to master. Be it speculation on currencies or speculation on stocks and shares, the world has become one big casino with gaming tables distributed along every latitude and longitude. The game and the bids, in which millions of players take part, never cease.

In many cases, the charging of interest is also demeaning. For example, if the loan is for procuring things necessary for survival, charging interest violates the nature of social life which requires cooperation, care and help of the needy by those who can spare some money.

Western views on interest

The practice of interest has been condemned by foremost thinkers in human history and by all divine religions. Under Judaism, Israelites were forbidden to demand any increase on the principal amount of the sum lent in transactions among themselves, although interest could be charged in dealings between Israelites and gentiles: 'Do not charge your brother interest, whether on money or food or anything else that may earn interest. You may charge a foreigner interest, but not a brother Israelite.'[5]

The reason for this distinction, according to many scholars of Judaism, was that there was no law at that time among the gentiles which prohibited the practice of interest, and it was not regarded as unfair that Jews be allowed to recover interest from people who charged interest from them.

In Christianity, the reported saying by Christ to 'lend freely, hoping nothing thereby' (Luke 6:35) is taken by many commentators as a condemnation of interest. However, the Church gradually changed its doctrine on the subject of interest. In any case, the divorce between religion and mundane affairs accepted by Christian societies after the Renaissance opened the door to a widespread practice of interest.

Mills and Presley (1999) have traced the history of prohibition of interest in Biblical texts and Western literature. Their findings can be summarized as follows:

1 Until approximately 1050, interest-taking was considered by the Church to be a sign of greed and lack of charity.
2 The harshest anti-usury Church legislation was passed by the Council of Vienna (1317). This not only called for the excommunication of usurers but also that of any ruler who sanctioned usury. To declare that interest-taking was not a sin was classed as heresy.
3 Within Catholic Europe, the usury prohibition continued to have some practical force until the late eighteenth century. (The Vatican only formally recognized the legitimacy of interest in 1917.[6])
4 In England, the last Act condemning all interest as contrary to God's law was passed in 1571.
5 From 1600 onwards, the debate was transformed from whether to proscribe interest altogether, to which rate it was most expedient to have as a legal maximum. Bowing to agrarian interests, the UK Parliament gradually reduced the legal maximum to 5 per cent by 1714.
6 Ultimately, the debate shifted to whether a legal maximum could be justified at all: for instance, Adam Smith supported the restriction of interest rates to just above the normal market rate.
7 It was Jeremy Bentham who argued in favour of interest. His arguments eventually carried the day. In Britain, the 1854 Money Lenders' Act abolished the 5 per cent usury law and allowed lenders to charge any rate. A limit of 48 per cent was reimposed in 1927 in an attempt to protect vulnerable borrowers. However, since the passage of the Consumer Credit Act (1974), no such restriction exists.[7]

Prohibition of *gharar*

The second important prohibition in exchange contracts is that of *gharar* trading. This prohibition is based on authentic *aḥādīth* of the Prophet (peace be upon him). Reliable sources have reported through a number of the Prophet's companions that the Prophet (peace be upon him) has forbidden *gharar* trading.[8]

Literally, *gharar* means to unknowingly expose oneself or one's property to jeopardy. In jurisprudential literature, *gharar* has been variously defined.

There are three main views which are summarized by Dhareer (1997) as follows. First, *gharar* applies exclusively to cases of doubtfulness or uncertainty, as in the case of not knowing whether something will take place or not. The definition by Ibn Abidin is a case in point: *gharar* is uncertainty over the existence of the subject matter of sale. A second view holds that *gharar* applies only to the unknown, to the exclusion of the doubtful. This view is adopted by the Zahiri school. Thus, according to Ibn Hazm, *gharar* in sales occurs when the purchaser does not know what he has bought and the seller does not know what he has sold. The third view is a combination of the two opinions; *gharar* here covers both the unknown and the doubtful, as exemplified by the definition proposed by Al-Sarakhsy which states that *gharar* obtains where consequences of a contract are not known. This is the view favoured by most jurists.

Gharar has been one of the most difficult Islamic juristic terms to understand. Perhaps the best way to visualize its true scope and import is to list some examples. The most important categories are the following:

1. Ignorance of the genus: for example, saying that A sells B 1 kilogram of apples for $5 involves *gharar* because it is not clear what type of apples are the subject of the sale.
2. Ignorance of the species: for example, saying A sells B his pet for $100.
3. Ignorance of the attributes: for example, saying A sells B his car for $5,000.
4. Ignorance of the quantity of the object: for example, saying A sells B a box of oranges for $20.
5. Ignorance about price: for example, saying A sells B a dress for a week's salary.
6. Ignorance of the specific identify of the object: for example, saying A sells B a flat for $50,000.
7. Ignorance of the time of payment in deferred sales: for example, saying A buys a house from B for $100,000 which A will pay later.
8. Inability to deliver the object: for example, saying A sells B a bird sitting on a tree in a park.
9. Contracting on a non-existent object: for example, saying A sells B the harvest of his farm from the next crop.
10. Not being able to inspect the object: for example, saying A sells B the contents of a carton for $50.
11. More than one option in a contract unless one is specifically chosen: for example, saying A can either take B's car for $10,000 or B's boat for $15,000. The sale would become valid only after A exercises his option and specifically chooses what he is buying.

These examples are not exhaustive but they should be sufficient to give a fairly good idea of what prohibition of *gharar* implies. In essence, *gharar* refers to acts and conditions in exchange contracts, the full implications of which are not clearly known to the parties (see Box 2.2). This is something very similar to 'asymmetric information'. Lack of knowledge with respect to all implications of a contract breaches the principle of voluntary consent of all parties which is a necessary condition in all contracts of exchange according to Islamic law. In the presence of asymmetric information, the agreement of the parties cannot be considered as voluntary consent. For the same reason, all kinds of cheating, fraud and dishonesty is covered by the prohibition of *gharar*. The objective is to minimize possibilities of *post facto* misunderstandings and conflicts between the contracting parties.

Box 2.2 Definition of *gharar*

Gharar refers to acts and conditions in exchange contracts, the full implications of which are not clearly known to the parties. This is something very similar to 'asymmetric information'. There are two kinds of *gharar: gharar fāḥish* (substantial) and *gharar yasīr* (trivial). The first kind is prohibited in Islam while the second is tolerated since this may be unavoidable without causing considerable damage to one of the parties. In many cases, it is simply not possible to reveal all information (not because the seller wants to hide anything, but because it is in the nature of the subject matter of the contract). Islamic jurisprudence relies on the general condition of trustworthiness of contracting parties to take care of this.

However, jurists make a distinction between two kinds of *gharar: gharar fāḥish* (substantial) and *gharar yasīr* (trivial). The first kind is prohibited while the second is tolerated since this may be unavoidable without causing considerable damage to one of the parties. In many cases, it is simply not possible to reveal all information (not because the seller wants to hide anything, but because it is in the nature of the product). The buyer has to trust the seller. For example, the buyer of a built house has to take the word of the seller as to what kind of material has been used in the foundations of the house. The seller obviously cannot dismantle the house to reveal the foundations to the buyer. Therefore, such lack of knowledge does not violate contracts. The principle in such cases is that the seller must act as a trustworthy person. Penalties may be imposed *ex post* if it is proved otherwise.

Basically, *ribā* and *gharar* are the only two prohibitions that have to be kept in view in financial contracts. Some other conditions are also mentioned sometimes (for example, prohibition of selling something before owning it, but that is really covered by the prohibition of *gharar*).

However, one special prohibition within the category of *gharar* may be noted separately, and that is *maysir* (gambling). It needs separate mention because of its wide application in modern times and also because its prohibition is based on Qur'ānic verses.

Prohibition of *maysir*

Islam prohibits all kinds of gambling and games of chance. This is based on clear texts in the Qur'ān. For example:

> O, you who believe! Intoxicants (all kinds of alcoholic drinks), and gambling, and Al-Ansāb (animals that are sacrificed in the name of idols on their altars) and Al-Azlām (arrows thrown for seeking luck or decision) are an abomination of Satan's handiwork. So avoid that (abomination) in order that you may be successful.
>
> (5:90)

However, it is important to draw a distinction between pure games of chance and activities that deal with uncertainties of life and business activities and involve an element of chance and risk-taking. Not all types of risk-taking are prohibited: as we will mention later, one of the distinguishing features of Islamic banking is risk-sharing between financiers and entrepreneurs. Due to the element of 'chance' in all insurance contracts, some Islamic scholars likened the insurance business to gambling which is prohibited in Islam. Other scholars have pointed out that the element of 'chance' emerges from the nature of risk. They further point out that all risks that one faces in life are not of the same kind. They make a distinction between three types of risk.

First, there is the risk that can be termed as 'entrepreneurial risk'. This risk is part of the normal course of business. Every economic activity involves uncertainty which generates risks. Some agents, called entrepreneurs, take those risks. An enterprising person makes profit, and on occasions incurs losses. However, the fact that society always has such enterprising people is testimony to the fact that, by and large, profit outweighs loss. Willingness to take such risks does not imply any moral evil; rather, it is a need that no society can do away with.

The second type of risk which is also part of life arises from the possibility of natural disasters and calamities occurring. People throughout history have sought ways and means to protect themselves from personal losses due to such calamities. This is the essence of insurance.

The third type of risk arises from uncertainties that are not part of everyday life. They arise from various types of 'games' that people create for themselves. These risks are unnecessary. They are unnecessary for the individual in the sense that if someone chooses not to participate in these 'games', that person will face no such risk. They are also unnecessary for society in the sense that they do not add any economic value to the wealth of the society. It is the third type of risk that is the essence of gambling which is prohibited by Islam. As to the other two types of risks, both are a natural part of everyday life and must be reckoned and dealt with.

In the light of the Doctrine of Universal Permissibility and the Golden Principle of Free Choice and the discussion of the few prohibitions, we can summarize the guidelines for financial engineering in what we call the 'Four Cs of Islamic Financial Engineering'. These are:

Consciousness: the parties should consciously and willingly agree on the conditions of contract without compulsion or duress. An implication of this is that any agreement made in a state of unconsciousness (such as under the influence of intoxicants or imposed by force) is not valid.

Clarity: the parties are fully aware of all the implications of the conditions laid down in a contract. Any ambiguity (with the exception of *gharar yasīr*) will make the agreement invalid.

Capability: the parties are reasonably certain that they are capable of complying with all conditions of the contract. An implication of this is that sale of any goods (or services) which are not owned and possessed by the seller at the time of the contract is not valid.

Commitment: the parties intend and are committed to respect the terms of a contract both in letter and spirit. An implication of this is that any subterfuge to evade any *Sharīʿah* condition through linguistic or legal tricks is not allowed.

We must note that these may not be all the conditions to be identified in designing financial contracts but we believe that they cover a very large portion (almost all) of the Islamic principles in the area of financial contracts.

Conclusion

Banks perform the very important function of financial intermediation for society and in the process improve allocation of resources. The financial intermediation function is required so that economic agents in any economy, savers and investors, can alleviate budget constraints. This involves creating a variety of financial assets with different characteristics that appeal to different savers and borrowers. Conventional commercial banks provide these services on the basis of rates of interest (both charged and paid) on their assets and liabilities. However, in Islam, both the giving and taking of interest is strictly prohibited. This prohibition provides the basic rationale for Islamic banking. As an alternative means of financial intermediation, Islamic banking is based on other mechanisms for providing financial services to the savers and borrowers without involving the interest rate mechanism.

In the Islamic theory of exchange contracts, the general rule is that of permission: that is, every contractual arrangement is permissible unless expressly prohibited by *Sharīʿah*. Based on Islamic juristic literature, in addition to the prohibition of interest, there are two other principles which are important for designing alternative financial instruments. The first of these is the prohibition of gambling and the second is the prohibition of *gharar*. Islamic banks and other financial institutions have developed several modes on both the assets and the liabilities sides which comply with the principles of Islamic finance mentioned above. Several of these will be discussed in the next chapter. Based on the Islamic theory of financial contracts, guidelines for Islamic financial engineering have been derived. These can be summarized in the four Cs of Islamic financial engineering: consciousness, clarity, capability, and commitment.

3
Development of the Islamic Banking Model

What is Islamic banking: the model

Islamic banking, like any other banking system, must be viewed as an evolving system. No one disputes that there is a definite desire amongst Muslim savers to invest their savings in ways that are permitted by the Islamic *Sharīʿah*. Nevertheless, they must be provided with *ḥalāl* returns on their investments. Islamic scholars and practical bankers took up that challenge and have made commendable progress in the last 30 years in providing a number of such instruments. However, the concepts of Islamic banking and finance are still in their early stages of development and Islamic banking is an evolving reality for continuous testing and refining of those concepts.

Islam fully recognizes the useful role that financial intermediation can play. It was not entirely unknown to Islamic society in its early centuries. Direct finance was no doubt the dominant mode of finance, but the practice of someone obtaining finance on the basis of profit-sharing and then giving it to another person, the actual user of the funds, on the basis of profit-sharing is also recognized. This is known as the principle of *al-muḍārib uḍārib* and it can be expressed as, *'the one who mobilizes funds, on a profit-sharing basis, extends these funds to the users on the same basis'*. In the early Islamic period, most caravan trades were financed by *muḍārabah* and *suftaja* (money transfer). Islamic scholars consider the earning of profits from an intermediary role as a genuine occupation. It is, however, noticeable that this concept of financial intermediation is interwoven with the production and exchange of real goods and services.

The functions of Islamic banks and other financial intermediaries are similar to their conventional counterparts. Muslim economists have shown that there are alternative Islamic modes and models through which these functions can be performed. In fact, they have shown that Islamic models can perform these functions in a better way. These models are briefly described below.

Two-tier *muḍārabah*

Under this model, a bank is organized as a joint stock company with the shareholders supplying the initial capital. It is managed by the shareholders through their representatives on the board of directors. Its main business is to obtain funds from the public on the basis of *muḍārabah* and to supply funds to businessmen on the same basis. Its gross income comprises the share in the actual profits of the fund users, in accordance with an agreed ratio of profit-sharing. That income, after deducting the expenses incurred in managing the funds, is distributed pro rata on share capital as well as deposits. The bank retains, in favour of its shareholders, part of the profits accruing to deposits in accordance with the predetermined profit-sharing ratio.

In addition to the general investment deposits mentioned above, there could also be specific investment accounts in which deposits are made for investments in particular projects. It is also possible to conceive of special investment accounts in which deposits are made on condition that they be invested in particular business activities (for example, trade financing on a *murābaḥah* (mark-up) basis, or leasing, and so on). Then, there could be current accounts in which deposits are made to be withdrawn at any time. These are current accounts on which banks pay no profit, but they are allowed to use these deposits profitably at their own risk. Demand deposits are regarded as loans to banks whose repayment is guaranteed. In sum, bank funds could comprise share capital, demand deposits, and various types of investment deposit.

The main feature of the model described above is that it replaces interest by profit-sharing on both the liabilities and the assets side of the bank's balance sheet. This change brings about a number of positive effects for the efficiency, equity and stability of the banking system.

One-tier *muḍārabah* combined with multiple investment instruments

This model visualizes the mobilization of savings on the basis of *muḍārabah* and the use of funds so acquired to earn profits through trade, commerce and industry. When academic work on Islamic banking as an alternative to interest-based banking first started, discussion essentially focused on the traditional forms of Islamic modes of finance such as *muḍārabah* and *mushārakah*. Subsequent writings, as well as the practice of Islamic banking, have made important contributions both to the evolution of new forms of Islamic business enterprises and also to the conceptual development of Islamic modes and financial instruments. The traditional modes of finance were based on either partnerships or the principle of deferred trading of goods and services. The practice of Islamic financial institutions has led to the evolution of different types of permanent, temporary as well as gradually diminishing partnerships based on the principles of *mushārakah* and *muḍārabah*, incorporating easily adaptable arrangements with respect to managerial responsibilities. Islamic banks have also developed various forms of price and object deferred sales, such as short-term *murābaḥah* (declared cost-plus-profit based financing), instalment sales (long- and medium-term *murābaḥah*); pre-paid or price-deferred manufacturing orders (*istiṣnāʿ*); and pre-paid or rent-deferred leasing (*ijārah*).

These developments have led to the emergence of a different model of Islamic banking. Under this model, the relationship between savers and the bank is organized on the basis of *muḍārabah*. However, in its relationship with the entrepreneurs, the bank uses a number of other financial instruments permissible from a *Sharīʿah* point of view, none of which involves interest. A wide variety of Islamic modes of financing is possible, and is now available. Some of these are described below.

Mushārakah (partnership)

Mushārakah literally means sharing. In the Islamic finance literature it refers to a joint enterprise in which all the partners share the profit or loss of the joint venture. The financial term is derived from the Islamic legal term *shirkah* with the same literal meaning but having a broader application. In the Islamic *fiqh* literature *shirkah* is of two kinds: the first is *shirkat-ul-milk*, which means joint ownership of two or more persons of a particular property which may come into existence either through inheritance or joint purchase. The second kind of *shirkah* is *shirkat-ul-ʿaqd*, which means a partnership established through a contract. Such contractual partnerships are usually established for commercial purposes and take several forms such as partnership in the capital of the enterprise, partnership in labour and management, common goodwill or a combination of these elements.

Mushārakah as a financial contract refers to an arrangement where two or more parties establish a joint commercial enterprise and all contribute capital as well as labour and management as a general rule. The profit of the enterprise is shared among the partners in agreed proportions while the loss is shared strictly according to capital contributions. The basic rules governing the *mushārakah* contract include the following:

1. Profits of the enterprise can be distributed in any proportion by mutual consent. However, it is not permissible to fix a lump sum profit for anyone.
2. In case of loss, it has to be shared strictly in proportion to the capital contributions.
3. As a general rule all partners contribute both capital and management. However, it is possible for any partner to be exempted from contributing labour/management. In that case, the share of profit of the sleeping partner has to be in strict proportion to his capital contribution.
4. The liability of all the partners is unlimited.

As a mode of finance, an Islamic bank can advance money to a client using the contract of *mushārakah*. Normally the bank will use the option of being a sleeping partner. The contract can be more widely used by Islamic funds with unit holders assuming the role of sleeping partners. The contract can also be used in securitized assets.

Muḍārabah (passive partnership)

Muḍārabah is a special type of partnership. This is a contract between two parties:[1] a capital owner (called *rabb al-māl*) and an investment manager (called *muḍārib*). Profit is distributed between the two parties in accordance with the ratio that they agreed upon at the time of the contract. Financial loss is borne by the capital owner, the loss to the manager being the opportunity cost of his own labour which failed to generate any income. Except in the case of a violation of the agreement or default, the investment manager does not guarantee either the capital extended to him or any profit generation. Some other important features of the *muḍārabah* contract include the following.

1 While the provider of capital can impose certain mutually agreed conditions on the manager, he has no right to interfere in the day-to-day work of the manager.
2 *Muḍārabah* is one of the fiduciary contracts (*ʿuqūd al-amānah*). The *muḍārib* is expected to act with utmost honesty, otherwise he is considered to have committed a grave sin (in addition to worldly penalties). This has important implications for the moral hazard problem.
3 The liability of the *rabb al-māl* is limited to the extent of his contribution to the capital.
4 The *muḍārib* is not allowed to commit the *muḍārabah* business for any sum greater than the capital contributed by the *rabb al-māl*.
5 All normal expenses related to *muḍārabah* business, but not the personal expenses of the *muḍārib*, can be charged to the *muḍārabah* account.[2]
6 The contract of *muḍārabah* can be terminated at any time by either of the two parties on giving a reasonable notice. (This condition may create serious problems in the context of modern commercial enterprises. However, using the Golden Principle of Free Choice,[3] the parties can agree on any conditions in the contract that will regulate the termination so as not to cause any damage to the enterprise.)
7 No profit distribution can take place (except as an ad hoc arrangement, and subject to final settlement), unless all liabilities have been settled and the equity of the *rabb al-māl* restored.

As a mode of finance applied by Islamic banks, on the liabilities side, the depositors serve as *rabb-al-māl* and the bank as the *muḍārib*. *Muḍārabah* deposits can be either general, which enter into a common pool, or restricted to a certain project or line of business. On the assets side, the bank serves as the *rabb-al-māl* and the businessman as the *muḍārib* (manager). However the manager is often allowed to mix the *muḍārabah* capital with his own funds. In this case profit may be distributed in accordance with any ratio agreed upon between the two parties, but the loss must be borne in proportion to the capital provided by each of them.

Diminishing partnership

This is a contract between a financier (the bank) and a beneficiary in which the two agree to enter into a partnership to own an asset, as described above, but on condition that the financier will gradually sell his share to the beneficiary at an agreed price and in accordance with an agreed schedule.

Bayʿ al-murābaḥah (sales contract at a profit mark-up)

In the classical *fiqh* literature, there is a sales contract called *bayʿ mu'ajjal* which refers to sale of goods or property against deferred payment (either by lump sum or instalments). *Bayʿ mu'ajjal* need not have any reference to the profit margin that the supplier may earn. Its essential element that distinguishes it from cash sales is that the payment is deferred. Strictly speaking, the deferred payment can be higher than, equal to or lower than the cash price.

There is another sale contract known as *bayʿ al-murābaḥah*, which refers to a sale in which the seller declares his actual cost and the parties agree on adding a specific profit margin. Basically, this is a two-party buying and selling contract; no financial intermediation is involved. The Islamic banks have created a mode of finance by combining the concepts of *bayʿ mu'ajjal* and *bayʿ al-murābaḥah*. They use this contract as a mode of finance in the following manner.

The client orders an Islamic bank to purchase for him a certain commodity at a specific cash price, promising to purchase such a commodity from the bank once it has been bought, but at a deferred price, which includes an agreed-upon profit margin (called a mark-up) in favour of the bank. Thus, the transaction involves an order accompanied by a promise to purchase and two sales contracts. The first contract is concluded between the Islamic bank and the supplier of the commodity. The second is concluded between the bank and the client who placed the order, after the bank has possessed the commodity, but at a deferred price which includes a mark-up. The deferred price may be paid as a lump sum or in instalments. In the contract between the Islamic bank and the supplier, the bank often appoints the person placing the order (the ultimate purchaser) as its agent to receive the goods purchased by the bank. The basic rules governing the *murābaḥah* contract are shown below:

1 The subject of the sale must exist at the time of sale.
2 The subject of the sale must be in the ownership of the seller at the time of sale.

3 The subject of the sale must be in the physical or constructive possession of the seller.
4 The delivery of the commodity sold to the buyer must be certain and should not depend on contingency or chance.
5 As in any sales contract the price must be specified and, once specified, it cannot be increased in case of default.
6 The time of delivery must be specified.
7 The payment schedule must be specified.

Ijārah (leasing)

In the simple lease contract the usufruct generated over time by an asset, such as machinery, aircraft, ships or trains, is sold to the lessee at a predetermined price. This is called an operating lease, as opposed to a financial lease. The operating lease has a number of features that distinguish it from other forms of leasing. First, the lessor is himself the real owner of the leased asset and therefore bears all the risks and responsibilities of ownership. All defects, which prevent the use of the equipment by the lessee, are his responsibility, even though it is possible to make the lessee responsible for the day-to-day maintenance and normal repairs of the leased asset. Second, the lease is not for the entire useful life of the leased asset but rather for a specified short-term period (for a month, a quarter, or a year) unless renewed by mutual consent of both the parties.

A lease ending in the purchase of the leased asset

Since the entire risk is borne by the lessor in the operating lease, there is a danger of misuse of the leased asset by the lessee. The financial lease helps take care of this problem by making the lease period long enough (usually the entire useful life of the leased asset) to enable the lessor to amortize the cost of the asset with profit. At the end of the lease period the lessee has the option of purchasing the asset from the lessor at its market value at that time. The lease is not cancellable before the expiry of the lease period without the consent of both the parties. There is, therefore, little danger of misuse of the asset.

A financial lease has other advantages too. The leased asset serves as security and, in the case of default on the part of the lessee, the lessor can take possession of the equipment without a court order. It also helps reduce the lessor's tax liability due to the high depreciation allowances generally allowed by tax laws in many countries. The lessor can also sell the equipment during the lease period such that the lease payments accrue to the new buyer.[4] This enables the lessor to get cash when he needs liquidity. This is not possible in the case of a debt because, while the *Sharīʿah* allows the sale of physical assets, it does not allow the sale of monetary debts except at their nominal value.

Some of the jurists have expressed doubts about the permissibility of financial leases. The rationale they give is that the long-term and non-cancellable nature of the lease contract shifts the entire risk to the lessee, particularly if the 'residual' value of the asset is also fixed in advance. The end result for the lessee may turn out to be worse than the outright purchase of the asset through an interest-bearing loan. A financial lease has thus the potential of becoming more exploitative than an outright purchase. Suppose the lease contract is for five years. The lessee would have to continue making lease payments even if he does not need the asset, say, after two years. In the case of a purchase through an interest-bearing loan, the purchaser can sell the asset in the market and repay the loan, thus reducing his loss. This cannot be done in a financial lease. If someone is unable to make lease payments, that person may lose his stake in the asset even though part payment of the asset price has been made beyond the rental charge he would normally pay in an operating lease.

However, there are jurists who consider financial leases to be permissible if certain conditions are satisfied. First, the lessor must bear the risks of leasing by being the real owner of the leased asset. The lessor cannot lease what he does not own and possess, and should be responsible for all the risks and responsibilities related to ownership. Therefore, a leasing contract where the lessor acts only as an intermediary between the supplier and the lessee and plays the role of a financier, with ownership of the asset being nothing more than a legal device to provide security for repayment of the loan and legal protection in case of default, is not allowed. In this case the lessor leases an asset before buying and taking possession and gets a reward without bearing any risk. Second, lease payments cannot start until the lessee has actually received possession of the leased asset and can continue only as long as it remains usable by him. Third, all manufacturing defects (and later damages which are beyond the control of the lessee) should be the lessor's responsibility.[5] The lessee can, however, be made responsible for the proper upkeep and maintenance of the leased asset.

As a form of financing used by Islamic banks in practice, the contract takes the form of an order by a client to the bank, requesting the bank to purchase a piece of equipment and promising, at the same time, to lease it from the bank after it has been purchased. Rent instalments are calculated in such a manner as to include, in reality, recovery of the cost of the asset plus the desired profit margin. Thus this mode of financing includes a purchase order, a promise to lease, and a leasing contract with a provision to transfer ownership of the leased asset to the lessee at the end of the lease agreement. This transfer of ownership is made through a new contract, in which the leased asset is either given to the lessee as a gift or is sold to him at a nominal price at the end of the lease agreement. According to a decision of the OIC Fiqh Academy, this second transfer-of-ownership contract should be signed only after termination of the lease term, on the basis of an advance promise to affect such a transfer of ownership to the lessee.

Salam

Salam is a sales contract in which the price is paid in advance at the time of contracting against delivery of the purchased goods/services at a specified future date. Not every commodity is suitable for a *salam* contract. It is usually applied only to fungible commodities. Some basic rules governing the *salam* sale are given below.

1 The price should be paid in full at the time of the contract.
2 Goods whose quality or quantity cannot be determined by specification cannot be sold through the contract of *salam*. An example is precious stones.
3 Goods can be sold only by specifying the attributes. They cannot be particularized to a given farm, factory or area.
4 The exact date and place of delivery must also be specified.

Islamic banks can provide financing by way of a *salam* contract by entering into two separate *salam* contracts, or one *salam* contract and an instalment sales contract. For example, the bank could buy a commodity by making an advance payment to the supplier and fixing the date of delivery as the date desired by its client. It can then sell the commodity to a third party either on a *salam* or sale by instalments basis. If the two were *salam* contracts, the second contract would be for delivery of the same quantity, description and so on as that constituting the subject-matter of the first *salam* contract. This second contract is often concluded after the first contract, as its price has to be paid immediately upon conclusion of the contract. To be valid from the *Sharīʿah* point of view, the second contract must be independent (i.e., not linked to the delivery in the first contract). Should the second contract consist of a sale by instalments, its date should be subsequent to the date on which the bank would receive the commodity.

Al-istiṣnāʿ (Contract of Manufacture) and al-istiṣnāʿ al-tamwilī (financing by way of istiṣnāʿ)

Al-Istiṣnāʿ is a contract in which a party orders another to manufacture and provide a commodity, the description of which, delivery date, price and payment date are all set in the contract. Any party can cancel the contract after giving notice to the other before the manufacturing work starts. However, after the manufacturing work has started, the contract cannot be cancelled unilaterally.

Istiṣnāʿ is similar to *salam* in the sense that both are exceptions to some general conditions of sale which prohibit the selling of something which is not owned and is not in the possession of the seller at the time of sale. However, there are some differences between the two which are summarized below.

1 The subject of *istiṣnāʿ* is always a thing which needs manufacturing, while *salam* can also be effected on things that do not involve manufacturing.
2 In the case of *salam* full payment of price is necessary, whereas in the case of *istiṣnāʿ* the payment can be delayed.
3 The time of delivery in case of *salam* must be specified at the time of the contract. In the case of *istiṣnāʿ* this is not necessary.

Al-Istiṣnāʿ al-tamwilī, which is used by Islamic banks, consists of two separate *istiṣnāʿ* contracts. The first is concluded between the beneficiary and the bank, in which the price is payable by the purchaser in future, in agreed instalments, and the bank undertakes to deliver the requested manufactured commodity at an agreed time. The second *istiṣnāʿ* contract is a subcontract concluded between the bank and a contractor to manufacture the product according to prescribed specifications. The bank would normally pay the price in advance or during the manufacturing process in instalments. The latter undertakes to deliver the product to the bank on the date prescribed in the contract, which is the same date as that stated in the first *istiṣnāʿ* contract. The original purchaser (i.e., the bank's client) may be authorized to receive the manufactured commodity directly from the manufacturer.

An Islamic bank working as an agent (*wakīl*)

It is also possible that Islamic banking is arranged on a basis of *wakālah* (agency) principle. *Wakālah* is a contract whereby somebody (the principal) hires someone else to act on his behalf (i.e., as his agent) for a specific task. The agent is entitled to receive a predetermined fee irrespective of whether or not, he is able to accomplish the assigned task to the satisfaction of the principal as long as he acts in a trustworthy manner. He would be liable to penalties only if it can be proved that he violated the terms of the trust or acted dishonestly.

In the case of a financial *wakālah* contract, clients give funds to the bank/company that serves as their investment manager. The bank/company charges a predetermined fee for its managerial services. The entire profit or loss is passed back to the fund providers after deducting such a fee.

This contract is used by some Islamic banks to manage funds on an off-balance sheet basis. The contract is more widely used by Islamic mutual funds and finance companies.

How Islamic banking works in practice

An Islamic bank, like other banks, is a company whose main business is to mobilize funds from savers and supply these funds to businessmen/entrepreneurs (see Box 3.1). It is organized as a joint stock company with the shareholders supplying the initial capital. It is managed by shareholders through their representatives on the Board of Directors. While a conventional bank uses the rate of interest for both obtaining funds from savers and supplying these funds to businessmen and others, an Islamic bank performs these functions using various financial modes described above. Banks utilize Islamic modes of financing on two sides of the balance sheet: first, on the side of liabilities or resource mobilization, and second, on the side of assets or resource utilization. On the resource mobilization side, the *muḍārabah*, either general or restricted (to a certain business line) is the mode most frequently used. The bank and the investment deposit holders share the realized profit in accordance with the ratios agreed upon between the parties at the time of contracting. The deposits in the current account are treated as if they are loans from the clients to the bank, and therefore they bear no yield to the account holders. However, being loans to the bank, their principal is guaranteed by the bank. Islamic banks have achieved significant success in attracting resources on the basis of the *muḍārabah* contract.

Box 3.1 How an Islamic bank works

An Islamic bank is a deposit-taking banking institution whose scope of activities includes all currently known banking activities, excluding borrowing and lending on the basis of interest. On the liabilities side, it mobilizes funds on the basis of a *muḍārabah* or *wakālah* (agent) contract. It can also accept demand deposits which are treated as interest-free loans from the clients to the bank and which are guaranteed. On the assets side, it advances funds on a profit-and-loss sharing or a debt-creating basis, in accordance with the principles of the *Sharīʿah*. It plays the role of an investment manager for the owners of time deposits, usually called investment deposits. In addition, equity holding as well as commodity and asset trading constitute an integral part of Islamic banking operations. An Islamic bank shares its net earnings with its depositors in a way that depends on the size and date-to-maturity of each deposit. Depositors must be informed beforehand of the formula used for sharing the net earnings with the bank.

When utilizing these resources for income generation, Islamic banks use both fixed return modes (such as *murābaḥah*) and leasing and variable return modes (such as *muḍārabah* and *mushārakah*). While, on the liabilities side, Islamic banks have made significant progress in using profit-sharing, this is not the case on the assets side. The share of profit-sharing modes in the total financing provided by Islamic banks is very small. Most of the financing is provided on a *murābaḥah* basis. A recent study found that the weighted average of the share of this mode in the total financing provided by

Islamic banks amounts to 66 per cent. The results of that study are reproduced in Table 3.1.

Rational behaviour in the financial market would lead Islamic banks as well as the users of their financing to strike a balance between the two modes of mark-up and profit-sharing. Many economists are of the opinion that the current combination of financing modes prevailing in the Islamic banking industry leaves something to be desired.

How is Islamic banking different from conventional banking: the salient features

While Islamic banks perform mostly the same functions as conventional banks, they do this in distinctly different ways. Some of the distinguishing features of Islamic banking are given below.

Risk-sharing

The most important feature of Islamic banking is that it promotes risk-sharing between the provider of funds (investor) and the user of funds (entrepreneur). By contrast, under conventional banking, the investor is assured of a predetermined rate of interest. Since the nature of this world is uncertain, the results of any project are not known with certainty *ex ante*, and so there is always some risk involved. In conventional banking, all this risk is borne by the entrepreneur. Whether the project succeeds and produces a profit or fails and produces a loss, the owner of capital gets away with a predetermined return.[6] In Islam, this kind of unjust distribution is not allowed. In Islamic banking both the investor and the entrepreneur share the results of the project in an equitable way. In the case of profit, both share this in pre-agreed proportions. In the case of loss, all financial loss is borne by the capitalist and the entrepreneur loses his labour.

Emphasis on productivity as compared to credit-worthiness

Under conventional banking, almost all that matters to a bank is that its loan and the interest thereon are paid on time. Therefore, in granting loans, the dominant consideration is the credit-worthiness of the borrower. Under profit-and-loss sharing (PLS) banking, the bank will receive a return only if the project succeeds and produces a profit. Therefore, an Islamic bank will be more concerned with the soundness of the project and the business acumen and managerial competence of the entrepreneur. This feature has important implications for the distribution of credit as well as the stability of the system.

Moral dimension

Conventional banking is secular in its orientation. In contrast, in the Islamic system all economic agents have to work within the moral value system of

Table 3.1 Distribution of financing provided by Islamic banks (average during 1994–6)

Institution	Total financing (million US$)	Murābaḥah (%)	Mushārakah (%)	Muḍārabah (%)	Leasing (%)	Other modes (%)	Total
Kuwait Finance House	2,454	45	20	11	1	23	100
Faisal Islamic Bank, Egypt	1,364	73	13	11	3	0	100
Dubai Islamic Bank	1,300	88	1	6	0	6	100
Faysal Islamic Bank, Bahrain*	945	69	9	6	11	5	100
Qatar Islamic Bank	598	73	1	13	5	8	100
Bank Islam Malaysia Berhad	580	66	1	1	7	24	100
Jordan Islamic Bank	574	62	4	0	5	30	100
Bahrain Islamīʿ Bank	320	93	5	2	0	1	100
Islamīʿ Bank Bangladesh	309	52	4	17	14	14	100
Al-Baraka Islamīʿ Investment Bank	119	82	7	6	2	3	100
Simple average	–	70	7	7	5	11	100
Weighted average		66	10	8	4	12	100

* In 1999 the Faysal Islamic Bank Bahrain merged with the Islamic Investment Company of the Gulf. The new name of the bank after the merger is Shamil Bank. However, since the data reported in this book pertain to the Faysal Islamic Bank Bahrain, the same name is used.
Source: Iqbal *et al.* (1998).

Islam. Islamic banks are no exception. As such, they cannot finance any project which conflicts with the moral value system of Islam. For example, they will not finance a wine factory, a casino, a night club or any other activity which is prohibited by Islam or is *known* to be harmful to society. In this respect Islamic banks are somewhat similar to the 'ethical funds' now becoming popular in the Western world.

Wider set of products

An important point to be noted in the way Islamic banking works is that it offers a wider choice of products. In addition to some fixed-return modes that can serve necessarily the same functions that interest serves in conventional banking, Islamic banks can use a variety of innovative profit-sharing financing techniques. The addition of various profit-sharing modes to the available menu of available financial products renders several advantages, including those listed below:

1. The allocation of financial resources on the basis of profit-and-loss sharing gives maximum weight to the profitability of the investment, whereas an interest-based allocation prioritizes credit-worthiness. We can expect that the allocation of resources made on the basis of profitability is likely to be more efficient than that made on the basis of interest and the ability to repay.
2. A system based on profit-sharing would be more stable compared to one based on a guaranteed interest rate on capital. In the case of conventional banking, the bank is obliged to pay a guaranteed return on its obligations (deposits) regardless of their fate, should economic conditions deteriorate. In profit-sharing, the return paid on the bank's obligations depends directly on the returns of its portfolio of assets. Consequently, the cost of capital would adjust itself automatically to suit changes in production and in other business conditions. Furthermore, any shock which might befall the obligations side of the balance sheet would be automatically absorbed. This flexibility not only prevents the failure of the enterprises seeking funds, but also ensures the existence of a necessary harmony between the firm's cash flow and its repayment obligations, an element which enables the financial system to work smoothly.
3. Since depositors of Islamic banks, except demand deposit holders, share in the actual performance of the banks, they are expected to remain more vigilant about the performance of banks. That will also contribute to financial stability.
4. Since bank assets are created in response to investment opportunities in the real sector of the economy, the real factors related to the production of goods and services (in contrast with the financial factors) become the prime movers of the rates of return to the financial sector.

5 The transformation of an interest-based system into one based on profit-sharing helps achieve economic growth as this results in increasing the supply of venture or risk capital and, consequently, encourages new project owners to enter the realm of production as a result of more participation in the risk-taking process.

Closer links between the monetary and real sectors

Another important feature of Islamic banking is that even in the case of fixed return modes that create debt, such as interest-based financing, there is a crucial difference. Debt creation in Islamic finance is generally not possible without the backing of goods and services, and the resultant debt instruments are not tradable except against goods and services. Monetary flows through Islamic financial modes are tied directly to the flow of goods and services, so there is little room for a sudden and mass movement of such funds as compared to the flow of interest-based short-term funds. Hence destabilizing speculation is expected to be significantly curtailed.

What does the Islamic banking model promise?

Economists usually evaluate any scheme on the basis of its allocative efficiency, equity, stability and growth implications. In this section we evaluate the Islamic banking model described in the previous section on these criteria.

More equitable

Islam is a religion which emphasizes justice to all parties. A contract based on interest involves injustice to one of the parties, sometimes to the lender and sometimes to the borrower. The *ribā* contract is unjust to the borrower because if somebody takes a loan and uses it in his business, he may earn a profit or he may end up with a loss. Now, in the case of loss, the person using that money, let us call him the entrepreneur, loses his labour. In addition to this loss, he has to pay interest and the capital to the lender. The lender, or the financier, in spite of the fact that the business of the enterprise has ended up making a loss, gets his money as well as his interest. Consequently it is unjust. Now, let us see how sometimes an interest contract can be unjust to the depositor. Many people do not realize that a *ribā* contract can be unjust to the depositor and not always so to the borrower. In most of the underdeveloped countries perhaps it is more unjust to the lender. This is because depositors may be paid a rate of interest that is in fact generating negative real returns if inflation is greater than the rate charged. If borrowers take out loans and invest these in successful projects that yield returns substantially greater than the rate of inflation then they benefit as they only have to make modest loan repayments that are not linked to the performance of the investment. In fact, they could be repaying at a rate that relates to negative levels of real interest while generating substantial positive real returns from their investment. In contrast, depositors may be rewarded with negative real return on their deposits. This would mean that depositors became relatively poorer and borrowers relatively richer in real terms, which contributes to greater financial and economic inequality in the system.

On the basis of economic reasoning, Islamic banking is superior to an interest-based arrangement because it ensures equity between the borrower and the lender. Both parties share the accrued return which the project generates. Let us also mention here that in most of the countries, even in a country such as the USA which is at the forefront of capitalist systems, there have been regulations which place upper limits on the rate of interest. One famous regulation of this kind was Regulation 'Q' in the USA which has now been scrapped, but there are still rules in many countries which place an upper limit on the rate of interest that the banks can pay. Now, we know that the rate of inflation in many countries is more than 50 per cent. In Latin America, sometimes the rate of inflation has been 1,000 per cent. In some Muslim countries also the rate of inflation is quite high. In the early 1980s, the rate of inflation in Turkey was 50–100 per cent, and most of the time the rate of interest paid on deposits did not match the rate of inflation. The rate of interest cannot adjust automatically with the rate of inflation and hence lenders are at a disadvantage. In the profit-sharing system, as prices increase, the rate of return of the projects also increases along with the rate of inflation. Thus the real rate of return does not become negative due to inflation. At the level of an economy the real rate of return is always positive. There may be a few enterprises which end up in a loss but, by and large, in a growing economy the rate of return remains positive. Therefore, both the borrowers and the depositors will share that rate of return in an equitable manner.

The distribution of credit in an Islamic banking system is also more equitable than in an interest-based economy, the reason being that in the case of profit-sharing banks are more interested in the results of the project. Of course, they are concerned with the safety of the capital itself but, in an interest-based system, the safety of the capital is the sole criterion because, with the rate of interest guaranteed, a bank's main concern is that it gets its principal as well as the interest back. In a profit-sharing arrangement, the banks as well as the entrepreneurs will try to maximize their profit, so their interests are the same. They are working for the same objective: that is, getting a better return which they will share. Even if a person's credibility may be low, if the potential of the project is high, the banks may be willing to finance that project because they will obtain a better return on their investment. Therefore, smaller savers and entrepreneurs who belong to the lower- and middle-class of the population get a better chance of obtaining finance from the banks as the criteria to lend are based on the profitable prospects of the investment project and not solely on the credit-worthiness of the borrower. In an interest-based system typically most of the funds flow to large industries, multinational corporations and big industrialists. Small savers and small middle-class entrepreneurs do not get sufficient finances even for their very best projects. This is not only a theoretical argument; it is an empirical fact. The distribution of credit in an interest-based system is skewed in favour of the wealthy and big industrialists, whereas in a profit-sharing system bank finances will be more equitably distributed.

Improved allocative efficiency

A profit-sharing system is also more efficient. It is more efficient because Islamic bank financing is solely based on the productivity of the project. In an interest-based system the sole criterion for the distribution of credit is the credit-worthiness of the borrower. In Islamic banking, the productivity of the project is more important, and so the finances will go to more productive projects. In this way the resources, instead of going to low-return projects belonging to credit-worthy clients, will flow to high-return projects even if the credibility of the borrower is lower. Therefore, the system is more efficient in its allocation of resources. It is also more efficient because the bank's return is now linked to the project. In case of interest-based systems, banks need not care much about project evaluation and may focus more on collateral and security. Their interest is with the borrower. In the case of profit-sharing, they have a much greater interest in the project itself so they will evaluate the project very carefully and allocate funds to more efficient projects. Third, since the return of Islamic banks depends on the success of the project, they may also contribute to the management of the project. Since they specialize in the area of finance and investment, their expertise will improve the profitability of the project.

Stability of the banking system

From the stability point of view also, the Islamic banking model is more stable than the conventional banking model. (Here, we are talking about the stability of the banking system and not of the economy.) In an interest-based system, there is a lack of symmetry in the cash flow of the banks and the cash flow of the enterprise. The entrepreneurs or the businessmen have to return a stipulated interest repayment to the banks that bears no relationship to the actual return of the project. Therefore, if the project is not going well in some stages of the project or in the entire life of the project, there develops an asymmetry between the cash inflow and cash outflow. That creates instability in the entire business sector. From the other side, the bankers also lack equilibrium in their assets and liabilities because their liabilities are fixed while their assets are variable. When there is any external shock, there is no automatic mechanism which can restore equilibrium between the assets and liabilities of the bank. In the case of an Islamic system, the liabilities of the bank are on the basis of *muḍārabah* and hence are also variable. If there is any shock, it affects the assets side as well as the liability side of the banks' balance sheet. For example, if recession occurs, banks' assets will go down, but, at the same time, their liabilities will also go down since they do not have to pay a fixed or guaranteed rate of return to the depositors. Even the principal is not guaranteed. Thus their liabilities are related to the actual performance of the projects they finance. The assets and liabilities are mutually linked and this mechanism restores equilibrium between the assets and liabilities of the Islamic banks, so there is a smaller likelihood of bank failure.

Promotion of growth

Another criterion on which economists usually judge a scheme is that of growth. From the growth point of view also the Islamic banking system is preferable to the conventional banking system for the following reasons. First, the Islamic banking model promotes innovation. Innovation is not something on which the big industrialists have a monopoly: anybody can be enterprising, and anybody can have a good idea. In Islamic banking, if a small or middle-class entrepreneur has a better project, he has (i) a possibility of getting it financed, and (ii) he will not be held back by the fear of tremendous risks. We know that innovations involve risks. Since risk is shared between the financier and entrepreneur, the Islamic banking system results in a better distribution of risk. Business risk is spread over a larger number of people. The entrepreneur is risking only his labour and the bank is risking its capital. Therefore, ingenious entrepreneurs will be forthcoming and innovation will be promoted. Second, conditions which dictate the cost of capital, one of the determinants of the rate of investment in any economy, are more favourable under the Islamic system. The cost of capital in an interest-based system, which is the rate of interest, is fixed in that the rate of interest paid or charged does not vary with the productivity of the projects which banks finance. In an Islamic economy, the cost of capital varies with productivity. There is no fixed cost of capital. In the periods when there is a recessionary trend in the economy, productivity goes down but, at the same time, the cost of capital for the clients of Islamic banks also goes down. Thus it does not have that deterrent effect on investment which a fixed cost of capital has. As a result, even in that period, relatively speaking, there will be greater investment in an Islamic economy or in the profit-sharing economy as compared to an interest-based economy. So, for these reasons, from the growth point of view the Islamic banking system fares better.

Conclusion

Prohibition of interest in Islam does not mean that savings will not be rewarded. It also does not mean that the cost of finance would be zero. Islam fully recognizes the useful role that financial intermediation plays in channelling resources from the surplus units in society to the deficit units. Islamic banks, though established in response to religious needs of Muslim clients, are by no means non-economic institutions: they are profit-seeking institutions. Islamic banking is just another way of performing the financial intermediation function. Instead of using the rate of interest to mobilize savings, Islamic banks mobilize funds on the basis of profit-sharing with the depositors. These funds are then passed on to corporate and other clients using sale-based or asset-based contracts. Several contracts of this kind are now available. The most important among these are *murābaḥah, muḍārabah, mushārakah, ijārah, salam* and *istiṣnāʿ*. The availability of these contracts not only fulfils the religious requirements of Muslim clients but also provides a wider set of products for all customers. Theoretical research has established that the contracts based on profit-sharing have several distinct economic advantages for society. They improve the allocation of resources; they ensure justice and fairness among the contracting parties; they lead to a more stable financial system; and they have a favourable impact on economic growth.

4
History and Growth of Islamic Banking and Finance

How Islamic banking started

From a very early stage in Islamic history, Muslims were able to establish a system without interest for mobilizing resources to finance productive activities and consumer needs. The system worked quite effectively during the heyday of Islamic civilization and for centuries thereafter. As recorded by Professor S. D. Goitein, partnership and profit-sharing rather than interest-based borrowing and lending formed the basis of commerce and industry in twelfth and thirteenth centuries in the Mediterranean region.[1] However, as the centre of economic gravity shifted over the centuries to the Western world, Western financial institutions (including banks) became dominant and the Islamic tradition remained dormant. In recent years, however, there has been a significant revival of interest in developing a modern version of the historic Islamic financial system in the wake of Muslims' desire to stay clear of interest.

When commercial banking emerged after the industrial revolution, a very large majority of Muslim scholars expressed their serious reservations with this model of financial intermediation due to its reliance on interest rate mechanism and they called for the development of alternative mechanisms to perform the financial intermediation function in Muslim societies. Muslim masses to a very significant extent refrained from dealing with commercial banks. However, the growing needs of traders, industrialists and other entrepreneurs in rapidly monetizing economies were pressing. The Muslim economists and banks took up the challenge of developing alternative models of financial intermediation. Valuable theoretical work was done in the early nineteenth century. At that time most of the Muslim world was under colonial rule. When Muslim countries gained their independence after the Second World War, practical experiments in interest-free financing started on a modest scale and gradually expanded in scope.

While credit societies and cooperatives (working on an interest-free basis) existed in several Muslim countries even during the colonial period, the semblance of banking institutions started emerging in the early 1960s. A pioneering experiment of putting the Islamic principles governing financial dealings into practice was conducted in Mit Ghamar, Egypt, from 1963 to 1967. Deriving inspiration from the idea of German saving banks, the Mit Ghamar initiative mobilized small savings from the rural sector largely through savings accounts. No interest was paid to the account holders. However, as an incentive they were eligible for small, short-term, interest-free loans for productive purposes. They were allowed to withdraw their deposits on demand. In addition, investment accounts on the basis of profit sharing were also introduced. The funds so mobilized were invested on the basis of profit-sharing with entrepreneurs.

The first interest-free institution with 'bank' in its name, Nasser Social Bank, was also established in Egypt in 1971. This was the first time that a government in a Muslim country had shown an interest in incorporating an interest-free institution. Even though the objectives of the Nasser Social Bank were mainly social, such as providing interest-free loans to the poor and needy, scholarships to students, and micro-credits to small projects on a profit-sharing basis, the involvement of a public authority in interest-free banking sent important signals to Muslim businessmen who had surplus funds. A group of such businessmen took the initiative of establishing the Dubai Islamic Bank in 1975 in Dubai in the United Arab Emirates (UAE). This was the first Islamic Bank established on private initiative. However, official support was crucial with the governments of the UAE and Kuwait contributing respectively 20 per cent and 10 per cent of the capital.

The most important development in the history of Islamic banking took place with the establishment of the Islamic Development Bank (IDB) in 1975. The IDB was established as an international financial institution in pursuance of the declaration of intent issued by a conference of finance ministers of Islamic countries held in Jeddah, Saudi Arabia, in December 1973. The declaration was signed by the representatives of 23 member countries of the OIC. The second conference of finance ministers, held in Jeddah in August 1974, adopted the Articles of Agreement establishing the Islamic Development Bank. The inaugural meeting of the Board of Governors of the IDB took place in Riyadh, Saudi Arabia, in July 1975 and it started functioning on 20 October 1975.

The period between 1975 and 1990 was the most important period in the history of development of Islamic financial industry. During this period, it matured into a viable alternative model of financial intermediation. It won respect and credibility in terms of both theoretical developments and practical experiences. On the one hand, several financial products compatible with the *Sharīʿah* were developed and, on the other hand, Islamic banks showed good results while using these products. The period was not only marked by the establishment of a large number of Islamic financial institutions in the private corporate sector under different socio-economic conditions, but also witnessed the expression of intent from three countries – Pakistan, Iran and Sudan – gradually to eliminate interest from their entire economies and substitute it with a complete banking system based on Islamic principles. Several practical steps were also taken in these countries towards achieving that objective. Even more important was the fact that several important multinational banks started offering Islamic financial products. That was a clear recognition of the viability of the new model and its acceptance by international players. The International Monetary Fund (IMF) and the World Bank also recognized Islamic financial products as a genuine means of financial intermediation and produced papers to that effect. In the 1990s, while the growth of the banking industry continued (though at a slower rate), attention was also given to non-bank financial institutions. Islamic financial institutions other than banks started coming on the scene in increasing numbers. These included insurance companies and investment funds. While the Islamic insurance sector has not registered sufficient growth, Islamic investment funds have witnessed significant progress.

Initiatives for the establishment of some of infrastructure institutions supporting the Islamic financial industry also started in the 1990s. At the beginning, Islamic banking institutions had to work within the institutional framework that supports conventional banking. They were at a comparative disadvantage because that framework was not specifically geared to their needs. A beginning has been made towards constructing a network of supporting institutions for the Islamic financial industry.

Various manifestations of the Islamic financial industry

The practice of Islamic banking as it has developed during the last 30 years has four main manifestations:

(a) banks and financial institutions in those countries where the promotion of an Islamic financial system is receiving active government support;
(b) Islamic banks and financial institutions in the private corporate sector working in a mixed environment;
(c) Islamic banking practices by some conventional commercial banks and non-bank financial institutions;
(d) multinational financial institutions working on *Sharīʿah* principles.

In the following sections, a brief account of each category is given, followed by a survey of other institutions.

Country experiences with Islamic banking

Pakistan

The process of economy-wide Islamization of the banking system in Pakistan was initiated soon after a declaration by the then President of Pakistan in February 1979 that the government planned to remove interest from the economy within a period of three years and that a decision had been taken to make a beginning in this direction with the elimination of interest from the operations of the House Building Finance Corporation, National Investment Trust and mutual funds of the Investment Corporation of Pakistan. Within a few months of this announcement, these specialized financial institutions took the necessary steps to reorient their activities on a non-interest basis.

The conversion of the operations of commercial banks to a non-interest basis was a much more complex task and took a longer time span. To begin with, steps were taken in January 1981 to set up separate counters for accepting deposits on a profit- and loss-sharing basis in all the domestic branches of the five nationalized commercial banks. The parallel system, in which savers had the option to keep their money with the banks either in interest-bearing deposits or PLS deposits, continued to operate until the end of June 1985. As of July 1985, no banking company was allowed to accept any interest-bearing deposits (except foreign currency deposits which continued to earn interest). As from that date, all deposits accepted by banking companies shared in the profit and loss of the bank, except deposits in current accounts on which no interest or profit was given and whose capital sum was guaranteed.

The central bank of the country issued instructions specifying twelve modes of financing in which funds mobilized by the banks can be employed. These were broadly classified into three groups: (i) loan financing; (ii) trade-related modes of financing; and (iii) investment modes of financing. Loan financing took the form either of *qarḍ al-ḥasan* loans given on compassionate grounds free of any interest or service charge (repayable if and when the borrower is able to repay) or of loans with a service charge not exceeding the proportionate cost of the operation.[2] Trade-related modes of financing included the following: (i) purchase of goods by banks and their sale to clients at an appropriate mark-up on a deferred payment basis, (ii) purchase of trade bills, (iii) purchase of moveable or immoveable property by the banks from their clients with buy-back agreement or otherwise, (iv) leasing, (v) hire-purchase, and (vi) financing for development of property on the basis of a development charge. Investment modes of financing included the following: (i) *mushārakah*, (ii) equity participation and purchase of shares, (iii) purchase of Participation Term Certificates[3] and *muḍārabah* certificates, and (iv) rent sharing.

The central bank of the country was authorized to fix the minimum annual rate of profit which banks should keep in view while considering proposals for provision of finance, and the maximum rate of profit they were allowed to earn. These rates were to be changed from time to time. It was also laid down that should losses occur, these must be shared by all the financiers in proportion to the respective finances provided by them.

A gesture towards introducing the *muḍārabah* technique of financing was made in June 1980 when a law was promulgated under which companies, banks and other financial institutions could register themselves as *muḍārabah* companies and mobilize funds through the issuance of *muḍārabah* certificates. Funds obtained through a *muḍārabah* could only be used in such businesses as were permitted under the *Sharīʿah*, and needed prior clearance from a Religious Board established by the government specifically for the purpose.

Though a number of steps were taken for the elimination of interest from the financial sector in Pakistan, the process of Islamization was slow and selective. Nothing was done to eliminate interest from government transactions. To begin with, commercial banks were precluded from investing PLS deposits in interest-bearing government securities. With the withdrawal of this restriction in August 1985, the movement towards an interest-free company suffered a serious retardation. Another disappointing feature of the situation was the lack of any notable progress in the transition to profit/loss sharing on the assets side of the banking system. The Islamization process was marked by another serious deficiency. No institutional mechanism was created for a continuous scrutiny of the operating procedures of banks and other financial institutions from the *Sharīʿah* point of view.

Individual scholars who examined these operating procedures pointed out several areas where the actual banking practices showed deviation from *Sharīʿah*. In December 1991, the Federal *Sharīʿah* Court, in one of its judgments, held that the system of mark-up financing as being practised by banks was not in conformity with the injunctions of Islam. It also took exception to a number of other practices prevailing in the banking sector. The court instructed the government to repeal/correct all un-Islamic provisions and practices. The government filed an appeal against this decision in the Supreme Court, the highest judicial body. After a long delay, the Supreme Court took up the hearing of this and some other similar appeals in 1998. In addition to the complainants, the court invited and heard a large number of economists, bankers and *Sharīʿah* scholars from both Pakistan and abroad. It gave its judgment in 1999, in which it rejected the government's appeal and endorsed most of the sections of the Federal *Sharīʿah* Court judgment. The court gave the government a time frame ending in June 2001 to correct objectionable practices identified by the Federal *Sharīʿah* Court and the Supreme Court itself while hearing the case.

Later, on an appeal from the government, the Court extended this deadline by one year. In compliance with that judgment, the government set up a Commission to devise a strategy for implementing the requirements of the judgment. The Commission submitted its report to the government, but in the meantime one bank affected by the Supreme Court decision filed a review petition. In 2002, the Court reversed its earlier decision and referred the case back to the Federal *Sharīʿah* Court for a fresh hearing which has not yet started (mid-2004).

Meanwhile, the government has decided to follow a model of a mixed system whereby conventional and Islamic banking can function side by side. Until the end of 2003, the Central Bank had given banking licences to three Islamic banks. In addition, all commercial banks are entitled to open Islamic windows, permission for which is granted on a case-by-case basis. In April 2004, the *Sharīʿah* Board of the Central Bank approved the essentials of Islamic modes of financing to ensure compliance with minimum *Sharīʿah* standards by banks conducting Islamic banking in Pakistan. In addition, model agreements for nine Islamic modes of financing were developed and announced with the dual objective of facilitating the existing Islamic banking sector and the potential market players to use Islamic banking products and to create general awareness about Islamic banking products. These include: (i) *murābaḥah* facility agreement, (ii) *musāwamah* facility agreement, (iii) lease agreement, (iv) *salam* agreement, (v) *mushārakah* investment agreement, (vi) *istiṣnāʿ* agreement, (vii) agreement for interest free loans, (viii) *muḍārabah* financing agreement, and (ix) syndicate *muḍārabah* agreement.

Iran

A new banking law, the Law for Usury-Free Banking Operations, was enacted in Iran in August 1983 to replace interest-based banking by interest-free banking. The law required the banks to convert their deposits to an interest-free basis within one year (and their other operations within three years) from the date of the passage of the law, and specified the types of transactions that must constitute the basis for asset and liability acquisition by banks. The law also specified the responsibilities of the central bank under the new system and the mechanics of the central bank's control over the banking system.

The law allows the banks to accept three types of deposits: *qarḍ al-ḥasanah* deposits, general term investment deposits and project-specific investment deposits. The *qarḍ al-ḥasanah* deposits comprise current as well as savings accounts which differ in their operational rules. The holders of current and savings accounts are guaranteed the safety of their principal amounts and are not entitled to any contractual return. However, banks are permitted to provide incentives to depositors through: (i) grant of prizes in cash or kind, (ii) reductions in or exemptions from service charges or agents' fees payable to banks, and (iii) according priority in the use of banking finances.

Holders of term investment deposits are entitled to receive a variable return, depending on the profitability of a bank's investments. The central bank fixes the minimum and maximum rates permissible. At the beginning of the year, 'expected' rates of profit are declared. However, the banks are required to calculate the 'actual' rates of return from their operations periodically and the difference between the 'actual' and 'expected' return is adjusted *post facto*. The law allows the banks to undertake and/or ensure the repayment of the principal amounts of term investment deposits.

The third type of deposit accounts are project-specific, in which banks mobilize savings for specific investment projects. In this type of account, the rate of return is calculated at the end of the project. The bank charges only an administrative fee for its intermediation between savers and investors. The rest of the profit received by the bank is distributed among the deposit holders.

On the asset side, the law provides thirteen different modes of contract, through which finance can be provided. These are: (i) *qarḍ-al ḥasanah,* (ii) *muḍārabah,* (iii) civil partnership (*musharakat madani*), (iv) legal partnership (*musharakat haqooqi*), (v) direct investment, (vi) instalment sales, (vii) hire-purchase, (viii) forward deals (*salaf*), (ix) *Juʿālah,* (x) *muzāraʿah,* (xi) *musāqah,* (xii) debt purchase, and (xiii) guarantee notes. However, in practice, instalment sales, civil partnerships and *muḍārabah* in trade activities are the most dominant modes of finance used.

One important feature of Islamic banking in Iran is that banks are obliged to earmark a portion of their resources for grants of *qarḍ al-ḥasanah* to help achieve the socio-economic objectives set out in the constitution of the country.[4] In addition to banks a number of charity organizations have also been established under government patronage to grant *qarḍ al-ḥasanah.* Besides *qard al-ḥasanah,* banks are authorized to extend financial assistance for productive ventures on a profit/loss sharing basis in accordance with the principles of *muḍārabah* and *mushārakah.* Banks are allowed to provide part of the capital of a new joint stock company and also to purchase shares of existing joint stock companies. Banks are authorized to provide working capital financing to productive units by purchasing raw materials, spare parts and other items on request for sale on the basis of deferred payment by instalments. Purchase of machinery and equipment for sale to their clients on a deferred payment basis is also allowed. Another mode is called *salaf* which is the same as *bayʿ salam,* and is used for meeting working capital requirements through advance purchase of output. Banks can engage in lease-purchase transactions. They can also provide finance on the basis of *juʿālah* (commission for working as agent), *muzāraʿah* (financing of agricultural production on a profit-sharing basis), or *musāqat* (financing of orchard production on a profit-sharing basis). In addition to these modes of financing, banks are permitted to purchase debt instruments of less than one year's maturity if these debts are issued against real assets.

Yasseri (2002) gives operational details of some of these modes. He points out that Iranian banks' most popular contract is instalment sales, followed by *mushārakah* (civil), *mushārakah* (equity), *muḍārabah, salaf* (*salam*), *qarḍ al-ḥasan,* direct investment, *juʿālah* and hire-purchase. He notes that it is evident from the provisions of these contracts that the state-owned nature of all banks in Iran is heavily reflected in the contracts, making them one-sided and in favour of the banks themselves. Furthermore, the drafters of the contracts were determined to preserve an intermediary role for Iranian banks, relieving them of the responsibility to engage in real, as opposed to financial, business. Iranian lawmakers have ensured that the Islamic banking contracts operate in a legally solid environment, free from ambiguous interpretations, and fully supported by binding legal measures.

Studies on the progress made in the implementation of the new system show that banks have, in general, adapted well to the new procedures. Problems have been encountered, however, in moving away from traditional short-term trade financing operations and towards profit-sharing medium- and long-term financing operations. It was expected that with the passage of time banks would increase their involvement in *muḍārabah* and *mushārakah* financing but this expectation has not been fulfilled. No attempt has been made so far to Islamize international banking and financial operations. In addition, the government continues to borrow from the banks on the basis of a fixed rate of return.[5] It has also been pointed out that some banking practices in Iran are at variance with the practice of Islamic banking in other countries.[6] A number of studies refer to conscious efforts made in recent years to reorient the activities of banks in Iran to achieve Islamic socio-economic objectives.[7] The banking system has been used as an instrument of restructuring the economy away from services and consumption, and towards production. Bank financing to the services sector has been drastically curtailed. Banks have reduced financing for the production of luxury goods and commodities with large import content, while financial assistance for the production of necessities and intermediate goods has been appreciably increased. Financing facilities for the agricultural sector have been considerably expanded. The banking system has also been used as an instrument of income redistribution through the provision of *qarḍ al-ḥasanah* loans to low-income groups, financing the building of low-cost houses, and provision of financing for small-scale agro business and industrial cooperatives often without stringent collateral requirements.

Sudan

The process of the economy-wide Islamization of the banking system in Sudan has not been smooth and steady. The first attempt to Islamize the entire banking system was made in 1984 when a presidential decree was issued directing all commercial banks to stop interest-based dealings with immediate effect and to negotiate the conversion of their then existing interest-bearing deposits and advances into Islamically acceptable forms. Foreign transactions were allowed to be continued on the basis of interest temporarily. It is reported that this sudden change forced the banks to adopt the nearest Islamic alternative available, *murābaḥah*, which soon constituted 90 per cent of their financial operations. It is also reported that the banks applied Islamic financing techniques only formally in their ledger books and in the reports submitted to the Central Bank of the country. Policy makers in the Central Bank were also discontented with the procedure of transforming the banking system. They considered it as a mere political decision imposed by the government which had not been prepared for adequately by detailed studies.[8] This experiment with economy-wide Islamization of the banking system came to an end in 1985 with the change in government. The government revived the process in May 1990 by reactivating an existing Islamic banking law. It issued a more comprehensive law in 1992 which envisioned an economy-wide Islamization of the financial system including the government sector. Reports indicate that the effort is much more earnest and much better organized this time. Now all banks are using Islamic modes of finance. An important development worth mentioning is the attempt being made to eliminate interest from the government sector, too. Other countries have found this a hard nut to crack. The government of Sudan has launched two funds based on the principle of *mushārakah* to mobilize resources for the public sector. The first is the Government *Mushārakah* Certificate (GMC). It is an instrument that enables the government to raise funds through issuing securities that promise the investor a negotiable return linked to developments in government revenue in return for their investment in the provision of general government services. The other is the Central Bank *Mushārakah* Certificate (CMC). This is an equity-based instrument that is issued against the government (or Central Bank) ownership in commercial banks. Under CMC, the Central Bank becomes a partner with the investors in profits of the underlying assets. The distribution of profit between the Central Bank and the investors is negotiable and the Certificate can be sold on the secondary market to another bank or the Central Bank. While GMC is still operating, CMC has been temporarily discontinued.

Bahrain

The Kingdom of Bahrain was amongst the first to recognize the importance of the concept of Islamic banking and finance and, as a consequence, has been both supportive of the development of the industry in general and welcoming to the new institutions in particular. As a result, Bahrain has gathered a concentration of specialist Islamic institutions on its shores. The first Islamic bank in Bahrain was established in 1979, when the Bahrain Islamic Bank was licensed. Since then, the sector has grown considerably. Now Bahrain has the largest number of Islamic financial institutions not only in the Gulf but anywhere in the world. The Kingdom is playing host to 26 Islamic banks and financial institutions, five industry-support organizations, six Islamic insurance companies and 34 Islamic mutual funds. A comprehensive prudential set of regulations for Islamic banks was introduced in early 2000 by the Bahrain Monetary Agency (BMA). This is referred to as the Prudential

Information and Regulations for Islamic Banks (PIRI) framework. The framework covers areas such as capital adequacy, asset quality, management of investment accounts, corporate governance and liquidity management.

Within such an environment, the Islamic financial industry in Bahrain will be able to enjoy sustainable growth based upon strong investor and customer confidence, attractive product design and expanding markets. Much is already in place. The Bahrain Monetary Agency's statutory responsibility as the sole regulator for the financial sector and the sector's adherence to the PIRI framework ensures that Islamic institutions will continue to operate according to standards comparable to those of the conventional financial sector.

Product innovation continues apace. The *ijārah* and *salam ṣukūk* are now firmly established and the Agency is fully committed to a rolling programme of further issues as an integral part of the development of Bahrain as an international Islamic bond market. These initiatives have been matched on their part by the private sector. The introduction of an Islamic credit card, and research into *takāful*, are two outstanding examples of the degree of innovative thinking coming from the industry that is driving forward the parameters of Islamic banking and finance.

Malaysia

In Malaysia, separate Islamic legislation and conventional banking regulations exist side by side. The Islamic financial system that has developed in Malaysia over the last two decades is emerging as a comprehensive Islamic financial system that operates in parallel with, and is able to compete on an even keel with, the more entrenched conventional financial system. The development of Islamic finance as an important niche activity in Malaysia's International Offshore Financial Centre in Labuan also complements the development of the domestic Islamic financial market.

The legal basis for the establishment of Islamic banks was the Islamic Banking Act (IBA) that came into effect on 7 April 1983. The IBA provides Bank Negara Malaysia (BNM) with powers to supervise and regulate Islamic banks, similar to the case of other licensed banks. The Government Investment Act 1983 was also enacted at the same time to empower the Government of Malaysia to issue Government Investment Certificates (GIC), which are government securities issued based on *Sharīʿah* principles. As the GIC are regarded as liquid assets, Islamic banks can invest in GIC to meet the prescribed liquidity requirements as well as to invest their surplus funds.

The first Islamic bank established in the country was Bank Islam Malaysia Berhad (BIMB), which commenced operations on 1 July 1983. After about two decades of operations, BIMB has proved to be a viable banking institution with its activity expanding rapidly throughout the country via a network of 80 branches and 1,200 employees. The bank was listed on the Main Board of the Kuala Lumpur Stock Exchange on 17 January 1992. On 1 October 1999, a second Islamic bank, Bank Muamalat Malaysia Berhad (BMMB), commenced operations. The establishment of BMMB was the effect of the spin-off following the merger between Bank Bumiputra Malaysia Berhad (BBMB) and Bank of Commerce (Malaysia) Berhad (BOCB). Under the merger arrangement, the Islamic banking assets and liabilities of BBMB, BOCB and BBMB Kewangan Berhad (BBMBK) were transferred to BBMB, while the conventional operations of BBMB, BOCB and BBMBK were transferred to the BOCB. In addition, BMMB was given 40 branches of BBMB and BBMBK in various locations throughout Malaysia.

Recognizing that, like any banking system, an Islamic banking system requires three vital elements to qualify as a viable system (i.e., a large number of players, a broad variety of instruments, and an Islamic money market), BNM has adopted a step-by-step approach to achieve the above objectives. The first step to spread the virtues of Islamic banking was to disseminate Islamic banking on a nation-wide basis, with as many players as possible so as to be able to reach all Malaysians. After a careful consideration of various factors, BNM decided to allow the existing banking institutions to offer Islamic banking services using their existing infrastructure and branches. The option was seen as the most effective and efficient mode of increasing the number of institutions offering Islamic banking services at the lowest cost and within the shortest time frame. Following from the above, on 4 March 1993 BNM introduced a scheme known as Skim Perbankan Tanpa Faedah (Interest-free Banking Scheme), or SPTF. More than 20 banks are now offering Islamic banking services. In addition, there are more than 50 Islamic investment funds. The Malaysian Financial Sector Master Plan launched in 2001 is the blueprint for the development of the financial sector over a 10-year period in Malaysia. The plan places importance on the development of Islamic banking and the *takāful* sector as an important component in the financial system.

To ensure the sound and stable development of the Islamic financial industry, it needs to be supported by a strong regulatory and supervisory framework. To fulfil this requirement, the Islamic Financial Services Board (IFSB) was established in 2002. The IFSB is an international body hosted by Malaysia. It has the important mandate of developing the prudential standards in accordance with the unique features of the Islamic financial institutions.

Islamic banks and financial institutions working in mixed environments

Islamic banks

There are around 70 Islamic banks working in the private sector, excluding those in Iran and Sudan, which have declared their intention to convert their entire banking sector to Islamic banking.[9] A list of these banks is given in Appendix 4.1. These institutions are spread across a number of countries and continents. The geographical distribution of these Islamic banks is given in Table 4.1. These figures show that the largest number of Islamic banks is in the GCC countries, followed by South-East Asian countries and then by other Middle Eastern countries. The share of the Arab world in the number of Islamic banks is about 60 per cent.

That is not the end of the story, however. While this gives us an idea about the 'spread' of Islamic banking, it does not reflect the relative 'strength' of Islamic banking in various regions because of the relative size of various institutions. In order to see the relative 'strength' of Islamic banking in various regions, the assets of a sample of 30 Islamic banks for which data are available for 2002 are shown in Table 4.2.

Table 4.1 Islamic banks by region (2002)

Region	**Number of institutions**	**%**
South and South-East Asia	22	31.9
GCC	26	37.7
Other Middle East	15	21.7
Africa	4	5.8
Rest of the world	2	2.9
Total	69	100

Source: Islamic Banking Information System (IBIS), under construction at the Islamic Research and Training Institute, Jeddah.

Table 4.2 Assets of Islamic banks by region (2002)*

Region	**Assets ($ million)**	**%**
South and South-East Asia	9,730	13.5
GCC	55,900	77.7
Other Middle East	6,180	8.6
Africa	NA	NA
Rest of the world	134	0.2
Total	71,944	100

* The data relate to 45 banks for which data were available. However, these banks comprise more than 80 per cent of the Islamic banks in the private corporate sector outside Iran and Sudan, since the other 24 banks are very small in size.

NA = not available.

Source: Islamic Banking Information System (IBIS), under construction at the Islamic Research and Training Institute, Jeddah.

It can be seen that the bulk of the Islamic banking activity is concentrated in the Middle East, especially GCC countries. This region accounts for 85 per cent of the total assets of Islamic banks. In addition, two major international holding companies – the Dar al-Māl al-Islamī and the Al-Baraka Group, each of which control about a dozen Islamic banks and finance companies, some of which operate outside the Middle East – are both controlled by Middle Eastern owners. Thus the real importance of the region in the Islamic banking industry is even higher.

Saudi Arabia is the largest market for Islamic finance in terms of size. The largest Islamic bank in the world, Al-Rajhi Banking and Investment Corporation, is based in Saudi Arabia. The bank had $15.8 billion in assets at the end of 2002. In addition, almost all other banks operating in Saudi Arabia are offering Islamic products besides their conventional operations. Saudi Arabia is also home to the largest concentration of Islamic funds. The most important Islamic banking institution, the IDB, is also headquartered in Saudi Arabia.

The Islamic Development Bank is a multilateral development bank serving the Muslim countries. Its present membership stands at 55 countries. Its purpose is to foster economic development and the social progress of member countries and Muslim communities, individually and collectively, in accordance with the principles of the *Sharīʿah*. In order to meet the growing and diverse needs of its member countries, the Bank has established a number of institutions and funds with distinct administrative arrangements and operational rules. These entities and funds, affiliated with the Bank, enable the IDB to mobilize supplementary financial resources in line with the *Sharīʿah* principles and to focus on those functions and activities which cannot be covered under its normal financing arrangements. With these affiliated entities and funds, the Bank has evolved over time into a group called the IDB Group.

Several other countries in the Arab world have a significant presence in Islamic finance. Kuwait is host to the second largest Islamic commercial bank, the Kuwait Finance House. In addition, there are 10 Islamic investment banks and finance companies working in Kuwait and Qatar, while Jordan and Yemen also have some Islamic banks and finance companies.

Growth of key variables

In this section we provide empirical evidence on the growth of the Islamic banking industry. For this purpose, a sample of twelve Islamic banks was chosen. These banks together account for more than 50 per cent of total capital as well as total assets of 'private' Islamic banks and thus form a very large sample from a statistical point of view. Therefore, the sample is representative and the conclusions drawn from this sample are likely to apply to the whole industry. The study covers the 1990–2002 period. Data were compiled from the annual reports of these banks.[10] Attempts have also been made to reconcile the data over the period as well as across the banks to construct a comparable series. The names of the banks included in the sample are given in Table 4.3.

Table 4.3 Sample of Islamic banks chosen for the study of growth

No.	Islamic Banks	Country
1	Al-Rajhi Banking & Investment Corporation	Saudi Arabia
2	Kuwait Finance House (KFH)	Kuwait
3	Al-Baraka Islamic Investment Bank (BKBN)	Bahrain
4	Bahrain Islamic Bank (BIB)	Bahrain
5	Faysal Islamic Bank (FIBB)	Bahrain
6	Faisal Islamic Bank (FIBE)	Egypt
7	Dubai Islamic Bank (DIB)	UAE
8	Jordan Islamic Bank (JIB)	Jordan
9	Qatar Islamic Bank (QIB)	Qatar
10	Islami Bank Bangladesh (IBBG)	Bangladesh
11	Bank Islam Malaysia Berhard (BIMB)	Malaysia
12	Al-Baraka Turkish Finance House (BKTF)	Turkey

Data on some key variables for the period 1990–2002 are given in Table 4.4 and analysed in the following paragraphs. The period has been divided into three subperiods to see the trends over time while minimizing yearly variations.

Total equity

Total equity, which is the most important variable by which to measure the strength of a company, grew at a rate of 9.9 per cent during 1990–2002 for the sample as a whole. Growth in equity has been continuous even though the rate of growth declined after reaching a peak around 1998. Consequently, the rate of growth for the 1996–2002 period was lower than that of 1990–6, but still a decent 9.27 per cent per annum. The continuous growth in equity has helped improve the capital to assets ratio over time.

There was considerable variation within the sample, with such variation being smaller in the second period as compared to the first, which is due to the fact that previously low-capitalized banks have improved their capital position. However, with the exception of one bank, all banks registered positive rates of growth in equity throughout the period. KFH showed the highest rate of growth in capital, followed by IBBG and BIMB.

Total deposits

During 1990–6, total deposits grew at an annual rate of 5.47 per cent. Other studies have shown that deposits of Islamic banks were growing at 15 per cent during the 1980s.[11] Against this background, the rate of growth for the 1990–6

Table 4.4 Average annual growth rates for some key variables (%)

	Total equity			Total deposits			Total investments			Total assets			Total revenue		
	1990–1996	1996–2002	1990–2002	1990–1996	1996–2002	1990–2002	1990–1996	1996–2002	1990–2002	1990–1996	1996–2002	1990–2002	1990–1996	1996–2002	1990–2002
Rajhi	7.82	6.22	7.02	10.94	11.79	11.37	9.58	10.12	9.85	9.74	11.13	10.43	5.4	6.7	6.0
KFH	40.16	9.83	22.70	2.38	9.47	6.19	8.05	10.14	9.19	4.64	9.98	7.52	11.9	4.8	8.0
DIB	16.54	17.11	16.83	15.18	17.81	16.49	12.83	20.07	16.39	13.87	18.40	16.11	13.7	10.6	12.1
QIB	1.94	10.44	6.11	6.01	8.65	7.32	4.87	9.61	7.21	6.78	9.13	7.95	1.4	5.5	3.4
BIMB	20.04	17.59	18.81	18.82	14.28	16.53	16.90	13.16	15.02	18.57	14.25	16.39	18.1	7.9	12.9
JIB	22.46	3.42	12.54	16.26	6.44	11.24	17.48	–0.32	8.22	15.43	4.57	9.86	11.6	–3.8	3.6
BIB	12.28	18.18	15.19	5.21	2.42	3.81	6.18	6.70	6.44	5.80	6.77	6.28	4.9	–1.7	1.5
IBBG	23.36	14.70	18.95	17.26	18.35	17.81	23.53	15.69	19.55	17.96	17.89	17.93	15.4	11.8	13.6
FIBE	–10.37	5.42	–2.79	0.46	5.26	2.84	6.57	5.02	5.79	1.49	3.87	2.67	5.9	–6.4	–0.4
FIBB	14.82	NA	NA	16.72	NA	NA	33.91	NA	NA	16.86	NA	NA	17.3	NA	NA
BKTF	2.98	21.17	11.71	18.34	–3.64	6.79	15.91	–12.21	0.88	11.85	–2.73	4.30	0.6	11.6	6.0
BKBN	1.09	0.39	0.74	12.97	16.44	14.69	6.27	10.94	8.58	7.63	11.91	9.75	24.7	2.5	13.1
Simple average	12.76	11.32	11.62	11.71	9.75	10.46	13.51	8.08	9.74	10.89	9.56	9.93	10.89	4.50	7.24
SD	13.27	6.89	8.04	6.56	6.88	5.39	8.66	8.60	5.33	5.70	6.28	5.02	7.39	6.23	5.03
Weighted average	10.52	9.27	9.89	5.47	11.21	8.30	8.58	10.44	9.50	8.16	10.93	9.54	7.56	5.68	6.61

NA = not available.
SD = standard deviation.
Source: Calculated from data in IBIS.

period was much lower than the 1980s rate. There are four possible reasons for this decline.

First, during the 1980s there were a lot of immobilized funds due to the fact that many Muslim clients did not want to be involved in any interest dealings. In the absence of a viable alternative, they were keeping their savings in private lockers (and so on). With the advent of Islamic banking in the late 1970s, these people started dealing with the new banks. As a matter of fact one of the biggest achievements of Islamic banking has been to bring this huge amount of funds into the formal sector. Over the next 10–15 years these savings found their way into the coffers of the Islamic banks. Accordingly the rate of growth of deposits started tapering off.

Second, in the early 1990s an increasing number of conventional banks started offering Islamic products. These banks offered a new kind of competition to existing Islamic banks that was hitherto unknown. Many of these Western multinational banks brought with them their marketing expertise, international connections, superior technology and better customer relations, and so some of the deposits must have been diverted to these banks. Due to the absence of any definite information, the extent of such diversion cannot be estimated, although some indication can be obtained by comparing the growth rates of deposits of such banks with those of Islamic banks.

Third, as the base gets bigger and bigger, it becomes increasingly difficult to maintain a given rate of growth.

The final reason for this trend was that in the 1990s a new trend in Islamic finance gained ground. This relates to the establishment of Islamic funds. Some of the deposits of the Islamic banks may have been diverted to these funds. In view of the evidence on the growth of Islamic funds, we believe this to be the most significant reason for the decline in the deposits of Islamic banks. This analysis is supported by the fact that due to a downward trend in the returns on stocks after 1999, Islamic banks regained some of the ground lost to Islamic funds. Consequently, the rate of growth of deposits for the 1996–2002 period worked out at 11.21 per cent.

The growth rate for the banks included in the sample for the entire period (1990–2002) was 8.3 per cent per annum, a relatively high annual growth rate for such a long period. Considering the fact that the Islamic funds and the Islamic branches of the conventional banks that offer Islamic products are both part of the Islamic financial industry, and the fact that new Islamic banks continued to be established during the 1990s, it is safe to conclude that the Islamic financial industry as a whole continued to enjoy double-digit growth rates during 1990s and beyond.

Total investment

The level of total investments is important because the overall profitability of the banks depends on the returns generated from such investments. The annual rate of growth for this variable for the entire period comes to

9.5 per cent. Over time the rate of growth of investment has improved, the rates of growth for the two subperiods being 8.58 and 10.44 per cent respectively. This is so because the growth in total investments depends on the growth in deposits and, as mentioned above, total deposits grew at a higher rate in the second period (1996–2002) than the first (1990–6).

However, the data show wide variations across the Islamic banks. In the case of two banks total investments actually decreased during 1996–2002. All other banks registered positive, though varying, rates of growth over both periods. For the entire period, the rates of growth ranged from a low of 0.88 per cent per annum in the case of Al-Baraka Turkish Finance House to a high of 19.55 per cent per annum in the case of Islami Bank Bangladesh.

Total assets

Total assets grew at 8.16 per cent during 1990–6. The industry witnessed an even higher growth of 10.93 per cent per annum during the later period, bringing the rate of growth for the entire period to 9.54 per cent per annum. Three banks achieved 15 per cent or more growth. As in the case of total deposits, the Islami Bank Bangladesh showed the most consistent performance, making progress at about 18 per cent per annum throughout the period, something rarely witnessed in the banking industry over such a long period.

Total revenue

Total operating revenue grew at a handsome rate of 7.56 per cent in 1990–6 but declined to a rate of 5.68 per cent in 1996–2002 giving an overall average rate of growth of 6.61 per cent for the entire period. It must be noticed that the growth rates of total investments for both the periods were higher than the growth rates of total revenue. Does this mean that the rate of return on investments was declining? That could be so; but another reason is probably due to the relative decline in fee-based operations. Other studies have shown that contra accounts (that are offset or deducted from other accounts) of Islamic banks have been declining over time.[12] This trend may also have to do with the entry of Western multinational banks into the Islamic banking industry. With their vast international networks, they may be siphoning off the letters of credit and letters of guarantee business away from Islamic banks. This is an important trend for Islamic banks to watch. Fee-based income is a relatively secure part of banks' income, and its decline may have important implications for the overall profitability of Islamic banks in the long run.

Islamic investment funds

Investment funds are considered as one of the most efficient and cost-effective ways of participating in stock markets. Though this investment vehicle suits all categories of investors in the medium- and long-term, they have several special advantages for small investors. These include, among others, economies of scale resulting in lower transaction costs, risk diversification over industries, countries and currencies, access to global markets, and professional portfolio management by expert fund managers.

Another reason in favour of establishment of investment funds is the need for long-term finance in all economies. In conventional systems, this is provided through long-term bonds and equities. Securities markets and specialized equity institutions perform this function. In addition to the general public, the most important sources of these long-term investments are investment banks, mutual funds, insurance companies and pension funds. Since in an Islamic economy use cannot be made of interest-bearing bonds, the need for equity-based institutions is much higher.

Therefore, the important question we need to ask is: can investment funds run on an Islamic basis? In addition, since in most Muslim countries (which are the natural domain of Islamic finance) security markets are not well established, another question needs to be posed. Can Islamic investment funds invest in international stock markets, and if so what *Sharīʿah* conditions need to be satisfied? We deal with these questions in turn.

The basic concept of investment funds, whereby funds are pooled from several investors and managed by others on their behalf is acceptable under the principle of *wakālah*. The fund promoter is the *wakīl* (agent) of the unit holders and charges a fixed fee for his services. He can in turn appoint a fund manager on a fixed salary or on profit-sharing basis. Both of these arrangements are acceptable from an Islamic point of view and are well established. Therefore, investment funds satisfy the fundamental principles of the Islamic theory of contracts. It is worth noting that investment funds are different from *muḍārabah* accounts in the Islamic banks. The basic difference between the two is that in the latter case the bank is *muḍārib* (working partner) and hence shares in the risk of investment.[13] In the case of investment funds all risk is borne by the unit holders. For the same reason, the fund promoters have no share in profits, all of which (after deducting fixed management fees of the promoters) is passed on to the unit holders. At the operational level, the basic concept of unit trusts is that risks and rewards are shared by investors (unit holders) who benefit from the expertise of professionals.

Therefore, from a contractual point of view, the case for investment funds is well established. However, since the fund promoter is only a '*wakīl*' of the unit holders, it is the unit holders' responsibility to ensure that the particular businesses in which fund money is invested do not violate any *Sharīʿah* principles. These conditions must be specified in the Agreement governing participation in the Fund. Once that is done, the Islamic responsibilities of a *wakīl* are well known. He is supposed to work according to the terms of the trust conferred on him. If he violates the terms of that trust, he is liable to penalties.

Once the funds are pooled, they can be used in any *ḥalāl* (Islamically permissible) business. Investment funds can take many forms. They can be 'income funds' targeting income growth, or 'growth funds' targeting capital gains. They can also be classified by type of business (e.g., lease funds), by industry (e.g., real estate funds) or by commodities (e.g., commodity funds or petroleum funds, etc.). All of these are permissible.

One important type of investment fund needs further comment. These are equity funds, whose main activity is buying and selling the shares of other companies. In this case, one has to ensure that the business activities of the companies whose shares are bought and sold are themselves acceptable from the *Sharīʿah* point of view. This is so because shareholders are the owners of the company and as such are collectively (as well as individually) responsible for its deeds. Islamic scholars have opined that investment in equity funds is permissible if certain conditions are satisfied. They have prescribed three minimum requirements: (i) the fund must not deal in equities of companies whose basic business activity is banned by the Islamic *Sharīʿah* (e.g., breweries, casinos, conventional banks, etc.); (ii) interest income earned by the fund must be negligible and separable so that the fund's income can be cleansed of it; (iii) since the sale of debt is not permissible except at face value, the proportion of debts receivable in the portfolio of the company should not exceed an 'acceptable' proportion. How these conditions can be complied with in practice is discussed below.

To ensure that the companies selected for the investment are acceptable from the perspective of the *Sharīʿah*, a fund management group can screen the prospective companies to be included in the portfolio. As with other types of ethical investment selection, both positive and negative criteria can be used. Negative criteria involve excluding companies whose major purpose is the production or distribution of alcohol or pork products or the management of gambling facilities or investment in *ribā*-based financial institutions. Some investors may prefer to avoid investing in airlines, hotels or supermarket chains which serve alcohol, even though this is a minor part of their business. This would, however, result in a much more restricted potential portfolio. Usually businesses are defined by their prime activity, which makes a hotel group or airline acceptable but a brewery unacceptable. There are parallels with ethical investment funds, which avoid investing in tobacco companies but may invest in retail groups selling cigarettes alongside other items.

Second, since according to *Sharīʿah* principles both giving and taking interest is forbidden, ideally it would be desirable to avoid investing in companies which have any dealing with *ribā*-based banks but, practically speaking, this would mean the exclusion of virtually all quoted companies, including those whose stocks are traded in the equity markets of Muslim countries. In practice fund management groups seeking to comply with the *Sharīʿah* adopt two criteria. First, they examine the extent to which a company's income is derived from interest (any proportion in excess of 10 per cent being unacceptable[14]). The second criterion is to consider the extent of debt to equity finance, a proportion in excess of one-third being unacceptable.

The *Sharīʿah* law itself does not specify ratios such as those suggested by some scholars, and neither does it establish what factors should be used in any calculations, such as debt to market capitalization versus debt to book values. The latter is arguably more stable as it is not subject to daily changes in market valuation, and there may be a case for using book values rather than market capitalization as the appropriate screening variable.

It is worth stressing that if all quoted companies that are leveraged are excluded there would be nothing left to include in any investment portfolio. There is also the issue of any interest that quoted companies obtain on their bank balances. Information on such receipts should be available in the annual reports of any quoted company and in the interim statements. One possible solution to this problem is for the fund manager to pay an amount equivalent to the proportion of any dividends derived from interest to charity in order to purify the income. Alternatively the income may be distributed, but the *Sharīʿah* committee advising the fund manager may make a recommendation to the investor about the amount he or she should donate to an appropriate charitable cause. It is worth stressing that any manager of a fund designated as Islamic should be able to draw on the services of a *Sharīʿah* adviser, or (even better) have the opinion of a *Sharīʿah* committee charged with overseeing all operations of the fund to ensure compliance with Islamic law.

Third, according to the majority of Islamic scholars, the sale of debt is not permissible except at face value. Now most companies have accounts receivable in their portfolios (i.e., debts). Can shares of these companies be bought and sold? Some *Sharīʿah* scholars have argued that the ruling of permissibility depends on what is the dominant component. If the ratio of debts receivable is less than 50 per cent in a company's portfolio, then buying and selling its shares would be permissible.

As to the practice, some Islamic investment funds were established in the early 1970s, and many of them did not survive. The real growth in this sector took place in the 1990s. While definite information on the number of Islamic funds and their size is not available, one source[15] gives a list of known Islamic funds that includes around 100 equity funds. *Islamic Banker* (July 2003) listed around 120 funds. None of these lists is exhaustive. If we also add other investment funds – for example, commodity funds, lease funds, *muḍārabas* and so on – the number of Islamic investment funds is somewhere around 200. However, there are about two dozen major players in this market. (The names of these major players are given in Appendix 4.2.)

Dow Jones and the FTSE (Financial Times Stock Exchange) have launched several Islamic indices which track more than 2000 companies world-wide. They use various screens to produce indices meeting Islamic criteria for holding equity in these companies. This has led to the involvement of several well-known Western fund managers in the Islamic fund management business.

Islamic insurance companies

Another segment of the Islamic financial industry relates to insurance. Unfortunately, due to juridical issues which have not been satisfactorily resolved, this segment has not shown enough growth. Due to the element of 'chance' in all insurance contracts, some Islamic scholars have likened the insurance business to gambling which is prohibited in Islam. Other scholars have pointed out that the element of 'chance' emerges from the nature of risk. They further point out that all risks that one faces in life are not of the same kind. They make a distinction between three types of risks.

First, there is the risk that can be termed 'entrepreneurial risk'. This risk is part of the normal course of business. Every economic activity involves uncertainty that generates risks. Some agents, called entrepreneurs, take those risks. An enterprising person makes a profit, as well as (on occasions) incurring losses. However, the fact that society has always had such enterprising people is testimony to the fact that, by and large, profit outweighs loss. Willingness to take such risks does not imply any moral evil; rather, it is a need that no society can do away with.

The second type of risk which is also part of life arises from the possibility of the occurrence of natural disasters and calamities. People throughout the history have sought ways and means to protect themselves from the occurrence of personal losses due to such calamities. This is the essence of insurance.

The third type of risk arises from uncertainties that are not part of everyday life. They arise from various types of 'games' that people create for themselves. These risks are unnecessary. They are unnecessary for the individual in the sense that if someone chooses not to participate in these 'games', he will face no such risk; they are also unnecessary for society in the sense that they do not add any economic value to the wealth of the community.

It is the third type of risk that is the essence of gambling which is prohibited by Islam. As to the other two types of risks, both are a natural part of everyday life and must be reckoned and dealt with. Once this is accepted, the concept of insurance becomes acceptable in principle. However, it must be noticed that there is an important difference between the first and second types of risk mentioned above. While the basic motivation for taking an entrepreneurial risk is 'profit', the basic motivation to seek protection against the second type of risk is 'fear'. The loss resulting from such calamities is often huge and may in many cases be beyond the capacity of the individuals who suffer them. By paying a small price, called a premium, one can buy 'protection' against such happenings.

Many Islamic scholars have pointed out that there is nothing wrong in seeking protection against suffering if one can manage to do that.

However, they have pointed out that nobody should make a profitable business out of the sufferings that naturally befall humanity. This has led to the development of Islamic insurance which is based on the concept of *takāful,* which means taking care of each other. Thus an Islamic insurance company, usually called *takāful,* has the following features:

1 The company is not the one who assumes risks nor the one taking any profit. Instead, it is the participants, the policy holders, who cover each other.
2 All contributions (premiums) are accumulated into a fund. This fund is invested using Islamic modes of investment and the net profit resulting from these investments is credited back to the fund.
3 All claims are paid from this fund. The policy holders, as a group, are the owners of any net profit that remains after paying all the claims. They are also collectively responsible if the claims exceed the balance in the fund.
4 The company acts as a trustee on behalf of the participants to manage the operations of the *takāful* business. The relationship between the company and the policy holders is governed by the terms of *muḍārabah* contract. Therefore, should there be a surplus from the operation, the company (*muḍārib*) will share the surplus with the participants (*rabb al-māl*) according to a pre-agreed profit-sharing ratio.

In practice, there are about 50 Islamic insurance companies operating in the world outside Iran and Sudan which, as mentioned before, are both attempting to Islamize their entire economies. The names of these companies are given in Appendix 4.3, while their geographical distribution is shown in Table 4.5.

South and South-East Asian countries host the largest number of Islamic insurance companies. Within this region, Bangladesh has the largest number of Islamic insurance companies while Malaysia is the largest market

Table 4.5 Islamic insurance companies by region (2002)

Region	Number of institutions	%
South and South-East Asia	23	48.93
GCC	18	38.30
Other Middle East	2	4.26
Africa	1	2.13
Rest of the world	3	6.38
Total	47	100

Source: Islamic Banking Information System (IBIS), under construction at the Islamic Research and Training Institute, Jeddah.

for Islamic insurance in terms of size. In GCC countries, Saudi Arabia and Bahrain have the largest number of Islamic insurance companies.

Islamic banking practices by conventional banks

Another achievement of Islamic banking may be gauged from the fact that many conventional banks have also started using Islamic banking techniques in the conduct of their business, particularly in dealing either with Muslim clients or in dominantly Muslim regions. At present, the number of such conventional banks may not be very large, but the very fact that some important and large multinational banks have also resorted to Islamic banking is itself a pointer of much significance. A Western observer of Islamic banking has aptly remarked that 'it is an excellent reflection on the success of Islamic banking that many conventional commercial banks are now offering their clients Islamic financial services'.[16]

The involvement of some Western conventional banks, particularly multinational banks, in Islamic banking started quite early, in the 1980s. In the early period of their establishment, Islamic banks were stuck with high liquidity which was the result of high deposit growth and very few investment opportunities. In such a situation, Islamic banks turned to Western institutions such as Citibank to find profitable avenues for the investment of their money. Most of the resources supplied by the Islamic banks went to commodity trade and trade finance deals. Since Islamic banks did not want any involvement of these funds in *ribā*-based transactions, the Western banks found themselves negotiating '*murābaḥah*' deals in which they arranged for a trader to buy goods on behalf of the Islamic bank and resell them at a mark-up. This prompted other Western commercial banks to follow suit.[17]

Although it is difficult to know with certainty how many conventional commercial banks around the globe practise Islamic banking techniques, even a randomly selected short list may contain some of the giants of the international banking industry such as Chase Manhattan, Citibank, the HongKong and Shanghai Banking Corporation (HSBC), ANZ Grindlays, along with other banks such as the Union Bank of Switzerland, Deutsche Bank of Germany, ABC International, the National Bank of Kuwait, the Saudi British Bank, National Commercial Bank, Riyadh Bank of Saudi Arabia and Bank Misr of Egypt. Islamic banking practice either takes the form of offering Islamic mutual fund services or fully-fledged Islamic banking windows. The list of banks offering such windows is given in Appendix 4.4. In addition to these banks, multinational banks located in certain Islamic countries, such as Iran and Sudan, also conduct their activities in accordance with the principles of Islamic banking because the local laws require them to do so. In the UAE and Pakistan all conventional banks are allowed in principle to open Islamic windows with the permission of the Central Bank.

International Islamic financial institutions

Some international financial institutions have also come on to the scene. Two major international holding companies, the Dar al-Māl al-Islamī and the Al-Baraka Group, control more than a dozen Islamic banks and finance companies each; but perhaps the most important multinational institution is the Islamic Development Bank. In the following paragraphs, brief profiles of some institutions established within the Islamic financial industry are given.

Islamic Development Bank

The Islamic Development Bank is a multilateral development bank serving Muslim countries. Its present membership stands at 55 countries. Its purpose is to foster economic development and the social progress of member countries and Muslim communities, individually and collectively, in accordance with the principles of the *Sharīʿah*. In order to meet the growing and diverse needs of its member countries, the Bank has established a number of institutions and funds with distinct administrative arrangements and operational rules. These entities and funds, affiliated with the Bank, enable the IDB to mobilize supplementary financial resources in line with *Sharīʿah* principles, and to focus on those functions and activities which cannot be covered under its normal financing arrangements. With these affiliated entities and funds, the Bank has evolved over time into a group called the IDB Group.

In 1995 IDB established the Islamic Corporation for Insurance of Investment and Export Credit (ICIEC). The objective of ICIEC is to enlarge the scope of trade transactions and the flow of investments among member states. In fulfilment of this objective ICIEC provides *Sharīʿah*-compliant export credit insurance and reinsurance to cover the non-payment of export receivables resulting from commercial (buyer) or non-commercial (country) risks; and foreign investment insurance and reinsurance against country risks, mainly the risks of exchange transfer restrictions, expropriation, war and civil disturbance and breach of contract by the host government. The safety-net provided by ICIEC is also expected to contribute positively to the development of the industry in the future.

In 1999 IDB established the Islamic Corporation for the Development of the Private Sector (ICD). The focused objectives of the ICD are to identify opportunities in the private sector that could function as engines of growth; to provide a wide range of *Sharīʿah*-compatible financial products and services; and to expand access to Islamic capital markets by private companies in IDB member countries. In the coming years, the operations of the ICD are expected to have a significant impact on the development of the member countries.

In order to promote the growth of Islamic financial industry, IDB supports the establishment of Islamic financial institutions licensed in various jurisdictions by participating in their equity capital, and also helps to introduce Islamic windows into traditional banks.

During the span of about three decades of existence, the Bank has made significant strides. It has not only successfully attained a respectable position among the multilateral development financing institutions, but has also proved to be a model emulated by other Islamic banks. At the end of February 2004 (corresponding to the latest accounting year of the Bank), the authorized capital of the Bank stood at 15 billion Islamic Dinars[18] (ID) (US$20.55 billion). Its subscribed capital amounted to ID8.1 billion (US$11.10 billion), whereas its paid-up capital amounted to ID2.68 billion (US$3.67 billion). The ordinary resources of the Bank consist of members' subscriptions (paid-up capital, reserves and retained profits), which amounted to ID3.98 billion (US$5.95 billion).

Unlike other financial institutions, the Bank does not support its financial resources by borrowing funds from conventional financial markets as this involves the payment of interest. For this reason, the Bank has developed new *Sharīʿah*-compliant financial schemes and instruments to support its ordinary financial resources. These schemes and instruments include the IDB Unit Investment Fund (IDB UIF), the Export Financing Scheme (EFS), which was formerly known as the Longer-term Trade Financing Scheme (LTTF), and the Islamic Banks' Portfolio (IBP). The Bank has so far raised about US$708 million through these schemes. In a major move in 2003, the Bank launched its debut *ṣukūk* issue (assets-based bond) worth US$300 million. The issue proved to be an overwhelming success and closed at US$400 million.

IDB extends financial support to the development projects of member countries. Unlike other multilateral financial institutions, the Bank finances its operations through a number of Islamic financing modes. Due to its operational needs, product development has been an important concern of the IDB. It has developed a number of innovative financial instruments. These include: instalment sales, and line of instalment sale, *ijārah* and line of *ijārah*, *murābaḥah*, financing based on service charges, and *istiṣnāʿ*. The IDB also has developed a Unit Investment Fund, the Islamic Banks' Portfolio, and the Infrastructure Fund. During 2003, the IDB launched the US$400 million Islamic Trust Certificates by pooled securitization of some of its *ijārah* assets, and instalment sales and *istiṣnāʿ* receivables.

The Accounting and Auditing Organization for Islamic Financial Institutions

The Accounting and Auditing Organization for Islamic Financial Institutions (AAOIFI) is an Islamic international autonomous non-profit making corporate body that prepares accounting, auditing, governance, ethics and *Sharīʿah* standards for Islamic financial institutions. It was established in accordance with the Agreement of Association which was signed by Islamic financial institutions on 26 February 1990 in Algiers. It was registered in the Kingdom of Bahrain on 27 March 1991. The objectives of AAOIFI include:

(a) develop accounting, auditing, governance and ethical ideas relating to the activities of Islamic financial institutions taking into consideration the international standards and practices which comply with Islamic *Sharīʿah* rules;
(b) disseminate the accounting, auditing, governance and ethical ideas relating to the activities of Islamic financial institutions and their application through training seminars, publication of periodical newsletters, preparation of reports, research and through other means;
(c) harmonize the accounting policies and procedures adopted by Islamic financial institutions through the preparation and issuance of accounting standards and the interpretations of the same to the said institutions;
(d) improve the quality and uniformity of auditing and governance practices relating to Islamic financial institutions through the preparation and issuance of auditing and governance standards and the interpretation of the same to the said institutions;
(e) promote good ethical practices relating to Islamic financial institutions through the preparation and issuance of codes of ethics to these institutions;
(f) achieve conformity or similarity – to whatever extent possible – in concepts and applications among the *Sharīʿah* supervisory boards of Islamic financial institutions to avoid contradiction and inconsistency between the *fatwās* and the applications by these institutions, with a view to activating the role of the *Sharīʿah* supervisory boards of Islamic financial institutions and central banks through the preparation, issuance and interpretations of *Sharīʿah* standards and *Sharīʿah* rules for investment, financing and insurance;
(g) approach the concerned regulatory bodies, Islamic financial institutions, other financial institutions that offer Islamic financial services, and accounting and auditing firms in order to implement the standards, as well as the statements and guidelines that are published by AAOIFI.

The AAOIFI standards were introduced for the first time in 1993 for Islamic financial institutions. Islamic financial institutions are adopting these standards in increasing numbers.

General Council for Islamic Banks and Financial Institutions

Founded in May 2001, the General Council for Islamic Banks and Financial Institutions (GCIBFI) is a non-profit association based in Bahrain with members from around the world including Islamic commercial banks, Islamic windows, investment banks, Islamic funds, Islamic *takāful* (insurance) companies and so on. Membership of the GCIBFI is available to any registered

Islamic bank or financial institution anywhere in the world that 'undertakes all activities in complete compliance with the tenets of Islam'. The GCIBFI represents Islamic banks and financial institutions on issues of international importance for these institutions and their customers. It also aims to increase understanding of Islamic banking and prevent misunderstandings that could inhibit its progress in the international banking sector. GCIBFI fulfils this role by hosting conferences in key centres around the world, and by finding ways to improve customer understanding of Islamic banking and finance. GCIBFI also acts as a resource for its members for employee training, technical assistance, conferences, and seminars.

International Islamic Financial Market

The Islamic financial services industry faces greater liquidity risk due to the absence of a secondary market for Islamic financial instruments. The non-existence of an inter-bank Islamic money market makes liquidity management a challenging task. The Islamic banks are thus under a constraint to maintain liquidity at higher levels than conventional banks. This adversely affects Islamic banks' competitiveness. The establishment of an International Islamic Financial Market (IIFM) in 2002 in Bahrain was thus an important building block for Islamic financial services infrastructure.

The IIFM is a non-profit international organization that aims to create an environment which will encourage cross-border trading of *Sharīʿah*-compatible instruments. The principal objectives of IIFM are to develop an active international financial market based on *Sharīʿah* rules and principles and to issue guidelines to market participants for the issuing of instruments and standardization of documentation for secondary market trading.

The core product of IIFM is the *Sharīʿah* endorsement of existing and new Islamic financial products and instruments which are offered by Islamic financial institutions, conventional banks with Islamic banking subsidiaries, windows and so forth. Through *Sharīʿah* endorsement, the IIFM intends to accomplish uniformity in Islamic products and instruments in order to have global reach and acceptance.

The Islamic Financial Services Board

Proper regulation and supervision of banks and financial institutions is also important for financial efficiency and stability. Some of the risks faced by the Islamic financial industry are unique due to the *Sharīʿah* compliance requirements. Bank supervisors utilizing the traditional standards cannot assess such risks. The need for special guidelines for the regulation and supervision of Islamic banks has long been felt. Some regulatory authorities have already introduced guidelines for Islamic banking supervision in their respective jurisdictions. With the active involvement of the IMF, the IDB and support from the Bahrain Monetary Agency, Bank Negara Malaysia and other central banks, an Islamic Financial Services Board was established in

Malaysia in November 2002 and has been in operation since March 2003. Its mandate is to serve as an international standard-setting body for the regulatory and supervisory agencies that have an interest in ensuring the soundness and stability of the Islamic financial services industry. It also strives to develop prudential standards in accordance with the unique features of Islamic financial institutions in coordination with the existing standard-setting bodies. The IFSB has begun the development of two prudential standards for the Islamic financial services industry: the Capital Adequacy and Risk Management standards. These two standards are expected to be issued by early 2005. Preparation of a standard on corporate governance is in the offing. The standards being prepared by the IFSB are to follow a lengthy process which involves, among others, the issuance of an exposure draft and, where necessary, the holding of a public hearing. Through this process IFSB expects to contribute towards the development of a robust and resilient Islamic financial system which can effectively preserve financial stability and contribute to balanced growth and development. That will also facilitate integration of the Islamic financial system as a viable component of the global financial system.

The International Islamic Rating Agency

Market discipline is important for an efficient and stable financial system. In this regard, external rating systems and accounting standards play a vital role in improving the availability of information to depositors, bankers and regulators. Existing conventional rating systems are primarily concerned with the financial strength of counterparties and ignore compliance with the *Sharīʿah* requirements. Since non-compliance of even a financially sound Islamic bank with the *Sharīʿah* requirements can be a serious cause of systemic instability, the need for an Islamic rating agency has always been felt necessary. Keeping this need in mind, an International Islamic Rating Agency (IIRA) was incorporated in Bahrain in October 2002. The IIRA will also scrutinize *Sharīʿah* aspects of financial institutions and products, which will be of major importance to the Islamic financial industry bearing in mind the global character/appeal of the new international agency. An internationally-recognized rating will give these institutions the credibility and the transparency they need to deal with the international market. As a specialized rating agency, the IIRA will be complementary to the existing agencies, adding value to the market. By assessing fiduciary relationships and the credit risk inherent in any instrument or issuer, the IIRA will help create a higher degree of confidence and acceptability of products among the players in the industry.

Other institutions

An account of the history of Islamic banking (see Box 4.1) would not be complete without mentioning various academic developments relating to

Box 4.1 **Time line for the development of the Islamic financial industry**

1940–	Critique of interest from Islamic perspective
1950–60	• Muslim economists offer ideas for interest-free banking possibilities • Non-bank applications of interest-free finance start
1960–70	• Profit-sharing models of interest-free banking defined • Experiments of bank-like institutions start (the Mit Ghamr experience in Egypt) • Trade-based modes of Islamic finance developed
1970–80	• First Islamic commercial bank (Dubai Islamic Bank) established • First Islamic international multilateral development finance institution (IDB) established in Jeddah • Pakistan declares its resolve to Islamize entire financial system • New modes of Islamic finance developed
1980–90	• Islamic banking industry witnesses very rapid growth; passes $100 billion mark • Two more countries (Iran and Sudan) declare intention to Islamize entire financial systems • Islamic investment funds start • Conventional banks including major international banks start Islamic products/windows • Development of new modes of Islamic finance continue • Academic institutions around the world start Islamic finance teaching • IMF, World Bank get involved
1990–00	• Islamic investment funds show phenomenal growth • Dow Jones announces Islamic indices • Existing Islamic banks grow and new ones established • Asset-based Islamic financial products developed • Islamic secondary markets start • Several support institutions established • Accounting standards for Islamic banks start
2000–	• Development of Islamic financial architecture continues • Accounting, regulatory and control issues gather steam • Islamic Financial Services Board (IFSB) established • First Islamic Rating Agency established • Public sector resource mobilization through Islamic modes gains momentum

study and research in the area. Interest in Islamic banking and finance is not limited to matters of practice only: an increasing number of universities are offering courses and in some cases full programmes in this field. These include universities in the Muslim world as well as other countries. Since the early 1980s, European and American academic circles have also been taking a keen interest in the subject. In the USA, Harvard University has an active research programme in this field. An annual Harvard Forum on Islamic Finance was initiated in 1998 to provide a forum for academic discourse to scholars coming from all over the world. Rice University, Houston in Texas, has established a Chair in Islamic Economics. In the UK, Loughborough University is offering an MSc in Islamic banking. Durham University also offers a Master's degree in Islamic finance. Portsmouth University has joined hands with the Markfield Institute of Higher Education established by the Islamic Foundation UK in offering Master's and PhD degrees in Islamic finance. A large number of PhD theses have been written on the subject in many Western universities. Prominent Western scholars and institutions are actively contributing books and articles in the area. Several professional journals are also being issued,[19] and several international seminars and conferences are held every year. Prominent professional associations, including the American Economic Association and the Western Economic Association, have also held dedicated sessions on Islamic economics and banking where important contributions have been made.

Conclusion

Serious research work in the past half-century has established that Islamic banking is not only feasible and viable; it is an efficient and productive way of financial intermediation. The theoretical development of the Islamic banking model in the 1950s and 1960s was followed by the establishment of Islamic financial institutions which began in the early 1960s. What started as a small rural banking experiment in the remote villages of Egypt in 1963 has now reached a level where almost all the major international banks are offering Islamic banking products. The practice of Islamic banking has spread east to Indonesia and Malaysia and west towards Europe and America. The Islamic financial industry is now worth hundreds of billions of dollars.

While the Islamic financial system is still in its early stages of development, various elements of the system and institutions are fast coming into existence. There are now about 70 Islamic banks working in different socio-economic milieus not including banks in Iran and Sudan, the two countries which have embarked upon the full Islamization of their financial systems. In addition, there are more than 40 conventional banks which are operating Islamic banking windows. Several prominent international banks are offering Islamic products, mostly in the form of mutual funds working on a *Sharīʿah*-compatible basis. Altogether, there are 200 Islamic investment funds. Some 70 Islamic insurance companies are also working around the globe. Many support institutions have recently started functioning. Thus, various components of the Islamic financial system are now available in different parts of the world in varying depth and quality. A detailed and integrated system of Islamic banking and finance is gradually evolving. It is now a reality accepted and respected by the international community.

Appendix 4.1 List of known Islamic banks (2004)*

#	Name of bank	Country
1	Arab Albanian Islamic Bank	Albania
2	Banque Al-Baraka D'Algérie	Algeria
3	ABC Islamic Bank (EC)	Bahrain
4	Al-Baraka Islamic Commercial Banks EC	Bahrain
5	Al-Khaleej Islamic Investment Bank (BSC) EC	Bahrain
6	Al-Amin Bank BSC (EC)	Bahrain
7	Al-Baraka Islamic Investment Bank BSC (EC)	Bahrain
8	Arab Islamic Bank EC	Bahrain
9	Bahrain Islamic Bank BSC	Bahrain
10	Citi Islamic Investment Bank EC	Bahrain
11	First Islamic Investment Bank EC	Bahrain
12	Gulf Finance House (BSC) EC	Bahrain
13	Gulf International Bank	Bahrain
14	International Investment Bank BSC (EC)	Bahrain
15	Investors Bank EC	Bahrain
16	Khaleej Finance & Investment BSC (C)	Bahrain
17	Kuwait Finance House (Bahrain) BSC (C)	Bahrain
18	Kuwait Turkish Evkaf Finance House	Bahrain
19	Noriba Bank BSC	Bahrain
20	Shamil Bank of Bahrain EC (previously Faysal Islamic Bank of Bahrain)	Bahrain
21	Al-Baraka Bank Bangladesh Ltd	Bangladesh
22	Al-Arafah Islami Bank Ltd, Dhaka	Bangladesh
23	Islami Bank Bangladesh, Dhaka	Bangladesh
24	Shahjalal Bank Ltd, Dhaka	Bangladesh
25	Shamil Bank of Bahrain, Dhaka	Bangladesh
26	Social Investment Bank Ltd, Dhaka	Bangladesh
27	The Oriental Bank Ltd, Dhaka	Bangladesh

#	Name of bank	Country
28	Islamic Bank of Brunei Berhad	Brunei Darussalam
29	Islamic Development Bank of Brunei Berhad	Brunei Darussalam
30	Egyptian Saudi Finance Bank	Egypt
31	Faisal Islamic Bank of Egypt	Egypt
32	Islamic International Bank for Investment & Development	Egypt
33	Arab Gambian Islamic Bank	Gambia
34	Banque Islamique de Guinée	Guinea
35	Bank Muʿāmalāt Indonesia	Indonesia
36	Bank Syariah Mandiri	Indonesia
37	Iraqi Bank for Investment & Development	Iraq
38	Islamic International Arab Bank PLC	Jordan
39	Jordan Islamic Bank for Finance and Investment	Jordan
40	Kuwait Finance House	Kuwait
41	Bank Islam Malaysia Berhad	Malaysia
42	Bank Muʿāmalāt Malaysia Berhad	Malaysia
43	Banque Islamique de Niger pour le Commerce et l'Investissement (BINCI)	Niger
44	Al-Baraka Islamic Bank	Pakistan
45	Faysal Bank Ltd	Pakistan
46	First Standard Investment Bank Ltd	Pakistan
47	Meezan Bank Limited	Pakistan
48	Al-Aqsa Islamic Bank	Palestine
49	Arab Islamic Bank	Palestine
50	Palestine Islamic Bank	Palestine
51	Qatar International Islamic Bank	Qatar
52	Qatar Islamic Bank	Qatar
53	Badr-Forte Bank	Russian Federation
54	Al-Rajhi Banking & Investment Corporation	Saudi Arabia
55	Bank Aljazira	Saudi Arabia
56	Islamic Bank of Senegal	Senegal
57	Beit et Tamweel Al-Saudi Al-Tunisi (BEST)	Tunisia
58	Al-Baraka Turk Ozel Finans Kurumu AS	Turkey
59	Anadolu Finans Kurumu AS	Turkey
60	Asya Finans Kurumu AS	Turkey
61	Family Finans Kurumu AS	Turkey
62	Kuwait Turkish Awqāf Finance House	Turkey
63	Abu Dhabi Islamic Bank	UAE
64	Dubai Islamic Bank	UAE

(Continued)

#	Name of bank	Country
65	National Bank of Sharjah	UAE
66	Islamic Bank for Finance and Investment	Yemen
67	Saba Islamic Bank	Yemen
68	Shamil Bank of Yemen & Bahrain	Yemen
69	Tadhamon International Islamic Bank	Yemen

* This list does not include Islamic banks in Iran and Sudan where all banks work according to the Islamic system. Islamic banking windows in conventional banks are listed separately in Appendix 4.4.

Appendix 4.2 List of major players in Islamic funds market (2004)

#	Name of company	Main domicile
1	Oasis Asset Management	Australia
2	Permal Group (Worms & Cie)	France
3	First Investment Company	Kuwait
4	Kuwait Finance House	Kuwait
5	National Bank of Kuwait	Kuwait
6	The International Investor	Kuwait
7	Amana Saham Kedah	Malaysia
8	Amānah Saham Darul Iman	Malaysia
9	BIMB Unit Trust Management Berhad	Malaysia
10	SBB Mutual Berhad (formerly known as BHLB Pacific Trust)	Malaysia
11	Qatar Islamic Bank	Qatar
12	Al-Rajhi Banking & Investment Corporation	Saudi Arabia
13	Al-Tawfeek Co. for Investment Funds (Al-Baraka Group)	Saudi Arabia
14	Faisal Finance Group	Saudi Arabia
15	National Commercial Bank	Saudi Arabia
16	Saudi Economic and Development Co. (SEDCO)	Saudi Arabia
17	UBS Global Asset Management	Switzerland
18	Saturna Capital Corporation	UAE
19	The Hongkong and Shanghai Banking Corporation (HSBC)	UK
20	Citibank NA	USA
21	Wafra Investment Advisors	USA
22	Wellington Fund Management	USA

Appendix 4.3 List of Islamic insurance companies (2004)

#	Name of company	Country
1	Australia Takāful Insurance Inc.	Australia
2	Al-Salam Islamic Takāful Company EC	Bahrain
3	Al-Dhaman Islamic (Insurance) Company EC	Bahrain
4	Bahrain Islamic Insurance Co.	Bahrain
5	Bahrain Takāful International Company	Bahrain
6	Islamic Insurance & Reinsurance EC	Bahrain
7	Takāful Islamic Insurance Company EC	Bahrain
8	Takāful International Company BSC	Bahrain
9	Far East Islami Life Insurance Company	Bangladesh
10	First Takāful Insurance Company	Bangladesh
11	Islami Commercial Insurance Company Ltd	Bangladesh
12	Islami Insurance Bangladesh Ltd, Dhaka	Bangladesh
13	Padma Islami Life Insurance Company Ltd	Bangladesh
14	Prime Islami Life Insurance Ltd	Bangladesh
15	Takāful Islami Insurance Ltd	Bangladesh
16	Takāful Islamic Bank of Brunei Berhad	Brunei
17	Takāful Islamic Development Bank of Brunei Berhad	Brunei
18	Insurance Islamic Taib Sendirian Berhad (IITSB)	Brunei
19	Metropolitan Insurance Company Ltd	Ghana
20	PT Asuransi Syariah Mubarakah	Indonesia
21	PT Asuransi Takāful Keluaga	Indonesia
22	PT Syarikat Takāful Indonesia	Indonesia
23	Islamic Insurance Company Plc	Jordan
24	Takāful Insurance Company	Kuwait
25	Takafol SA, Luxembourg	Luxembourg
26	Mayban Takāful Berhad	Malaysia
27	MNI Takāful Sdn Berhard	Malaysia
28	Syarikat Takāful Malaysia Berhad	Malaysia
29	Takāful Ikhlas Sdn. Berhad	Malaysia
30	Takāful Nasional Sdn. Berhad	Malaysia
31	Qatar Islamic Insurance Company	Qatar
32	Al-Rajhi Islamic Company for Co-operative Insurance EC	Saudi Arabia
33	Islamic Arab Insurance Company EC	Saudi Arabia
34	Islamic Corporation for the Insurance of Investment and Export Credit	Saudi Arabia
35	Islamic Takāful & Retākaful (Bahamas) Ltd	Saudi Arabia
36	National Company for Cooperative Insurance	Saudi Arabia

(Continued)

#	Name of company	Country
37	Takāful Islamic Insurance Company	Saudi Arabia
38	Ampro Holdings, Singapore	Singapore
39	Arabian Malaysia Takāful Company EC	Singapore
40	Keppel Insurance (Singapore)	Singapore
41	Syarikat Takāful Singapura	Singapore
42	Beit Laadat Ettameen Tounsi Saudi	Tunisia
43	Abu Dhabi National Takāful Co.	UAE
44	Dubai Islamic Insurance and Reinsurance Company (AMAN)	UAE
45	Islamic Arab Insurance Company of Saudi Arabia	UAE
46	Takāful UK Ltd	UK
47	Yemen Islamic Insurance Company	Yemen

Appendix 4.4 List of Islamic banking windows in conventional banks (2004)

#	Name of bank	Country
1	Arab Bangladesh Bank Ltd, Dhaka	Bangladesh
2	The City Bank Ltd, Dhaka	Bangladesh
3	Prime Bank Ltd, Dhaka	Bangladesh
4	Southeast Bank Ltd, Dhaka	Bangladesh
5	Dhaka Bank Ltd, Dhaka	Bangladesh
6	Exim Bank Ltd, Dhaka	Bangladesh
7	The Premier Bank Ltd, Dhaka	Bangladesh
8	Bosna Bank International	Bosnia and Herzegovina
9	Bank Misr	Egypt
10	Bank Al-Nile	Egypt
11	Bank Qanat Al-Suwais	Egypt
12	National Bank of Egypt	Egypt
13	National Bank for Development	Egypt
14	Bank for Trade and Development	Egypt
15	United Egyptian Bank	Egypt
16	Port Said National Development Bank	Egypt
17	Gulf Egyptian Bank	Egypt
18	United Arabic Bank for Investment & Development	Egypt
19	PT Bank BNI	Indonesia

#	Name of bank	Country
20	PT Bank IFI	Indonesia
21	PT Bank Jabar	Indonesia
22	PT Bank Bukopin	Indonesia
23	PT Bank Danamon Indonesia, Tbk	Indonesia
24	PT Bank Rakyat Indonesia (Persero)	Indonesia
25	PT Bank International Indonesia	Indonesia
26	The Hongkong and Shanghai Banking Corporation Ltd (HSBC)	Indonesia
27	Affin Bank Berhad	Malaysia
28	Alliance Bank Malaysia Berhad	Malaysia
29	Am Bank Berhad	Malaysia
30	Citibank Berhad	Malaysia
31	EON Bank Berhad	Malaysia
32	Hong Leong Bank Berhad	Malaysia
33	HSBC Bank Malaysia Berhad	Malaysia
34	Malaysian Banking Berhad	Malaysia
35	OCBC Bank (Malaysia) Berhad	Malaysia
36	Public Bank Berhad	Malaysia
37	RHB Bank Berhad	Malaysia
38	Southern Bank Berhad	Malaysia
39	Standard Chartered Bank Malaysia Berhad	Malaysia
40	Muslim Commercial Bank Ltd	Pakistan
41	Cairo-Amman Bank	Palestine
42	National Commercial Bank	Saudi Arabia
43	The Hongkong and Shanghai Banking Corporation Ltd (HSBC)	UAE

5
The Performance of Islamic Banks

There are several aspects of a firm's operations that need to be watched by financial managers, who commonly use many ratios. In this chapter we employ some of these ratios to evaluate the performance of Islamic banks. For this purpose, the same sample of twelve Islamic banks as was chosen for the analysis in Chapter 4 will be employed. We will attempt to evaluate Islamic banks with respect to their soundness, prudence, effectiveness in the use of funds, economy and profitability.

Soundness

The soundness of a bank depends on its ability to meet its obligations in a crisis situation. This is usually measured by the capital–assets ratio. There are three major reasons for a bank to monitor its capital–assets ratio. First, regulatory authorities require a minimum amount of bank capital. Second, the size of the bank capital has some safety implications as it provides some cushioning, albeit limited, against the possibility that the bank cannot satisfy its obligations to its creditors. Third, the amount of capital affects the rate of return to the bank equity holders. There is a trade-off between the return to the owners and the safety of the bank; given return on assets, the smaller the bank capital, the higher the rate of return to the owners of the bank. Therefore, the owners of the bank have a natural tendency to keep lower capital–asset ratios. However, the lower capital–asset ratios increase the risk of bank failures. It is for this reason that the regulatory agencies prescribe certain minimum capital–asset ratios. According to the Basel Agreement (1988), the Basel Committee on Banking Supervision has defined international standards on banks' capital adequacy. According to these standards, a bank must meet two capital requirements: it must have a 'core' or Tier 1 capital (stockholder equity capital) of at least 4 per cent of total risk-adjusted assets, and total capital (Tier 1 capital plus Tier 2 capital, which is made up of loan loss reserves and subordinated debt)[1] of at least 8 per cent of total risk-adjusted assets.

In the absence of data on loan loss reserves and subordinated debt in the case of Islamic banks, and also the 'risk adjustment' calculations, it is not possible to reach a judgement with respect to 'total capital' requirements. Therefore, for our purposes we assume that the ratio of total assets to the sum of paid-up capital, reserves and undistributed profit should lie in between Tier 1 and Tier 2 capital standards (i.e., 6 per cent). Against this standard, the overall capital assets ratio for Islamic banks was 10.5 per cent during 1990–6 and 12.2 per cent during 1996–2002. Not only is this figure well above the Basel Standards, but it has been increasing over time as the average for the later period is higher than the former. However, not all the banks are as sound as these figures would have us believe. The disaggregated figures given in Table 5.1 present a slightly different picture.

Two things need special mention: first, in the case of two banks, the Al-Baraka Investment Bank, Bahrain (BKBN) and the Faysal Islamic Bank,

Table 5.1 Capital–asset ratios for Islamic banks (1990–2002)

	Abbreviation	Average (%)		
		1990–6	1996–2002	1990–2002
Al-Rajhi Banking & Investment Corporation, Saudi Arabia	Al-Rajhi	14.73	13.61	14.09
Kuwait Finance House, Kuwait	KFH	9.17	17.06	12.87
Dubai Islamic Bank, UAE	DIB	6.29	7.59	6.85
Qatar Islamic Bank, Qatar	QIB	6.83	7.36	7.09
Bank Islam Malaysia Berhad, Malaysia	BIMB	8.20	10.82	9.69
Jordan Islamic Bank, Jordan	JIB	5.71	6.95	6.27
Bahrain Islamic Bank, Bahrain	BIB	8.60	14.02	11.41
Islami Bank Bangladesh, Bangladesh	IBBG	4.40	5.90	5.00
Faisal Islamic Bank, Egypt	FIBE	3.95	3.47	3.77
Faysal Islamic Bank, Bahrain	FIBB	31.32	NA	NA
Al-Baraka Turkish Finance House, Turkey	BKTF	3.61	5.66	4.75
Al-Baraka Islamic Investment Bank, Bahrain	BKBN	37.05	28.22	32.34
Simple average		11.65	10.97	10.38
SD		11.01	7.08	8.05
Weighted average		10.49	12.23	11.28

SD = standard deviation; NA = not available.
Source: Calculated by authors. Source data are from annual reports.

Bahrain (FIBB), the ratio is 30 per cent or more which is unusually high. The reason for this is that these banks 'manage' a large amount of *muḍārabah* funds that are treated as an off-balance sheet item. Though the owners of these funds are liable to share losses, some equity is still being kept to support the assets generated by these funds. If we exclude these two banks and calculate the average ratio for the other ten banks, it comes to 7.15 and 9.22 per cent respectively for the two subperiods, which is still above the Basel Standard.[2]

Second, the overall satisfactory ratio conceals the fact that there are several banks for which this ratio is below the minimum international standard. The number of such banks during 1990–6 was four. The situation is better in the second period when only two banks appear undercapitalized. From these numbers and the increase in total ratio over time, we can conclude that, in general, Islamic banks are well-capitalized and/or are becoming increasingly so.

Prudence

Banks, like other corporations, are profit-seeking institutions. However, unlike other corporations they cannot put all their money into profit-earning assets.[3] Banking business crucially depends on the confidence of the depositors in the ability of banks to meet their demands if and when they want to withdraw their deposits; the inability of the banks to do so can lead to a crisis of confidence and consequent failure. Therefore banks, unlike other corporations, are legally required to keep a certain portion of their deposits in 'liquid' form. In most cases, banks would like to keep some extra reserves in addition to legal reserve requirements. Since liquidity and profitability are two divergent objectives, 'prudence' demands a delicate balancing act. In the following paragraphs we judge Islamic banks on this criterion.

For balance sheet analysis of corporations one of the ratios usually measured is the 'current ratio'. This ratio measures the ability of a firm to meet its current liabilities. In the case of banks, the current liabilities are the demand deposits. Therefore, in the case of banks, the equivalent of what is known as the 'current ratio'[4] in financial statement analysis would be the 'liquidity ratio': that is, the ratio of liquid assets to demand deposits. However, since time deposits could also be of short maturity and (in many cases) withdrawals from such accounts are possible by means of a short advance notice of withdrawal, we have calculated the liquidity ratio as follows:

$$\text{Liquidity ratio} = \frac{\text{Cash and accounts with banks}}{\text{Total deposits}}$$

There is a general impression that Islamic banks have excess liquidity. In a survey of opinions of practical bankers and scholars of Islamic banking conducted by this author in 1998, more than 60 per cent of the respondents believed that Islamic banks were suffering from excess liquidity, implying that they do not have enough investment opportunities. Similarly, Babikir (2001) argues that apart from legal reserve requirements, Islamic banks have large amounts of short-term idle balances which earn no return. In order to check the hypothesis that Islamic banks have excess liquidity, we need first to determine what 'excess' liquidity means.

As stated above, unlike other firms, banks are legally required by the regulating agencies to keep a minimum amount of liquidity. These are known as 'legal reserve requirements'. The ratio of legal reserves varies from country to country. In the case of countries from where our sample is drawn, this ratio on average is around 12 per cent of deposits.[5] In addition, it is customary for all banks to keep some more liquid assets as 'prudent reserves'. Therefore, for the purpose of this study we can set the desired liquidity ratio at around 15 per cent depending upon the ratio of current deposits to total deposits. Within this range, the higher the ratio of current deposits to total deposits for a bank, the higher the desired liquidity ratio.

As shown in Table 5.2, the industry average for Islamic banking during 1990–6 works out at 18.47 per cent, which seems to lend some support to the excess liquidity hypothesis. However, one cannot say the same for the 1996–2002 period when the ratio was 15.83 per cent. Moreover, we need to

Table 5.2 Liquidity ratios for Islamic banks (1990–2002)

	Average (%)		
	1990–6	**1996–2002**	**1990–2002**
Al-Rajhi Banking & Investment Corporation, Saudi Arabia	16.89	16.10	16.51
Kuwait Finance House, Kuwait	14.38	7.81	11.32
Dubai Islamic Bank, UAE	15.81	11.60	13.53
Qatar Islamic Bank, Qatar	8.74	12.48	10.52
Bank Islam Malaysia Berhad, Malaysia	12.78	28.72	20.56
Jordan Islamic Bank, Jordan	38.16	39.30	39.63
Bahrain Islamic Bank, Bahrain	4.86	5.60	5.32
Islami Bank Bangladesh, Bangladesh	32.96	30.75	32.65
Faisal Islamic Bank, Egypt	28.59	11.73	20.23
Faysal Islamic Bank, Bahrain	132.31	NA	NA
Al-Baraka Turkish Finance House, Turkey	12.91	16.25	14.85
Al-Baraka Islamic Investment Bank, Bahrain	26.52	25.68	26.05
Simple average	28.74	18.73	19.20
SD	34.15	10.77	10.18
Weighted average	18.47	15.83	17.28

NA = not available; SD = standard deviation.
Source: Calculated by authors. Source data are from annual reports.

consider the fact that in the case of Islamic banks the possibilities of borrowing from the central bank in case of need are either not available or not desirable due to involvement of interest, so it is prudent for them to remain relatively more liquid. Considering these factors, we do not find any strong support for the 'excess liquidity hypothesis' even for the first period. It may also be noted that Islamic banks have clearly improved their liquidity management over time. More importantly, the excess liquidity phenomenon is not as widespread as believed. While the industry average was a little higher than desired during 1990–6, most of the banks were either close to the desired level or even lower. In the next section we will employ a simple 'benchmarking technique' to examine the hypothesis from another angle; therefore, let us delay a final judgement on this matter until then.

Effectiveness

Another aspect of performance evaluation is to see how best a bank is using its resources. In order to evaluate Islamic banks on this score, we have calculated what we call the 'deployment ratio', which is defined as follows:

$$\text{Deployment ratio} = \frac{\text{Total investment} + \text{Total deposits}}{\text{Total equity}}$$

Estimates for this ratio are given in Table 5.3.

The industry average for Islamic banks as whole has been around 90 per cent throughout the period, which is quite impressive. Even for the banks taken individually, the ratio is quite high for a vast majority of them. This is a clear proof that the absence of the interest rate mechanism is not hindering Islamic banks in making effective use of the resources at their disposal. Once again, in the next section we will see how these ratios compare with conventional banks.

Economy

Cost efficiency is one of the important criteria for the evaluation of banks' performance. For this purpose we use the standard cost to income ratio. Theoretically, no standard for this ratio is available in the academic literature. However, *The Banker* magazine publishes a list of the top 1,000 banks in the world every year, and has reported this ratio since 1997. We calculated the average ratios for the 1,000 banks for 1997–2002 to arrive at a benchmark indicator. These are given in Table 5.4.

Considering the figures given in Table 5.4, we can use 62 per cent as a simple 'benchmark' indicator for bank cost-efficiency. Against this standard, the overall weighted cost/income ratio for Islamic banks during 1990–6 was 53.51 per cent (see Table 5.5). It deteriorated to 58.28 per cent in the

Table 5.3 Deployment ratio for Islamic banks (1990–2002)

	Average (%)		
	1990–6	**1996–2002**	**1990–2002**
Al-Rajhi Banking & Investment Corporation, Saudi Arabia	98.46	95.07	96.80
Kuwait Finance House, Kuwait	90.25	97.21	93.71
Dubai Islamic Bank, UAE	91.73	93.18	92.90
Qatar Islamic Bank, Qatar	100.33	95.99	98.57
Bank Islam Malaysia Berhad, Malaysia	89.63	78.45	84.23
Jordan Islamic Bank, Jordan	74.95	77.75	75.75
Bahrain Islamic Bank, Bahrain	96.78	103.99	100.63
Islami Bank Bangladesh, Bangladesh	75.39	77.87	75.63
Faisal Islamic Bank, Egypt	85.11	100.80	92.44
Faysal Islamic Bank, Bahrain	65.78	NA	NA
Al-Baraka Turkish Finance House, Turkey	95.79	77.63	86.27
Al-Baraka Islamic Investment Bank, Bahrain	90.63	91.35	91.08
Simple average	87.90	89.94	89.82
SD	10.70	10.11	8.48
Weighted average	92.29	91.45	91.76

NA = not available; SD = standard deviation.
Source: Calculated by authors. Source data are from annual reports.

Table 5.4 Cost to income ratios for the top 1,000 banks in the world (1997–2002)

Year	**Mean cost to income ratio (%)**
1997	62.00
1998	60.47
1999	62.10
2000	60.88
2001	61.77
2002	63.71
Average	61.82

1996–2002 period. It is the latter figure that is closer to the period for which the top 1,000 banks' figure has been presented. It is still lower than the benchmark. However, when we look at the ratios for individual banks a different picture emerges. Only two out of twelve banks were up to (or better than) the standard. The overall average is pushed down largely because of the low ratio for Al-Rajhi which, being the largest bank in the sample, carries a lot of weight. The ratio for Al-Rajhi, in turn, is unusually low because it has no (or negligible) cost of funds. Almost all of its funds come

Table 5.5 Cost to income ratios for Islamic banks (1990–2002)

Bank	Cost/income ratio (%)		
	Average 1990–6	Average 1996–2002	Average 1990–2002
Al-Rajhi Banking & Investment Corporation, Saudi Arabia	35.27	32.09	33.98
Kuwait Finance House, Kuwait	77.23	60.36	69.37
Dubai Islamic Bank, UAE	72.11	77.96	74.89
Qatar Islamic Bank, Qatar	67.30	66.88	67.36
Bank Islam Malaysia Berhad, Malaysia	78.79	81.88	80.47
Jordan Islamic Bank, Jordan	75.12	76.48	75.86
Bahrain Islamic Bank, Bahrain	79.89	77.78	79.09
Islami Bank Bangladesh, Bangladesh	51.81	75.64	64.75
Faisal Islamic Bank, Egypt	61.53	82.20	73.51
Faysal Islamic Bank, Bahrain	56.47	77.86	68.33
Al-Baraka Turkish Finance House, Turkey	47.41	89.08	67.92
Al-Baraka Islamic Investment Bank, Bahrain	45.43	76.52	62.14
Simple average	62.36	72.89	68.14
SD	14.99	14.76	12.14
Weighted average	53.51	58.28	56.22

SD = standard deviation.
Source: Calculated by authors. Source data are from annual reports.

from current accounts on which no return is paid. When we look at the simple average figures for the ratio, these were considerably higher, 62.36 and 72.89 respectively for the two periods, both of which are higher than the benchmark. Therefore, we conclude that, in general, Islamic banks do not seem to be working in a cost-effective manner. However, one should bear in mind that Islamic banks are relatively small compared with the aforementioned comparator group, so if banking is characterized by scale economies they may be at a disadvantage on the cost side. Later in the chapter we will compare Islamic banks with a 'peer group' which should perhaps give us a better idea of the efficiency of Islamic banks as this peer group are of similar size.

Profitability

There are several ratios that are typically used to measure the profitability of firms. The two most often used are the rate of return on assets (ROA) and the rate of return on equity (ROE). We will now analyse the profitability of Islamic banks on the basis of these two measures.

Rate of return on assets

The average rate of return on assets for the period 1990–6 for the Islamic banks was 1.63 per cent. The same rate stood at 1.29 per cent during the 1996–2002 period, indicating a decline in profitability. In order to make some judgement on the performance of Islamic banks, once again we need an objective benchmark. For this purpose, we calculated the ROA for the top 1,000 banks. It worked out at 1.0 per cent during 1990–6 (see Table 5.6). When we compare the performance of Islamic banks against this benchmark, we find that six out of the twelve Islamic banks posted higher rates than this (see Table 5.7). Similarly, the ROA for the top 1,000 banks in the world during 1996–2002 was 1.1 per cent. During this period, five out of the twelve Islamic banks posted higher returns than this. Overall, the average for Islamic banks in both periods was higher than the world average.

Rate of return on equity

The average rate of return on equity for the period 1990–6 for the Islamic banks was 15.3 per cent. During the second period it decreased to 13.3 per cent. As for benchmark, the rate of return on equity for the top 1,000 banks in the world was 15.7 per cent during 1990–6. Five out of the twelve Islamic banks scored higher rates than that. In the second period, the average for the top 1,000 banks in the world was 14.4 per cent. In this period there were only

Table 5.6 Profitability ratios for the top 1,000 banks in the world (1990–2002)

Year	ROA (%)	ROE (%)
1990	0.8	15.3
1991	0.9	14.2
1992	0.9	15.1
1993	1.1	16.7
1994	1.1	16.4
1995	1.1	16.0
1996	1.1	16.4
1997	1.1	15.7
1998	0.9	10.9
1999	1.2	15.2
2000	1.1	15.2
2001	1.1	13.9
2002	1.1	13.2
Average (1990–6)	1.0	15.7
Average (1996–2002)	1.1	14.4
Average (1990–2002)	1.0	14.9

Source: Calculated by authors.

Table 5.7 Profitability ratios for Islamic banks (1990–2002)

Bank	ROA (%)			ROE (%)		
	1990–6	Average 1996–2002	1990–2002	1990–6	Average 1996–2002	1990–2002
Al-Rajhi	3.87	3.49	3.66	25.92	25.52	25.69
KFH	0.73	2.43	1.52	–0.78	14.25	6.10
DIB	0.77	0.96	0.87	12.05	3.90	7.83
QIB	0.55	1.51	0.98	2.58	20.52	10.49
BIMB	1.12	0.50	0.79	14.14	6.45	9.96
JIB	0.92	0.46	0.67	17.55	6.56	12.00
BIB	0.94	1.25	1.09	10.99	9.66	10.21
IBBG	1.51	1.04	1.24	33.66	18.14	25.86
FIBE	0.15	0.22	0.20	2.55	5.98	4.49
FIBB	5.66	NA	3.93	18.05	NA	NA
BKTF	1.61	1.02	1.31	42.43	28.60	35.01
BKBN	1.67	1.37	1.43	4.76	4.83	4.49
Average	1.63	1.29	1.47	15.33	13.13	13.83

NA = not available.
Source: Calculated by authors. Source data are from annual reports.

four Islamic banks with ROE higher than this. Overall, the rate of return on equity achieved by Islamic banks was slightly lower than the world average. Also note the substantial variation among the Islamic banks over the period, perhaps reflecting markedly different operating environments in the various countries in which the banks operated.

From the evidence given above, it appears that Islamic banks' performance, in terms of profitability in general, at least meets (or even surpasses) international 'standards'. However, it should be noted that conventional banks' depositors are guaranteed their principal amounts, and hence bear less risk than Islamic banks' depositors, and so the depositors of Islamic banks would genuinely expect a higher rate of return to compensate for the extra risk. The current rates of profit on assets of the Islamic banks may not be enough to meet that expectation. As a matter of fact, if one looks at the rates of return offered to depositors, it can be seen that in general these are not attractive. In many cases these rates are even lower than the market rate of interest. Therefore, we can conclude that while Islamic banking is quite attractive as a business, there is a need to make the rates of return paid to depositors more attractive. In the long run Islamic banks cannot and should not rely merely on the 'loyalty' of their customers for religious reasons. They must be able to pay them more than the market rate of interest by an amount equivalent to a risk premium for sharing risk with the bank.

Islamic and conventional banks: a comparative analysis

In this section the performance of Islamic banks has been evaluated *vis-à-vis* conventional banks. In section 5.6.2, the performance of the top ten Islamic banks is compared with the top ten banks in the world, and four regions.

Peer group comparison

For the peer group analysis, a sample of twelve conventional banks was chosen for comparative analysis. The banks were chosen from the same countries as the sample of Islamic banks and in the same number. An attempt was also made to choose banks of roughly similar size. In this way both geographical and size considerations were controlled. The names of the banks chosen for the comparison are given in Table 5.8.

Since the data for the peer group banks has been taken from a secondary source, *The Banker's Almanac*, the data were not as detailed as in the case of Islamic banks. The income statements' data were not available before 1993. Therefore, for cost and profit ratios, the first period for comparison was adjusted to 1993–6 instead of 1990–6.

Growth analysis

The rates of growth for four important variables are shown in Table 5.9. It may be noted that in the case of all variables, the rates of growth achieved

Table 5.8 Sample for peer group comparison

No.	Islamic banks	Conventional banks
1	Al-Rajhi Banking & Investment Corporation, Saudi Arabia	Riyadh Bank, Saudi Arabia
2	Kuwait Finance House, Kuwait	National Bank of Kuwait SAK, Kuwait
3	Al-Baraka Islamic Investment Bank, Bahrain	Arab Banking Corporation (BSC), Bahrain
4	Bahrain Islamic Bank, Bahrain	Bank of Bahrain and Kuwait BSC, Bahrain
5	Faysal Islamic Bank, Bahrain	National Bank of Bahrain BSC, Bahrain
6	Faisal Islamic Bank, Egypt	Egyptian American Bank, Egypt
7	Dubai Islamic Bank, UAE	Mashreq Bank PSC, UAE
8	Jordan Islamic Bank, Jordan	Bank of Jordan plc, Jordan
9	Qatar Islamic Bank, Qatar	Qatar National Bank SAQ, Qatar
10	Islami Bank Bangladesh, Bangladesh	Arab Bangladesh Bank, Bangladesh
11	Bank Islam Malaysia Berhad, Malaysia	Malayan Bank Berhad, Malaysia
12	Al-Baraka Turkish Finance House, Turkey	Finansbank AS, Turkey

Table 5.9 Comparative annual growth rates (%)

	Total equity		Total deposits		Total investments		Total assets	
	Islamic banks	Peer group	Islamic banks	Peer group	Islamic banks	Peer group	Islamic banks	Peer group
1990–6	10.52	7.07	5.47	6.29	8.58	5.15	8.16	7.66
1996–2002	9.27	4.15	11.21	5.08	10.44	7.03	10.93	4.70
1990–2002	9.89	5.60	8.30	5.68	9.50	6.09	9.54	6.17

Source: Calculated by authors. Source data are from annual reports for the Islamic banks and *The Banker's Almanac* for the peer group banks.

by Islamic banks are higher than conventional banks in the peer group during the two subperiods as well as for the entire period, with the exception of only one entry.

The rate of growth of total equity for the whole period was 9.89 per cent per annum in the case of Islamic banks as against 5.6 per cent for the peer group. The rate of growth of total deposits in the case of peer group banks was 6.29 per cent per annum during 1990–6, whereas the same rate was 5.47 per cent in the case of Islamic banks. This is the only exceptional case where the rate of growth achieved by the conventional banks was higher than the Islamic banks. However, the rate of growth in deposits declined to 5.08 per cent in the case of conventional banks for the second period while that of the Islamic banks increased to 11.21 per cent, suggesting the increased attractiveness of Islamic deposit services over the period.

A similar trend is observed in the case of total investments, which grew at a rate of 8.58 per cent during 1990–6 for the Islamic banks while the peer group banks witnessed a rate of growth of only 5.15 per cent. During the second period growth in investment in the case of Islamic banks improved for both groups, to 10.44 per cent and to 7.03 per cent for Islamic and conventional banks respectively. Yet Islamic banks outperformed conventional banks throughout the period.

In the case of total assets, the Islamic banks again posted a higher rate of growth in both periods. During 1990–6, it was 8.16 per cent as against 7.66 per cent, while during 1996–2002 it was 10.93 per cent for Islamic banks, as against only 4.7 per cent for the conventional banks.

Ratio analysis

Some of the key ratios used in the balance sheet analysis have been computed for both the groups and are reported in Table 5.10.

The first of these ratios is the capital to asset ratio, which measures the strength of the banks. The weighted average capital to asset ratio for the Islamic banks for the 1990–6 period works out at 10.49 per cent, while this ratio for the same period was 8.72 per cent for the conventional banks.

Table 5.10 Comparative ratios (%)

Ratio	Islamic banks	Peer group
Capital to asset ratio		
1990–6	10.49	8.72
1996–2002	12.23	8.66
1990–2002	11.28	8.71
Liquidity ratio		
1990–6	18.47	31.25
1996–2002	15.83	31.10
1990–2002	17.28	30.60
Deployment ratio		
1990–6	92.29	73.62
1996–2002	91.45	77.07
1990–2002	91.76	75.59
Cost to income ratio		
1993–6	49.14	62.87
1996–2002	58.28	65.53
1993–2002	55.28	64.81
ROA		
1993–6	2.16	1.28
1996–2002	2.21	1.36
1993–2002	2.17	1.33
ROE		
1993–6	19.29	14.99
1996–2002	18.06	15.69
1993–2002	18.34	15.40

Source: Calculated by authors.

There has been no change in this ratio for the second period in the case of conventional banks, while in the case of Islamic banks the ratio has increased to 12.23 in the second period, widening the lead of Islamic banks over time.

With regard to liquidity, the comparative analysis given below allows us to conclusively reject the hypothesis that Islamic banks are suffering from excess liquidity. The liquidity ratio is in fact lower for the Islamic banks as compared to the peer group banks. This ratio for the whole period was 17.28 per cent in the case of Islamic banks as against 30.60 per cent for the peer group.

The Islamic banks also appear to have made a better use of resources. The deployment ratio is higher for the Islamic banks as compared to the conventional banks throughout the 1990–2002 period. Therefore we can conclusively state that the absence of the interest rate mechanism does not limit the Islamic banks when they are trying to make effective and profitable use of resources put at their disposal.

In terms of cost-effectiveness also the Islamic banks as a group perform better than the conventional banks, the cost to income ratio being 55.28 per cent for the Islamic banks as against 64.81 per cent for the conventional banks for 1993–2002. However, as noted earlier, the ratio for the Islamic banks is unduly pushed down because of the high weighting attached to Al-Rajhi Bank.

Both profitability ratios, ROA and ROE, were higher for Islamic banks throughout the period of analysis. However, the margin of difference was smaller during 1996–2002 as compared to 1993–6.

Top ten comparison

In this section, we present a brief comparison of the performance of the top ten Islamic banks with the top ten banks in terms of capital in the world and four regions. The data for conventional banks have been taken from *The Banker* magazine. Some key financial indicators for the year 2002 are given in Table 5.11 and discussed in the following paragraphs.

Capital–asset ratio

The capital–asset ratio for the top ten Islamic banks in 2002 was 11.12 per cent. While this average compares favourably with the top ten banks worldwide as well as in the four regions, it must be noted that bigger banks, in general, can afford to keep a lower capital–assets ratio because they have a lower risk of a run on the bank. Partly for the same reasons, regulators typically force smaller banks to hold more capital irrespective of minimum requirements. It should also be noted that under conventional banking systems, in addition to minimum capital–assets ratios, the depositors are protected (at least partially) by deposit insurance. Under the Islamic banking system, there is no deposit insurance in general. Therefore, the capital–asset ratio needs to be kept higher.[6] On the other hand, it must also be noted that higher capital adequacy ratios are needed to protect the rights of depositors in case of insolvency. One should keep in mind the fact that with Islamic banking only demand deposits are guaranteed, while investment deposits are not. Investment depositors are required to share in the loss of the bank,

Table 5.11 Key financial ratios: top ten banks, 2002 (%)

Region	Capital to asset ratio	Cost to income ratio	ROE	ROA
Top ten World	3.60	75.08	3.88	0.25
Top ten Asia	3.38	84.34	–14.06	–0.38
Top ten GCC	9.51	42.83	18.47	1.76
Top ten other Middle East	4.55	56.65	13.24	0.50
Top ten Europe & America	3.96	68.35	16.79	0.80
Top ten Islamic banks	11.12	43.83	15.56	1.75

Source: Calculated by authors from raw data in *The Banker*, July 2003.

if any,[7] so the liabilities of Islamic banks are automatically reduced in difficult periods. It should also be noticed that the capital–asset ratio for the top ten banks in the GCC region, the region where the bulk of Islamic banking resides, is fairly close to that of the top ten Islamic banks. Considering all relevant factors, we can conclude that the capital–asset ratio for Islamic banks as a group meets international standards. If anything, they are better capitalized.

Profit on assets

The average rate of return on assets for the top ten Islamic banks was 1.75 per cent in 2002. Though much higher than the world and three other regions' average, the rate is comparable to the corresponding rate for the commercial banks in the GCC region. However, it should be noted that conventional banks' depositors are guaranteed, and hence bear less risk than Islamic banks' depositors. Therefore, the latter would expect a higher rate of return to compensate for the extra risk. The current rate of profits on assets for the Islamic banks may not be enough to meet that expectation. Nevertheless, in a comparative framework, the performance of Islamic banks is not bad, though there seems to be a need for improvement. It should also be noted that the lower rates of profit for the top ten banks in the world as well as in Asia are due to Japanese banks posting losses, bringing the average rates down. These losses were mainly caused by bad debts. Therefore, one may conclude that Islamic banking as a model performs relatively well because its 'bad debts' problem is at least lower than that in various interest-based systems.

Return on equity

The average rate of return on capital for Islamic banks during 2002 was 15.56 per cent. This also compares quite favourably with the conventional banks. In addition to a better rate of return on capital, if one considers the fact that the capital–asset ratio of Islamic banks is higher than their counterparts, as mentioned above, one can conclude that Islamic banking as a business is doing reasonably well. We must, however, notice that the rate of return on equity for the top ten banks in the GCC region is higher than that of Islamic banks. With ROA roughly the same, this result emerges from higher capital in Islamic banks. Are they overcapitalized? Some of them might be, but one should not draw such a conclusion from the aggregate data, and the question of overcapitalization needs to be dealt with on a case-by-case basis.

Conclusion

The practice of Islamic banking over the last 30 years or so has shown that the model is not merely a theoretical construction in abstraction. All empirical studies to date show that in terms of performance, Islamic banks are by no means inferior to their conventional counterparts. As a matter of fact, most studies conclude that they usually show better results than conventional banks. Empirical analysis in this chapter confirms such findings. Islamic banking has shown tremendous growth throughout its existence. The high rates of growth witnessed by the industry are not based on any emotional reasons; the growth is derived from economic and financial fundamentals. Analysis of key performance ratios measuring soundness, effective use of resources, prudence, cost-efficiency and profitability shows that Islamic banks meet, and in several cases surpass, international standards. Benchmarking exercise for many performance measuring variables shows that Islamic banks have outperformed their conventional peers.

Several new results have emerged from this chapter. The following major conclusions need to be noted:

(1) The trend analysis points to a general and gradual slowdown in the growth of Islamic banking industry as compared to the 1980s. This is not unexpected. As any industry matures, its rate of growth usually tapers off. Four reasons have been identified for this trend. First, during the 1980s there were a lot of immobilized funds due to the fact that many Muslim clients do not want to be involved in any interest dealings. In the absence of a viable alternative, they were keeping their savings in private lockers, or similar. However, over the next 10–15 years, these savings found their way into the coffers of the Islamic banks. Accordingly the rate of growth of deposits started tapering off. Second, during 1990s an increasing number of conventional banks started offering Islamic products. It is quite likely that some of the deposits of the Islamic banks were diverted to these banks. Third, in the 1990s there was a trend for establishing Islamic mutual funds. Some of the deposits of the Islamic banks may have been diverted to these funds too. Finally the decline in the rate of growth is merely a statistical phenomenon. As the base gets bigger and bigger, it becomes increasingly difficult to maintain a given rate of growth. In absolute terms, the industry is still expanding at a handsome rate of about 10 per cent per annum.

(2) The evaluation of the performance of Islamic banks through a number of key ratios yields fairly satisfactory results. In general, Islamic banks are well-capitalized, profitable and stable.

(3) They also seem to be making an effective use of the resources at their disposal. We can conclusively state that the absence of an interest rate mechanism does not prevent the Islamic banks making effective and profitable use of resources put at their disposal.

(4) While their profitability ratios compare favourably with international standards, it should be noted that conventional banks' depositors are guaranteed their principal amounts, and hence bear less risk than Islamic banks' depositors. Therefore, the depositors of Islamic banks would genuinely

expect a higher rate of return to compensate for the extra risk. The current rate of profit on the assets of the Islamic banks may not be enough to meet that expectation.

(5) The study does not lend any support to the general belief that Islamic banks are suffering from excess liquidity.

(6) When compared with conventional banks, Islamic banks as a group outperformed the former in almost all areas and in almost all years. However, there are considerable variations among Islamic banks in terms of growth as well as performance. Therefore, results based on average figure must be taken with caution.

This chapter reports new empirical evidence on the experience of Islamic banking. However, empirical research in Islamic banking is still new and the quality of the data leaves much to be desired. Therefore, the results should be taken only as indicative rather than conclusive. It is hoped that further empirical research will be undertaken to arrive at more definitive results and empirical realities.

6
Efficiency in Islamic Banking

This chapter provides an overview of the literature that deals with measuring bank efficiency and shows recent empirical evidence that has sought to compare cost and profit efficiencies of Islamic and conventional banks. The first part of the chapter deals with the main methodological issues associated with estimating bank efficiency and outlines the main parametric and non-parametric approaches currently used in the literature. It then goes on to discuss features of the bank production process and finishes off with a review of recent studies that compare the banking sector efficiency of Islamic banks in GCC countries, Egypt, Jordan, Turkey and Sudan. Other studies that solely focus on Islamic banks are also briefly discussed. The main finding from this (albeit recent and limited) literature is that Islamic banking as a production process is almost always found to be more cost and profit efficient than conventional banking. This is perhaps due to the lower funding costs and loan-loss levels in Islamic banking as compared with other types of banking operation. This phenomenon, amongst others, may explain why we continue to see high growth rates of Islamic banking practice internationally.

Why study Islamic bank efficiency?

The question that might be asked is, why is the concept of efficiency important in understanding the performance of Islamic banks? The following may provide an answer to this question:

> For financial institutions, efficiency would imply improved profitability, greater amounts of funds intermediated, better prices and service quality for consumers, and greater safety and soundness if some of the efficiency savings are applied towards improving capital buffers that absorb risk. Of course, the opposite is the case if structural changes result in less efficient

intermediaries, with the additional danger of taxpayer-financed bailouts if substantial losses are sustained.

(Berger, Hunter and Timme, 1993, p. 221)

In general, the study of the efficiency of Islamic banks is important for three reasons. First, an improvement in cost efficiency means achieving higher profits and increasing the chance of survival in deregulated and competitive markets. This is particularly relevant for Islamic banks as they compete head-on with conventional commercial banks in many jurisdictions. Second, customers are interested in knowing the prices and the quality of bank services as well as new services that banks could offer, and these are strongly influenced by a bank's overall efficiency of operations. Third, an awareness of efficiency features is important to help policy makers formulate policies that affect the banking industry as a whole.

Moreover, for competition and mergers analysis it is important to know the effects of market concentration and past mergers on banking efficiency; whether one type of organizational form (such as Islamic banking) is more efficient than another; and whether inefficiency manifests itself in the form of poor production decisions, risk management decisions, or both. From a public policy perspective, concern about the economic efficiency of banks is also rationalized on the grounds that the efficiency of individual banks may affect the stability of the banking industry and, in turn, the effectiveness of the whole monetary system. The information obtained from the evaluation of Islamic banks' performance can also be used to improve managerial performance by identifying best and worst practice firms.

Measuring bank efficiency

Before we discuss recent empirical evidence on the efficiency of Islamic banks it is important to outline the way in which bank efficiency has been measured in the literature. Several approaches have been developed in the banking literature for measuring bank (firm) level efficiency, ranging from simple financial ratios to complex econometric models. Berger and Humphrey (1997) note that efficiency estimation techniques can be broadly categorized into parametric and non-parametric methods. However, no consensus exists as to the preferred method for determining the best-practice frontier against which relative efficiencies are measured. The most commonly used non-parametric methods are known as Data Envelopment Analysis (DEA) and the Free Disposable Hull (FDH). On the other hand, the most commonly used parametric methods are the Stochastic Frontier Approach (SFA), the Thick Frontier Approach (TFA) and the Distribution Free Approach (DFA). These approaches differ primarily in the assumptions imposed on the data in terms of the functional form of the best-practice frontier.

Frontier approaches are considered to be superior to standard financial ratio analysis because they use programming or statistical techniques that remove the effects of differences in input prices and other exogenous market factors affecting the standard performance of firms. This provides more accurate estimates of the underlying performance of firms and their managers. Therefore, frontier efficiency has been used extensively in the extant banking literature to measure the effects of mergers and acquisitions, capital regulation, deregulation of deposit rates, removal of geographic restrictions on branching and holding company acquisitions, and on financial institution performance in general.

In addition, frontier efficiency models are preferred by researchers over other performance indicators primarily because these models result in an objectively determined quantified measure of relative performance that removes many exogenous factors. This permits the researcher to focus on quantified measures of costs, inputs, outputs, revenues, profits, and so on to impute efficiency relative to the best practice institutions in the population.

Overall, the use of frontier efficiency techniques yields useful comparative and benchmarking information that can provide the impetus for significant improvements and can alert institutions to new business practices. Simple ratio-based analyses can be used for benchmarking and provide important insights, but these may be limited in scope because they take a one-dimensional view of a service, product or process and ignore any interactions, substitutions or trade-offs between key variables. Thus, a more inclusive multiple-input, multiple-output framework for evaluating productive efficiency, which provides benchmarking information on how to become a well-managed bank, seems essential to improve decision-making processes (especially at poorly managed banks).

Parametric versus non-parametric approaches to measuring efficiency

The choice of bank efficiency estimation method has been debated for some time with some researchers preferring the parametric approach (e.g., Berger, Hunter and Timme, 1993) and others the non-parametric approach (e.g., Seiford and Thrall, 1990). Despite a dispute over the preferred methodology, an emerging view suggests that it is not necessary to have a consensus as to one single (best) frontier approach for measuring bank efficiency. Instead, there should be a set of consistency conditions to be met for the efficiency measures derived from various approaches. If efficiency estimates are consistent across different methodologies then these measures will be convincing and therefore valid (or believable) estimates (Bauer *et al.*, 1998).

Efficiency estimates derived from different approaches should be consistent by generating analogous efficiency levels and rankings concerning the identification of best and worst firms. These should also be consistent over time and in line with the competitive conditions of the market, and also with standard non-frontier measures of performance. These consistency conditions measure the degree to which different approaches are mutually consistent and the degree to which the efficiencies generated by the different approaches are consistent with reality.

In brief, both parametric and non-parametric approaches to estimating bank efficiency have advantages and disadvantages. While the parametric approach has the virtue of allowing for noise in the measurement of inefficiency, this method requires assumptions about the particular form of the cost or profit function being estimated and the distribution of efficiency. The non-parametric linear programming approach requires no such specification of the functional form. However, the non-parametric approach suffers from the drawback that all deviations from the frontier are attributed to inefficiency with no allowance made for noise in the standard models.

The stochastic frontier approach and other parametric methods

This section outlines the main features of the most widely used parametric approach that has been used to estimate bank efficiency. The SFA was independently proposed by Aigner, Lovell and Schmidt (1977), and Meeusen and Van den Broeck (1977); it postulates that firms face various technical inefficiencies in producing a particular level of output. For a given combination of input levels, it is assumed that the realized production of a firm is bounded by the sum of a parametric function of known inputs, involving unknown parameters, and a random error, associated with measurement error of the level of production or other factors. The more the realized production falls below the production frontier, the greater the level of inefficiency.

The frontier approach labels a bank as inefficient if its costs (profits) are higher (lower) than those predicted for an efficient bank producing the same input/output combination, and the difference cannot be explained by statistical noise. The cost frontier is obtained by estimating a cost function with a composite error term, the sum of a two-sided error term representing random fluctuations in cost and a one-sided positive error term representing inefficiency. The single-equation stochastic cost function model can be given as:

$$TC = TC(y_i, w_i) + \varepsilon_i$$

where TC is observed total cost, y_i is a vector of outputs, and w_i is an input-price vector. Note the cost (or profit) function can take various forms, the most common being the translog specification, although recent studies tend to use the more flexible Fourier functional form. An example of a standard translog cost function using a two-output (loans and securities), three-input (wages, interest costs and other operating costs) specification is shown as:

$$\ln TC = \alpha_0 + \tau_1 t + \frac{1}{2}\tau_1 t^2 + \sum_{i=1}^{2} (\alpha_i + \varphi_i t)\ln Q_i + \sum_{h=1}^{3} (\beta_h + \theta_h t)\ln P_h$$
$$+ \frac{1}{2}\left[\sum_{i=1}^{2}\sum_{j=1}^{2} \delta_{ij}\ln Q_i \ln Q_j + \sum_{h=1}^{3}\sum_{m=1}^{3} \gamma_{hm}\ln P_h \ln P_m\right]$$
$$+ \sum_{i=1}^{2}\sum_{m=1}^{3} \rho_{im}\ln Q_i \ln P_m + \varepsilon$$

where:

$\ln TC$ = the natural logarithm of total costs (operating and financial cost);
$\ln Q_i$ = the natural logarithm of bank outputs, total loans and total securities ;
$\ln P_h$ = the natural logarithm of *i*th input prices (i.e., wage rate, interest cost and physical capital price)

Following Aigner, Lovell and Schmidt (1977), the error of the cost function is:

$$\varepsilon = u + \nu$$

where u and ν are independently distributed; u is assumed to be distributed as half-normal; $u = N(0, \sigma_u^2)$: that is, a positive disturbance capturing the effects of inefficiency; and ν is assumed to be distributed as two-sided normal with zero mean and variance, σ_ν^2, capturing the effects of the statistical noise.

Observation-specific estimates of the inefficiencies, u, can be estimated by using the conditional mean of the inefficiency term, given the composed error term, as proposed by Jondrow *et al.* (1982). The mean of this conditional distribution for the half-normal model is shown as:

$$E(u_i/\varepsilon_i) = \frac{\sigma\lambda}{1+\lambda^2}\left[\frac{f(\varepsilon_i\lambda)/\sigma}{1 - F(\varepsilon_i\lambda)/\sigma} + \left(\frac{\varepsilon_i\lambda}{\sigma}\right)\right]$$

where $\lambda = \sigma_u/\sigma_\nu$ and total variance, $\sigma^2 = \sigma_u^2 + \sigma_v^2$ $F(.)$ and $f(.)$ are the standard normal distribution and the standard normal density function, respectively; (u_i/ε_i) is an unbiased but inconsistent estimator of u_i since, regardless of the number of observations, N the variance of the estimator remains non-zero (see Greene, 1993, pp. 80–2). Jondrow *et al.* (1982) have shown that the ratio of the variability (standard deviation, σ) for u and v can be used to measure a bank's relative inefficiency, where $\lambda = \sigma_u/\sigma_v$ is a measure of the amount of variation stemming from inefficiency relative to noise for the sample.

Estimates of this model can be computed utilizing maximum likelihood procedures.

Bauer *et al.* (1998) refer to Greene's (1990) argument that alternative distributions for inefficiency may be more appropriate than the half-normal, and the application of different distributions sometimes 'do matter' to the average efficiencies for financial institutions. If panel data are available, however, some distributional assumptions can be relaxed, and the DFA may be used. The distribution-free method assumes that there is a core efficiency or average efficiency for each firm over time. The core inefficiency is distinguished from random error (and any temporary fluctuations in efficiency) by assuming core inefficiency as persistent over time, while random errors tend to average out over time. In particular, a cost or profit function is estimated for each period of a panel data set. The residual in each separate regression is composed of both inefficiency ($\ln u$) and random error ($\ln v$), but the random component is assumed to average out over time. Furthermore, an adjustment (called truncation) is assigned to the average of a bank's residuals from all of the regressions ($\ln \hat{u}$). This is done so as to assign less extreme values of $\ln \hat{u}$ to these banks, since extreme values may indicate that random error has not been completely purged by averaging. The resulting $\ln \hat{u}$ for each bank is used to compute its core efficiency.

Other parametric approaches used to measure efficiency in banking markets include the TFA and the DFA. The TFA divides banks in a sample into four quartiles based on the total cost per unit of assets. The estimated cost function for banks in the lowest average cost quartile is used to construct the cost frontier (the banks in this quartile are assumed to be the most cost efficient), while the estimated cost function for banks in the highest average cost quartile are assumed to have lower than average efficiency. The difference between the cost functions estimated for banks in the lowest average cost quartile and banks in the highest average cost quartile are assumed to reflect differences in efficiency alone.

The DFA specifies a functional form for the cost function but it does not impose a specific shape on the distribution of efficiencies. It assumes that there is a core efficiency or average efficiency for each firm that is constant over time, while random error tends to average out over time (Bauer *et al.*, 1998). Unlike the other approaches, a panel data set is required, and therefore only panel estimates of efficiency over the entire time interval are available.

Data Envelopment Analysis and other non-parametric approaches to measuring bank efficiency

The DEA non-parametric or mathematical programming approach is an alternative method to help estimate productive efficiency in the financial sector. DEA is non-parametric in the sense that it simply constructs the frontier of the observed input–output ratios by linear programming techniques. This procedure is not based on an explicit model of the frontier, or the relationship of the observations to the frontier, other than the fact that observations cannot lie below the frontier. This approach shows how a particular bank operates relative to other banks in the sample and so it provides a benchmark for best practice technology based on the experience of the banks in the sample.

DEA can estimate efficiency under the assumption of constant returns to scale (CRS) and variable returns to scale (VRS). The CRS assumption is only appropriate when all banks are operating optimally. However, factors such as imperfect competition and constraints in finance may cause banks not to operate optimally. As a result, the established bank literature that uses linear programming techniques to estimate efficiency tend to use the VRS approach as suggested by Banker, Charnes and Cooper (1984) where they propose a variable returns to scale measure using an output-oriented model.

Bauer *et al.* (1998) note that the DEA estimates are based on technological efficiency where efficient firms are those for which no other firm or linear combination of firms produces as much or more of every output (given inputs), or uses as little or less of every input (given outputs). The efficient frontier is composed of these undominated firms and the piecewise linear segments that connect the set of input/output combinations of these firms yield a convex production possibility set.

To match firms in so many dimensions, other constraints are often imposed on DEA linear programming problems. The constraints that may be specified in banking studies can include such factors as quality controls (e.g., the number of branches or average bank account size) or environmental variables (e.g., bank ownership or state regulatory controls). However, matching firms in so many dimensions can result in firms being measured as highly efficient solely because no other firms or few other firms have comparable values of inputs, outputs or other constrained variables. That is to say, some firms may be self-identified as 100 per cent efficient not because they dominate other firms, but because there are only a few other observations with which they are comparable. The problem of self-identifiers or near self-identifiers most often arises when there are a small number of observations relative to the number of inputs, outputs, and other constraints, so that a large proportion of the observations are difficult to match in all dimensions.

Other non-parametric approaches that have been used to estimate bank efficiency include the Free Disposal Hull approach (FDH), developed by Deprins, Simar and Tulkens (1984), which is a special case of DEA. Here the hypothesis of convexity of the production possibility set (PPS) is abandoned, and the PPS is composed only of the DEA vertices and the free disposal hull points interior to these vertices. Because the FDH frontier is either congruent or interior to the DEA frontier, FDH will typically generate larger efficiency estimates than DEA. DEA is a more efficient estimator than FDH, but only if the assumption of convexity is correct.

A major drawback of the non-parametric approach is that it considers any deviations from the efficient frontier as inefficiencies given the absence of random error. In addition, this approach also suffers from the difficulty of drawing statistical inference and the lack of a definite functional form encapsulating the production technology.

Specification of a bank's inputs and outputs

So far we have discussed different ways in which bank efficiency can be estimated but have said little about the actual bank production process. This involves the choice of bank inputs and outputs. Banks are entities engaged in the intermediation of services between borrowers and lenders. These services are related directly or indirectly to the financial assets and liabilities held by this firm, such as loans and deposits. In addition, financial institutions such as banks are naturally multi-product firms: many of their services are jointly produced and so certain kinds of costs are jointly related to production of a variety of services. Furthermore, financial firms provide services rather than readily identifiable physical products, and there is no consensus as to the precise definition of what banks produce and how service output can be measured.

Intermediation theories do not provide a clear-cut view regarding banks' output and input and therefore do not present precise indication as to how to define banks' costs. Allen and Santomero (1998) argue that many current theories of intermediation are too narrow and focus on functions of institutions that are no longer crucial in many developed financial systems. Bhattacharya and Thakor (1993) provides a review of the relevant literature where such theories are often unable to account for those activities that have become more central to many institutions, such as risk management and cost-reduction oriented activities.

Casu and Molyneux (2001) note that the earliest cost studies in banking applied a variety of different banking output indicators. Some early studies proxied bank services by a single index that combined all services into a unidimensional measure; others measured each bank service separately. In addition, some researchers chose to measure output in terms of bank assets and liabilities by focusing either on only one side of the balance sheet, or on both sides at the same time. Others have used bank revenues to measure bank output. Greenbaum (1967), for example, used the dollar market value of services rendered to measure output in an attempt to estimate the real social value of banking services.

While the multi-product nature of the banking firm is recognized, there is still no agreement as to the definition and measurement of bank inputs and outputs. The banking literature is divided concerning the issue of bank cost and there is no agreement concerning the variables that provide a good proxy for bank costs. Benston, Hanweck and Humphrey (1982) have summarized the issue into three viewpoints: economists tend to view a bank's output as dollars of deposits or loans; monetary economists see banks as producers of money-demand deposits; while others see banks as producing loans, with demand and time deposits being analogous to raw materials. In general, researchers take one of two approaches, labelled the 'intermediation approach' and the 'production approach'.

The intermediation approach views the bank as an intermediator of financial services. This approach was suggested by Sealey and Lindley (1977) and assumes that banks collect funds (deposits and funds purchased with the assistance of labour and capital) and transform these into loans and other assets. The deposits are treated as inputs, along with capital and labour, and the volumes of earning assets are defined as measures of output. Consistent with this approach, costs are defined to include both interest expense and total costs of production. Some authors support the exclusion of interest expense from total costs, reasoning that interest costs are purely financial and not pertinent in measuring efficiency. Others have argued that excluding interest costs disregards the process of financial technology by which deposits are transformed into loans.

The production approach views banks as producers of loan and deposit services using capital and labour. The number of accounts of each type is the appropriate definition of outputs. The total costs under this approach are exclusive of interest expense, and thus consider only operating but not interest costs; outputs are measured by the number of accounts serviced as opposed to dollar values.

In addition, there are three other forms of the intermediation approach suggested by Berger and Humphrey (1992). These forms define bank inputs and outputs according to bank activities. The first is the assets approach which considers banks as financial intermediaries between liability holders and those who receive funds. The outputs are defined as various types of assets, while inputs include deposits and other liabilities. The main shortcoming of this approach is that it does not take into account the other services, such as fee-based off-balance sheet services provided by banks. The second version is known as the value-added approach where both assets and liabilities are considered to have some output characteristics, and bank inputs and outputs are defined based on their share of value added. Outputs are classified from activities that create high value-added such as loans, demand deposits and time and saving deposits. Other outputs may be regarded as unimportant, intermediate products or inputs. The third approach is known as the user-cost approach, which determines whether the final product is an input or an output based on its contribution to bank revenue. On this basis, transactions are defined as outputs if the financial return (e.g., return on assets or equity) exceeds the opportunity cost of funds, or defined as a cost (liability) if the financial cost is less than the opportunity cost of those funds. The drawback of this approach is that it is often difficult to obtain accurate data on prices and revenues associated with different areas of banks' business. Finally, some researchers model bank inputs and outputs according to assumed bank objectives. For example, Leightner and Lovell (1998) specified outputs such as net interest income and non-interest income, assuming that banks' main objective is to maximize revenue.

Overall, both the intermediation and production approaches have received significant attention in the banking efficiency literature but there is no consensus as to the 'best' approach to defining the bank production process. Berger and Humphrey (1997) indicate that both approaches are imperfect because neither fully captures the dual role of financial institutions, which includes both the provision of transaction and document processing services, and the transfer of funds from savers to borrowers. The 'production approach' may be somewhat better for evaluating the efficiencies of branches of financial institutions, because branches primarily process customers' documents for the institution as a whole, and branch managers typically have little influence over bank funding and investment decisions. On the other hand, the 'intermediation approach' may be more appropriate for evaluating entire financial institutions because this approach is inclusive of interest and/or funding expenses, which often account for between half and two-thirds of total costs. Moreover, the 'intermediation approach' may be superior for evaluating the importance of frontier efficiency for the profitability of financial institutions, since the minimization of total costs (and not just production costs) is needed to maximize profits.

Difficulties associated with defining the production features of Islamic banks is further compounded by the fact that their outputs can be viewed as different from conventional commercial banks. For instance, Hussein (2003) in his study on Islamic banks in Sudan uses investment in *murābaḥah* and other modes of Islamic finance (leasing, *mushārakah* and *istiṣnā*ʿ) as two of his main bank outputs (the third being off-balance sheet activity). Of course, if one wishes to compare Islamic banks with conventional banks one has to choose output measures that apply to both types of banks, such as a standard balance sheet measure (El-Gamal and Inanoglu (2003) used total loans in their analysis of Turkish banking). Having said this, however, studies that investigate Islamic bank efficiency typically use standard definitions for inputs: cost of physical capital, labour and funds.

Empirical evidence on efficiency in Islamic banking

While there has been extensive literature examining the efficiency features of US and European banking markets over recent years, the work on Islamic banking is still in its infancy. Typically, studies on Islamic bank efficiency have focused on theoretical issues and the empirical work has relied mainly on the analysis of descriptive statistics rather than rigorous statistical estimation (El-Gamal and Inanoglu, 2003). However, this is gradually changing as a number of recent studies have sought to apply the approaches outlined above to estimate bank efficiency using various frontier techniques. These will now be discussed.

Al-Shammari (2003) uses the translog stochastic cost and alternative profit frontier approaches to estimate bank efficiency in GCC countries and compare Islamic bank efficiency with other types of banks. The cost efficiency estimates are shown in Tables 6.1 and 6.2. Cost efficiency estimates for banks in the countries under study averaged 88 per cent. These estimates improved over time from 84 per cent in 1995 to 91 per cent in 1999. This suggests that the same level of output could be produced with approximately 88 per cent of current inputs if the banks being studied were operating at the most efficient level. This level of technical inefficiency is similar to the range of 10–15 per cent found in the survey of 130 studies undertaken by Berger and Humphrey (1997). The results appear slightly lower than the levels of inefficiency found in European banking (see Goddard, Molyneux and Wilson 2001).

The efficiency scores based on geographical location ranged from 83 per cent in Qatar to 92 per cent in Saudi Arabia. Referring to Table 6.2, the average cost efficiency based on bank specialization ranged from 84 per cent for investment banks to 91 per cent for Islamic banks. It seems that Islamic banks have higher cost efficiency because of their generally lower cost of funds compared to commercial and investment banks.

The bank efficiency literature considers the estimation of both cost and profit efficiencies to reveal more accurate information about firm-level performance. Profit inefficiency depends both on the production structure and on the composition of the product portfolio, which has to be updated by banks at the pace required by general macroeconomic and other trends in the economy. In addition, profit efficiency incorporates both the cost and revenue sides of a bank's operations and therefore can be considered a more encompassing measure of firm performance. For instance, just looking at cost efficiency may be misleading as one may find cost-efficient banks that are highly efficient but earn low revenues. Profit efficiency estimates therefore encompass bank cost and revenue features in the optimization process. As such, Al-Shammari (2003) repeats the aforementioned analysis and estimates alternative profit efficiency for the same sample. (This is done by estimating the translog stochastic cost frontier, but using profits instead of total costs as the dependent variable.) The results of the alternative profit efficiency estimates are shown in Table 6.3. Here one can see that for different bank types the profit efficiency scores ranged from 64 per cent for investment banks to 73 per cent for the Islamic banks. Al-Shammari concludes that in the GCC countries, Islamic banks are the most cost and profit efficient while investment banks are the least efficient. He suggests

Table 6.1 GCC banks' cost X-efficiency scores (%) over 5 years

Year	Bahrain		Kuwait		Oman		Qatar		Saudi Arabia		UAE		GCC	
	Score	No .of banks	Score	No. of banks	Score	No. of banks	Score	No. of banks	Score	No. of banks	Score	No. of banks	Score	No. of banks
1995	82	17	84	12	83	7	81	6	88	10	83	20	84	72
1996	82	17	84	12	85	7	83	6	91	10	85	20	86	72
1997	83	17	85	12	85	7	84	6	90	10	87	20	87	72
1998	84	17	88	12	86	7	84	6	92	10	90	20	89	72
1999	86	17	90	*12*	89	*7*	85	6	93	*10*	91	*20*	91	72
Average	84	85	87	60	86	35	83	30	92	50	90	100	88	72

Source: Adapted from Al-Shammari (2003), pp. 279–86.

Table 6.2 Cost X-efficiency (%) and bank type organizational form (commercial, investment and Islamic)

Year	Islamic banks		Commercial banks		Investment banks	
	Cost x-eff.	No. of obs.	Cost X-eff.	No. of obs.	Cost X-eff.	No. of obs.
1995	90	10	84	47	83	15
1996	91	10	86	47	84	15
1997	91	10	86	47	84	15
1998	92	10	87	47	85	15
1999	92	10	88	47	86	15
Average	91		86		84	

eff. = efficiency; obs. = observations.
Source: Adapted from Al-Shammari (2003), pp. 279–86.

Table 6.3 Alternative profit efficiency in GCC member states, 1995–9 (based on geographical location) (%)

Country	1995	1996	1997	1998	1999	All
Bahrain	63	66	69	70	71	69
Kuwait	64	68	69	71	72	70
Oman	62	66	66	67	67	64
Saudi Arabia	68	70	70	72	74	72
Qatar	63	67	68	69	70	67
UAE	64	67	69	71	72	69
All	64	68	69	70	72	68
According to bank's organizational form						
Commercial	64	67	68	68	70	69
Investment	62	64	65	66	66	64
Islamic	68	72	73	74	75	73
All	64	68	69	70	72	68

Source: Adapted from Al-Shammari (2003), pp. 279–86.

that the motives behind the increase in Islamic banking activities over the past few years is due to the fact that Islamic banks appear to have a cheaper source of funds than other types of financial institution.[1]

The finding that Islamic banks are more cost and profit efficient than conventional banks is a finding confirmed in a similar study by Al-Jarrah and Molyneux (2003). They also use the stochastic frontier approach, with the Fourier-flexible functional form, and estimate cost and profit efficiency estimates for banks operating in Bahrain, Jordan, Egypt and Saudi Arabia. Table 6.4 shows that the average cost efficiency for different types of banks

Table 6.4 Cost efficiency in Jordan, Egypt, Saudi Arabia and Bahrain banking over 1992–2000 (%)

	1992	1993	1994	1995	1996	1997	1998	1999	2000	All
Bahrain	100	100	100	100	100	99	99	99	99	99
Egypt	94	94	94	94	94	93	93	93	93	94
Jordan	90	89	89	89	89	89	89	88	88	89
Saudi Arabia	97	97	97	97	97	97	97	97	96	97
Commercial	95	95	95	95	94	94	94	94	94	94
Investment	93	93	93	93	93	93	93	93	93	93
Islamic	98	98	98	98	99	99	98	98	98	98
Other	97	96	96	96	96	96	96	96	96	96
All	95	95	95	95	95	94	94	94	94	95

Source: Adapted from Al-Jarrah and Molyneux (2003).

ranged from 93 per cent for investment banks to 98 per cent for Islamic banks.

Al-Jarrah and Molyneux (2003) extend their analysis by also estimating both standard and alternative profit efficiency for their sample of banks and the results are around 66 per cent and 58 per cent respectively over the period 1992–2000. It should be noted that these levels of efficiency are similar to that found in US studies, which is about half of the industry's potential profits according to Berger and Humphrey (1997). While over the period 1993–9 the efficiency estimates derived from both profit function specifications fluctuated slightly around their average, the year 2000 exhibits falls in profit efficiency across the banks under study. This might reflect the response of economic and financial activities to the instability in the oil prices and the political instability arising from recent conflict in Palestine and the Gulf.

Tables 6.5 and 6.6 report the standard and alternative profit efficiency estimates, respectively. Based on specialization the results show that the standard profit efficiency scores ranged from 56 per cent for investment banks to 75 per cent for the Islamic banks. Similar results are found from the alternative profit function estimates, where Islamic banks are again the most profit efficient.

Majid *et al.* (2003) used the stochastic cost frontier approach to estimate the cost efficiency of Malaysian banks over the period 1993–2000. Their data set included 34 banks (24 local and 10 foreign) from a total of 55 commercial banks in operation during the period of study. They used translog cost function to arrive at inefficiency measures. Their results are reported in Table 6.7.

The results show that Islamic banks did marginally better than conventional banks in terms of efficiency, although both produce at a cost that is

Table 6.5 Standard profit efficiency in Jordan, Egypt, Saudi Arabia and Bahrain banking over 1992–2000 (%)

	1992	1993	1994	1995	1996	1997	1998	1999	2000	All
Bahrain	69	78	67	71	66	72	67	68	57	68
Egypt	66	64	66	70	66	64	65	73	63	66
Jordan	84	60	61	61	63	56	56	59	50	61
Saudi Arabia	67	68	66	69	69	65	59	63	63	65
Commercial	70	67	68	72	69	65	62	68	62	67
Investment	65	69	55	55	48	51	57	60	43	56
Islamic	83	73	78	79	75	80	67	67	76	75
Other	64	58	57	61	64	73	74	78	55	65
All	70	67	65	68	66	65	63	68	59	66

Source: Adapted from Al-Jarrah and Molyneux (2003).

Table 6.6 Alternative profit efficiency in Jordan, Egypt, Saudi Arabia and Bahrain banking over 1992–2000 (%)

	1992	1993	1994	1995	1996	1997	1998	1999	2000	All
Bahrain	58	72	60	66	58	64	51	61	58	61
Egypt	65	58	60	62	59	60	56	68	55	60
Jordan	59	51	54	53	49	39	42	52	46	49
Saudi Arabia	56	56	54	51	61	59	51	61	61	57
Commercial	60	59	61	63	63	58	53	62	56	60
Investment	55	61	52	50	43	46	46	62	44	51
Islamic	76	57	60	64	54	63	51	55	78	62
Other	69	62	47	53	48	63	56	67	47	57
All	61	60	58	60	58	57	52	62	55	58

Source: Adapted from Al-Jarrah and Molyneux (2003).

respectively 30.2 per cent and 28 per cent higher than necessary. The slight edge achieved by the Islamic banks over conventional banks is not, however, statistically significant, and it can be safely concluded that Islamic banks are at least as efficient as their conventional counterparts despite a more restrictive business environment.

It is also interesting to note that foreign banks are generally more efficient than local banks. Further tests suggest that the difference is statistically significant at the 5 per cent level.

El-Gamal and Inanoglu (2002) used the stochastic cost frontier approach to estimate the cost efficiency of Turkish banks over the period 1990–2000. The study compared the cost efficiencies of 49 conventional banks with four Islamic special finance houses (SFHs). The Islamic firms comprised around

Table 6.7 Descriptive statistics for inefficiency measures for various bank categories

	Mean	Std dev.	Minimum	Maximum
Conventional	0.302	0.240	0.030	1.230
Islamic	0.280	0.162	0.090	0.600
Local	0.321	0.248	0.050	1.230
Foreign	0.254	0.199	0.030	1.080
Asset size > RM12 billion	0.319	0.209	0.110	0.860
Asset size RM6–12 billion	0.290	0.269	0.090	1.200
Asset size RM3–6 billion	0.409	0.338	0.120	1.230
Asset size < RM3 billion	0.226	0.206	0.030	0.810

RM = Malaysian Ringgit.
Std dev. = standard deviation.

3 per cent of the Turkish banking market. Overall, the authors found these firms to be the most efficient and this was explained by their emphasis on Islamic asset-based financing which led to lower non-performing loan ratios. It should also be noted that the SFHs achieved high levels of efficiency despite being subject to branching restrictions and other self-imposed constraints, such as the inability to hold government bonds. El-Gamal and Inanoglu (2004) substantially extend their earlier study by providing an alternative method for evaluating bank efficiency scores. Again, they examine the cost efficiency of Turkish banks throughout the 1990s. They distinguish between groups of banks that have different production technologies, and find that the Islamic financial firms have the same production technology as conventional (mainly domestic) banks. By using standard stochastic cost frontier estimates they show that the Islamic firms are among the most efficient. In addition, they use a new labour efficiency measure, and again Turkish Islamic special finance houses are found to be among the most efficient.

Hussein (2003) provides an analysis of the cost efficiency features of Islamic banks in Sudan between 1990 and 2000. Using the stochastic cost frontier approach, he estimates cost efficiency for a sample of 17 banks over the period. The interesting contribution of this paper, as noted earlier, is that specific definitions of Islamic financial products are used as outputs. In addition, the analysis is also novel as Sudan has a banking system based entirely on Islamic banking principles. (Of course, the drawback is that we cannot compare the efficiency of Islamic with conventional banks.) Nevertheless, the results show large variations in the cost efficiency of Sudanese banks, with the foreign-owned banks being the most efficient. State-owned banks are the most cost inefficient. The analysis is extended to examine the determinants of bank efficiency. Here, Hussein finds that smaller banks are more efficient than their larger counterparts. In addition, banks that have a higher proportion of *mushārakah* and *muḍārabah* finance relative to total assets also have efficiency advantages. Overall, the substantial variability in efficiency estimates is put down to various factors, not least the highly volatile economic environment under which Sudanese banks have had to operate over the last decade or so.

While the above outlines the literature that uses advanced modelling techniques to evaluate bank efficiency one should also note that there is a substantial body of literature that covers the general performance features of Islamic banks. Such studies include those by Hassan and Bashir (2003), who look at the determinants of Islamic bank performance and show Islamic banks to be just as efficient as conventional banks if one uses standard accounting measures such as cost-to-income ratios. Other studies that take a similar approach are those by Sarker (1999), who looks at the performance and operational efficiency of Bangladeshi Islamic banks; Bashir (2000), who examines the performance of Islamic banks across eight countries between 1993 and 1998; Bashir (1999), who examines the risk and profitability features of two Sudanese banks; Samad (1999), who compares the performance of one Malaysian Islamic bank to seven conventional banks; and Iqbal (2001b) who analyses the performance of various groups of conventional and Islamic banks within various countries. Overall, the general finding from this literature is that Islamic banks are at least as efficient as their conventional bank competitors and, in most cases, are more efficient.

Conclusion

The review of the extant literature which compares the efficiency of Islamic with conventional banks strongly suggests that the former is a more cost and profit efficient form of banking organization. Evidence from the GCC countries, Egypt, Jordan and Turkey that uses cost frontier approaches to model bank efficiency suggests that Islamic banking is a more efficient organization form than other types. Other evidence where ratio analysis is used also tends to find the same result, particularly in the case of cost efficiency. While the consensus of opinion seems to reveal substantial efficiency advantages, it is not absolutely clear why these exist; some put it down to lower funding costs and others to lower loan-losses. This area deserves further investigation. Nevertheless, the broad findings do strongly suggest that Islamic banks can act as effective competitors to conventional banks and operate with at least the same (if not better) technology. We suggest that the identified efficiency advantages of Islamic banking are another reason that have helped the development of this type of banking business over recent years.

7
Challenges Facing Islamic Banking

As mentioned in Chapter 4, serious research work of the past half-century has established that Islamic banking is a viable and efficient way of financial intermediation. A number of Islamic banks have been established during this period under heterogeneous, social and economic conditions. Recently, many conventional banks, including some major multinational Western banks, have also started using Islamic banking techniques. All this is encouraging. However, the Islamic banking system, like any other system, has to be seen as an evolving reality. This experience needs to be evaluated objectively and the problems ought to be carefully identified and addressed. In this chapter we review some of the challenges being faced by Islamic banks.

Theoretical challenges: unresolved issues

Theory precedes practice in almost all cases. Islamic banking is no exception, and in this case there is an additional aspect: no product can be launched until it is cleared by *Sharīʿah* scholars. This process has been very slow although, during the last 30 years, considerable progress has been made. However, there are a number of issues which still remain unresolved. These issues are constraining further progress of the Islamic financial industry. In the following paragraphs, we discuss some of these issues.

Conditions of participation in equity markets

In all businesses there is need for long-term finance. In a conventional system, this is provided through long-term bonds and equities. This function is performed by securities markets and specialized equity institutions. In addition to the general public, the most important sources of these investments are investment banks, mutual funds, insurance companies and pension funds. Islamic banks do not deal with interest-bearing bonds and therefore the need for equity markets is much higher in an Islamic framework. It may be mentioned here that even in conventional finance, there is an increasing trend towards the use of equities as a source of business finance.

Islamic financial institutions need to be involved in equity markets. However, there are some unresolved *fiqh* issues that are hampering this trend. What conditions must be satisfied before participating in equity funds is a subject that is still unsettled. The Islamic Fiqh Academy has ruled that equity investments are permissible under *Sharīʿah* within certain parameters.[1] However, it has deferred a decision on specifying those parameters until further studies have been performed. Some Islamic scholars have prescribed three minimum requirements: (i) the fund must not deal in the equities of companies whose business activity is banned by the Islamic *Sharīʿah* (for example, breweries, casinos, conventional banks etc.); (ii) interest income earned by the fund must be negligible[2] and separable so that the fund's income can be cleansed of it; and (iii) since the sale of debt is not permissible except at face value, the proportion of debts receivable in the portfolio of the company should not exceed an 'acceptable'[3] proportion. The scholars who have laid down these conditions have done so in their individual capacities or as members of the *Sharīʿah* Boards of some Islamic funds. However, as stated above, the OIC Fiqh Academy, after deliberating on this issue on several occasions, has not issued a final ruling. In view of the increasing importance that equity markets are gaining day by day, and considering the 'need' of individuals and institutions to invest in these markets, the issue needs to be resolved as soon as possible.

Delinquent borrowers and the issue of penalties

By using fixed rate modes of financing, Islamic banks have been able to minimize the impact of business risks on their cash flows. But precisely because of the same reason (i.e., the use of debt as compared to equity), they can land themselves in serious problems. *Murābaḥah* deals create debt obligations against buyer firms. Now, while it is permissible to charge a higher price in credit sales as compared to cash sales, the wherewithal of the *murābaḥah* mode of financing, once the deal has been entered into, it creates a fixed liability. If the buyer defaults on his payment, banks cannot charge anything extra because that would mean taking *ribā*. Thus there is a built-in incentive for immoral buyers to default.

Islamic jurists have been discussing this problem. It is generally agreed that penalties, both physical and financial, can be imposed on defaulters but the bank cannot receive any benefit from these penalties. Some contemporary scholars have argued that the banks can be compensated because the defaulter has caused damage and Islam permits, and even encourages, compensation for damages. However, the issue still remains unresolved due to a lack of consensus among jurists. Furthermore, the award of compensation is not automatic. This has to be done by a judge, which makes this option both time-consuming and uncertain. The issue needs to be looked at in its modern perspective and a solution compatible with *Sharīʿah* needs to be found.

Indexation

The question of indexation is often raised in the presence of a sustained high rate of inflation. The *Sharīʿah* aspect of indexation is still under the consideration of the *fuqahā'*, especially at the OIC Fiqh Academy. While the Academy has so far allowed indexation in the case of wages and some other contracts fulfilled over a period of time, provided that this does not harm the economy, it has not allowed it in the case of monetary debts. However, it has ruled that the creditor and debtor may agree, on the repayment day and *not* before, to settle the debt in a currency other than that in which the debt has been contracted, and at the prevailing exchange rate. It is also permissible to specify payment of a deferred price in a specific currency, a basket of currencies, a commodity or a basket of commodities, and the debtor should, in this case, abide by such an agreement and repay the amount in the unit agreed.

As an example, the Articles of Agreement[4] of the Islamic Development Bank provide for the use of the ID in its transactions. The ID is the Bank's accounting unit, having the same value as one Special Drawing Right, which is also used as an accounting unit by the International Monetary Fund. IDB's instalment sale and lending operations are denominated in ID, and are repaid in a freely convertible currency on which the two parties agree on the repayment day in accordance with the prevailing exchange rate on that specific day. However, the IDB dinar is a notional currency. Since no real currency can be indexed, creditors still find it impossible to protect the real value of their loans. The matter is still being debated and needs to be settled.

Financial engineering

Innovation is a necessary condition for the survival of any industry, and Islamic banking is no exception. Until now, Islamic financial tools have essentially been limited to conventional instruments developed centuries ago and their variants. Classical instruments were developed to meet the needs of those societies. Financial markets are now becoming more and more sophisticated. In order to exploit the fast changing market environment and face increasing competition, financial engineering and innovation is imperative. While classical contracts may serve as useful guidelines for new Islamic financial instruments, there is no reason to be restricted only to these types of contracts. In the Islamic theory of contracts, parties are free to agree on any terms as long as known Islamic rules and principles are not violated. There is a well-known *ḥadīth*[5] stating: 'All the conditions agreed upon by the Muslims are upheld, except a condition which allows what is prohibited or prohibits what is lawful.'

In the light of the principles of *ijtihād*, a 'needs approach' to financial engineering is desirable (keeping, of course, within the known principles of Islamic finance). In this regard, the example of *bayʿ salam* is very important. In general, it is not allowed to sell anything that is not in one's possession but, in the case of *salam*, the Prophet (peace be upon him) allowed such a sale because of the 'need' of the people, but laid down clear rules to protect the interests of both parties. The financial needs of both individuals and businesses, however, have now changed. Engineers in modern finance have designed several new instruments such as options, derivatives, hedging, insurance pension plans, credit cards and new mortgage products to meet these needs. Islamic banks must examine what needs are being fulfilled by these instruments. If the needs are genuine, Islamically speaking, then they must either adapt them for their purposes or invent Islamic alternatives for them.

However, because of the religious dimension of Islamic banking and finance, no new product can be adopted until it is cleared by *Sharīʿah* scholars. Even after a new product is put into use, *Sharīʿah* auditing of the operations of financial institutions is very important to ensure that the actual practice complies with the requirements of *Sharīʿah*. This is important not only for religious reasons but also for purely business considerations because the clients of Islamic banks will not have confidence in their operations unless *Sharīʿah* scholars clear their activities. Against this background, the expertise of *fiqh* scholars in understanding the prerequisites of modern financial products and in evaluating these products becomes very important.

Almost all Islamic banks have their own *Sharīʿah* boards or *Sharīʿah* advisers. A survey of the members of these boards would reveal that hardly any of these scholars has a formal training in modern finance. This puts a serious constraint on the ability of *Sharīʿah* scholars to issue well-informed rulings on financial products and activities. The *Sharīʿah* scholars themselves are conscious of this difficulty. They are using a number of ways to acquire the necessary background information before issuing a *fatwā*. One way is to discuss an issue in meetings/workshops attended by both *Sharīʿah* scholars and financial experts. Institutions such as the Islamic Research and Training Institute and Islamic universities are playing an active role in organizing such workshops. However, these workshops have no mandate to issue a *fatwā*. For that purpose, the meetings of the Fiqh academies, the most prominent among which is the OIC Fiqh Academy in Jeddah, play a more important role. These academies also commission a number of studies by specialized experts on specific issues before discussing them and taking a decision. In the absence of the required expertise in the field of finance among *Sharīʿah* scholars, this approach of group *ijtihād* is playing an important role in safeguarding against serious mistakes in adopting doubtful instruments.

The situation is, however, far from being ideal. As any participant at the workshops and meetings of the Fiqh academies may easily see, the interaction between Fiqh scholars and the experts of modern economics and finance does not proceed smoothly. They have such different backgrounds and speak such different technical languages that communication between them is very difficult. It is, therefore, quite understandable that the *Sharīʿah* scholars are very cautious in giving their rulings. The result has been that the decision-making process has become extremely slow and tends to be overconservative.

The past record shows that *Sharīʿah* bodies have done a commendable job in evaluating the applications of traditional contracts and safeguarding against the use of some and the misuse of others. However, when it comes to evaluating modern financial contracts or Islamic substitutes for them, *Sharīʿah* bodies have found it quite difficult to issue verdicts. This is basically due to an acute shortage of scholars with dual specialization, or at least working knowledge of modern finance and *Sharīʿah* at the same time (see Box 7.1).

Box 7.1 The need for an autonomous *Sharīʿah* Supervisory Board

Banking supervision is needed as much for Islamic banks as conventional banks. However, because of the special nature of operations of Islamic banks, it has different control and supervisory requirements. There is also an additional dimension of supervision in the case of Islamic banks. This relates to *Sharīʿah* supervision of their activities. At present, most Islamic banks have their own *Sharīʿah* Boards. Questions have been raised about the autonomy and powers of these Boards. *Sharīʿah* Boards of different banks could issue different rulings on similar practices which may raise doubts in the minds of clients. Minimum *Sharīʿah* standards for each type of contract issued by an autonomous body will go a long way to assure customers of the '*Sharīʿah* compatibility' of those contracts as well as actual operations. This need becomes more important in the wake of the entry of several Western banks into Islamic banking.

In view of these considerations, an autonomous *Sharīʿah* Board for supervising the *Sharīʿah* side of Islamic banks needs to be constituted. However, it must be mentioned here that since Islamic banks do not fall under the jurisdiction of a single government, such a Board can be constituted only if the Islamic banks agree to abide by a common discipline. They must realize that doing so will be in their own long-term interest. If Islamic banking is not perceived to be 'Islamic', it will not be long before the existing Islamic banks lose much of their market.

Risk management[6]

A number of risks are inherent in the banking business. These include credit risks, market risks, liquidity risks and operational risks. Islamic banks face these risks just as conventional banks do. There are, however, some special considerations for Islamic banks. Some of these are set out below:

1 According to some *fuqahā'*, including the OIC Fiqh Academy, the *murābaḥah* contract is binding on only the seller and not the buyer.[7] By contrast, some *fuqahā'* consider it binding on both parties, and most Islamic banks operate on the basis of this latter verdict. This difference of opinion may cause some problems.
2 There are a number of counterparty risks in the *salam* contract. These range from the failure to supply on time, or even at all, to the failure to supply the agreed quality or quantity. These risks arise not only due to factors that are in the suppliers' control, but also due to factors that are beyond their control, such as natural disasters and climatic and other reasons for crop failure.
3 While entering into an *istiṣnāʿ* contract, an Islamic bank assumes the roles of a manufacturer and supplier and then subcontracts. This exposes the bank to a two-way counterparty risk. One of these is the risk of default by the bank's client. This is the same as that in *murābaḥah*. In addition, there is the risk of the subcontractor's failure to fulfil his obligations efficiently and on time.
4 Since Islamic banks use LIBOR (London Inter Bank Offered Rate) as a benchmark, it is natural for the assets of these banks to be exposed to the risk of changes in the LIBOR rate. A rise in LIBOR will automatically lead to a rise in the mark-up and, in turn, lead to the payment of higher profits to future depositors compared with those received by the banks from the users of long-term funds.
5 The nature of investment deposits on the liabilities side of Islamic banks adds an additional dimension to this risk. Profit rates to be paid to *muḍārabah* depositors by the Islamic bank will have to respond to changes in the market rate of mark-up. However, profit rates earned on assets cannot be raised because most of these are *murābaḥah* receivables and the price has been fixed on the basis of the mark-up rates of the previous period.
6 Conventional banks try to manage interest rates, exchange rates, and commodity and equity price risks by using futures, forwards, options and swap contracts. However, no agreement has yet taken place among the *fuqahā'* on the permissibility of these instruments.
7 There are a number of reasons that may lead to liquidity risks for Islamic banks. First, most of them rely largely on current accounts, that can be withdrawn on demand. Second, there is a *fiqhī* restriction on the sale of debts, which constitute a major part of their assets. Third, due to the slow development of Islamic financial instruments, Islamic banks are not able to raise funds quickly from the markets. The non-existence of an Islamic inter-bank money market tends to make this problem a little

more difficult. Fourth, the Lender of Last Resort (LLR) facility is also not available at present except on the basis of interest.

Issues such as these need to be discussed and debated.

Practical challenges: operational problems

Islamic banks generally operate under conventional legal frameworks and institutional arrangements. In many cases, these are not suitable for their operations. Islamic banks have struggled for more than a quarter of a century, gaining some success yet facing many operational problems. Islamic banking institutions all over the world try to benefit from the legal and institutional framework that supports conventional banking. However, they suffer from a lack of institutional support specifically geared to their needs. Building a proper institutional set-up is perhaps the most serious challenge for Islamic finance. To face this challenge, a 'functional approach' towards building this set-up is needed. The functions being performed by various institutions in the conventional framework should be examined and attempts should be made to modify the existing institutions in a way that enables them to provide better support, or establish new ones as needed. Some areas that need immediate attention are discussed below.

Appropriate legal framework and supportive policies

The commercial, banking and company laws in most Islamic countries are fashioned on the Western pattern. Those laws contain provisions that narrow the scope of activities of Islamic banking within conventional limits. While parties can structure their agreements according to an Islamic contract, the enforcement of those agreements in courts may require extra effort and costs. Those conditions, among others, necessitate that special laws for the introduction and practice of Islamic banking be put in place. Such laws would facilitate the operation of Islamic banks side by side with conventional banks.

In addition, laws are needed to allow financial institutions to operate according to Islamic rules and to give room in financial markets for Islamic financial transactions. In that context, the legal framework of Islamic banking and finance might include the following.

Islamic banking laws

This set of laws will be concerned with the establishment, functioning and supervision of Islamic banking in the country. In several Muslim countries such laws already exist and have provided a framework for the working of various Islamic banks. In many others, only small modifications in existing laws can be sufficient.

Laws concerned with financial institutions

Islamic non-banking financial institutions can operate with reasonable ease within the legal framework existing in many Islamic countries. In some others, some modifications are required to widen the scope of operations to cover Islamic financial operations.

Regulation and supervision

There are three main reasons why regulation and supervision of the banking industry are important: to increase the information available to investors (transparency), to ensure the soundness of the financial system, and to improve control of monetary policy. In the case of Islamic banks, there is an additional dimension of supervision which relates to *Sharīʿah* supervision of their activities. Therefore regulation and supervision of Islamic banks is as important as, if not more so than, that of the conventional banks.

Asymmetric information in financial markets exposes investors to many risks and hazards. It can also lead to widespread collapse of financial intermediaries, referred to as financial panic. Because depositors may not be able to assess whether the institutions holding their funds are financially sound or not, if they have doubts about the overall health of the financial intermediaries they may want to pull their funds out of both sound and unsound institutions. The possible outcome is a financial panic that produces large losses for the public and causes serious damage to the economy.

Asymmetric information also leads to the problems of moral hazard and adverse selection in financial markets. In this regard, there is a need to make the activities of the banks as transparent as possible. The present situation of Islamic banks leaves a lot to be desired in this respect. In many cases the most essential information is not made public. More transparency in various aspects of the activities of the Islamic banks will increase the confidence of clients and will help in avoiding panics.

To protect the public and the economy from financial panics, most governments have created elaborate regulatory bodies. As a result, the banking industry has become one of the most heavily regulated industries all over the world. In most countries Islamic banks are put under the supervision of the central bank of the country and are given the same treatment as is given to conventional commercial banks. Some countries issue special Islamic Banking Acts to govern the operations of specific Islamic banks and their relationship with the central bank.[8] Some others issue laws that set general rules for the operations of Islamic banks side by side with conventional banks.[9] The regulatory and supervisory framework prevailing at present for Islamic banks in a cross-section of Muslim countries is summarized in Table 7.1.[10]

It may be noticed that by and large regulatory authorities subject Islamic banks to the same controls, conditions and regulations that they apply to the interest-based banks. However, there are certain factors which require that

Table 7.1 Salient features of Islamic banking and supervisory systems in some Muslim countries

Country	Salient features of Islamic banking supervisory systems
Bahrain	Regulated by the BMA ◆ BMA regulates both commercial banks and investment banks (securities firms); insurance companies are under separate regulatory authority ◆ Dual banking (Islamic and conventional) banking system; Basel capital requirements and core principles adopted for both groups ◆ Four Islamic banking groups: (a) Islamic commercial banks, (b) Islamic investment banks, (c) Islamic offshore banks, and (d) Islamic banking windows in conventional banks ◆ Consolidated supervision ◆ International Accounting Standards adopted ◆ Each Islamic bank must have a *Sharīʿah* board ◆ Compliance with AAOIFI standards under active consideration ◆ Investment deposits, current accounts and capital allocation for assets must be declared ◆ Mandatory liquidity management by adopting the standardized maturity buckets of assets ◆ Islamic and conventional mixed system
Gambia	Regulated by the Central Bank of Gambia (CBG) ◆ Islamic banking law exists ◆ Dual system ◆ Separate *Sharīʿah* board required ◆ Compliance with Basel capital requirements and core principles and International Accounting Standards not clear
Indonesia	Regulated by the Central Bank of Indonesia (Bank Sentral Republik Indonesia, or BSRI) ◆ Separate regulatory bodies for banks and securities firms ◆ Separate Islamic banking law does not exist; Islamic (*Sharīʿah*) banking is covered by section added to banking law (Act No. 10 1998 and Act No. 23 1999) ◆ Separate *Sharīʿah* board required ◆ Islamic windows allowed ◆ Consolidated supervision ◆ Basel capital requirements and core principles adopted ◆ International Accounting Standards adopted ◆ Major financial transformation in process to strengthen bank capital and solvency ◆ Active *Sharīʿah* bank development strategy in place by the government
Iran	Regulated by the Central Bank of Iran (Bank Jamhuri Islami Iran) ◆ All banks in the public sector with a plan for minority privatization ◆ Bank regulation and supervision is strongly affected by monetary as well as fiscal and other government policies ◆ Single (Islamic) banking system under the 1983 Usury Free Banking Law ◆ Modes of finance are defined by this Law ◆ Recent policy orientation towards adopting the Basel capital and supervisory standards and International Accounting Standards ◆ No *Sharīʿah* board for individual banks ◆ Onsite and offsite supervisory methods and objectives defined and applied ◆ Banks and insurance companies are supervised by different regulatory authorities

Table 7.1 (Continued)

Country	Salient features of Islamic banking supervisory systems
Jordan	Regulated by the Central Bank of Jordan (CBJ) ◆ Separate regulatory bodies for banks and securities firms ◆ Islamic banking law exists ◆ Dual system ◆ Separate *Sharīʿah* board required ◆ Consolidated supervision ◆ Basel capital requirements and core principles adopted ◆ International Accounting Standards adopted
Kuwait	Supervised by the Central Bank of Kuwait (CBK) ◆ CBK regulates both commercial banks and investment banks (securities firms); insurance companies are under separate regulatory authority ◆ Dual banking system ◆ Two Islamic banking groups: (a) Islamic commercial banks, and (b) Islamic investment banks. Conventional banks not allowed to have Islamic banking windows ◆ Consolidated supervision ◆ Basel capital requirements and supervisory standards adopted ◆ International Accounting Standards adopted ◆ Separate Islamic banking law under active consideration ◆ Separate *Sharīʿah* board for each bank necessary
Malaysia	Regulated by the Central Bank of Malaysia (Bank Nagara Malaysia, or BNM) ◆ Insurance companies and banks under same regulatory authority; securities firms under separate authority ◆ Private banks ◆ Dual banking system ◆ Islamic windows allowed in conventional banks ◆ Consolidated supervision ◆ Basel capital requirements and core principles adopted ◆ International Accounting Standards adopted ◆ CAMELS rating system adopted ◆ Onsite and offsite supervision well defined with clear objectives ◆ Separate *Sharīʿah* boards at institutional level in the BNM and Securities Exchange Commission ◆ Islamic money market and liquidity arrangement exists ◆ Ministry of Finance closely associated with the supervision of Islamic banks
Pakistan	Regulated by the Central Bank of Pakistan (State Bank of Pakistan, or SBP) ◆ Securities firms and insurance companies are regulated by separate regulatory bodies ◆ Major banks in the public sector; bank regulation and supervision effected by government policies ◆ Islamic banking law does not exist ◆ *Muḍārabah* Companies Law exists ◆ *Sharī'ah* Board concept does not exist ◆ Islamic banks are not identified distinctly ◆ Basel capital requirements and supervisory standards adopted ◆ Bank merger is on cards to strengthen capital ◆ Concept of onsite and offsite supervision exists ◆ Major financial transformation is called for by the Supreme Court of Pakistan to introduce Islamic banking and financial system; a Financial Services Transformation Committee has been established by the SBP

Qatar	Regulated by the Central Bank of Qatar (CBQ) ◆ Dual banking and separate regulatory system ◆ No separate Islamic banking law exists ◆ Islamic banks supervised by special directives of CBQ ◆ Separate *Sharīʿah* boards for banks required ◆ Standardized transparency requirements for Islamic banks exist
Sudan	Regulated by the Central Bank of Sudan (CBS) ◆ Single (Islamic) system ◆ Islamic banking law in place ◆ Separate *Sharīʿah* boards for banks required, and the Central Bank also has a *Sharīʿah* Supervisory Board ◆ Substantial public sector control; supervision and regulation is effected by other government policies ◆ Evolution of financial instruments under way ◆ Compliance with the capital adequacy and supervisory oversight standards of the Basel Committee not clear ◆ Major bank merger is planned to strengthen bank capital
Turkey	Regulated by the Central Bank of Turkey (Turkeyi Cumhuriyet Merkez Bankasi, or TCMB) ◆ Banks and securities firms regulated by separate bodies ◆ Law about Special Finance Houses covers Islamic banks ◆ Dual system; no Islamic windows allowed ◆ Basel Committee capital adequacy requirements and supervisory standards recently introduced ◆ Major financial transformation under way ◆ Onsite and offsite supervision concepts and methods exist
UAE	Regulated by the Central Bank of UAE ◆ Islamic banking law exists ◆ Dual system ◆ Islamic banking windows allowed ◆ Separate *Sharīʿah* boards required ◆ Basel Committee capital adequacy requirements and supervisory standards in place ◆ International Accounting Standards in place
Yemen	Regulated by the Central Bank of Yemen (CBY) ◆ Islamic banking law exists ◆ Dual system ◆ Islamic banking windows allowed ◆ Separate *Sharīʿah* Board required ◆ Major policies and standards set by the CBY are equally applicable to all banks ◆ Separate supervisory office for Islamic banks inside the CBY under active consideration ◆ Compliance with the Basel standards not clear

Note: CAMELS stands for:
C: Capital adequacy
A: Asset quality
M Management quality
E: Earnings quality
L: Liquidity
S: Sensitivity to market risks
Source: Chapra and Khan (2000).

Islamic banks should be treated on a different footing. Some of these factors are listed below:

1 Islamic banks, like all other commercial banks, are required to keep some of their deposits with central banks. Central banks usually pay interest on those deposits which Islamic banks cannot accept. An alternative is needed to ensure that Islamic banks get a fair return on their deposits with the central banks.
2 Central banks function as lenders of last resort to commercial banks, providing loans at times of a liquidity crunch. Although most Islamic banks function under the supervision of the central bank, they cannot legitimately benefit from such a facility because such funds are usually provided on the basis of interest. It is understandable that such assistance cannot be free of cost. However, there is a need to devise and implement an interest-free framework for such assistance. The Pakistan Council of Islamic Ideology suggested a profit-sharing mechanism whereby profit can be calculated on a 'daily-product' basis.[11] Another suggestion is for Islamic banks to build a 'common pool' under the supervision of central banks to provide relief to one another in case of liquidity problems on a cooperative basis.[12]
3 Legal reserves imposed on deposits with conventional banks are meant to meet possible withdrawals, whose rates vary between demand, saving and time deposits. This may apply to the same extent only in case of Islamic banks' demand deposits. However, the *muḍārabah* deposits are like bank equity, so Islamic banks should not be required to maintain reserves against them just as equity capital is not subject to those reserves.[13]
4 In countries where the central bank conducts open market operations, Islamic banks are not able to participate in these operations because of the interest-based nature of the securities bought and sold. Thus Islamic banks are constrained by the fact that financial assets which could be liquidated quickly are not available to them. This introduces some rigidity in the asset structure of Islamic banks.
5 Lack of understanding of the correct nature of Islamic financing techniques may also be partially responsible for rather inappropriate policies of the central banks towards Islamic banks. This is particularly true of *mushārakah* and *muḍārabah*. In debt financing, a loan being granted by a bank is a one-off activity, no matter what the size of the loan. But *mushārakah* and *muḍārabah* are on-going activities and the participation of an Islamic bank in these activities continues as long as the project financed is in operation. This may have important implications for reporting as well as control and regulation of Islamic banks by the central banks.
6 Central bank regulators are sometimes unclear about the exact role of the *Sharīʿah* Boards. It is sometimes felt that these Boards may interfere in the banks' decisions with regard to monetary policy tools such as reserve

requirements, open market operations, and so on. It would be desirable to determine the exact role of the *Sharīʿah* Boards and take the central bankers into confidence.

After the Asian financial crisis of 1997–8, the regulation and supervision of financial firms has assumed greater importance. New regulatory standards are being actively discussed. It is important at this stage that Islamic financial institutions are also integrated into the international financial system. However, due to the unique nature of Islamic banking, the regulatory and supervisory standards applied to conventional banking would, therefore, be insufficient to provide the necessary safeguards for Islamic banking. Ignoring such a fact would leave the whole banking sector exposed, simply because a part of it is not supervised properly. Countries that host Islamic banking and financial institutions have a real interest in closing this hole. This can only be done through a coordinating body which produces and enforces sound regulatory and supervisory standards, and which would be tailored to the needs of Islamic banking and finance. In this regard, the establishment of the IFSB is a step in the right direction. It is important that the IFSB works in close coordination and understanding with international standard-setters, such as the Basel Committee, to develop standards that are suitable for supervision of Islamic banks, yet acceptable to international bodies.

In the aftermath of September 11, some misgivings have emerged in certain quarters with respect to the possible role of Islamic banks in the financing of terrorism. All these are ill-founded. No evidence has ever been produced to that effect. Islamic banking is a dependable, well-regulated and supervised activity. There is no reason for the international financial community to have any fears with respect to its possible use for some illegal activities. Like traditional banks, Islamic financial institutions are simply profit-seeking businesses. They are subject to essentially the same regulations as traditional banks. Compliance therewith is monitored by central banks and other financial regulatory authorities. These regulations are set in accordance with international best practice, and assign prime importance to the 'know thy customer' rule. Like other countries, Muslim countries are also updating their laws so as to be in full compliance with the recommendations of the Financial Action Task Force (FATF) on money laundering and terrorist financing. While on these types of issue Islamic financial institutions have the same legal and regulatory obligations as traditional banks, their overall law and compliance environment is more stringent, insofar as Islamic financial institutions are also subject to the additional self-regulation needed to comply with the Islamic rules.

Of course, without the knowledge of the management or owners, and despite the best efforts of management in applying the 'know thy customer' rule, any financial institution, whether traditional or Islamic, might be misused as a transaction channel by terrorists or other criminals. But we should always bear in mind that Islamic finance has noble objectives and principles, and Islamic banks should be treated accordingly.

All the international financial community has a common cause in fighting money laundering and other financial crimes. This requires developing uniform, non-discriminatory standards and procedures to monitor the working of all financial institutions. There is a need to improve the supervisory and regulatory environment for both conventional and Islamic banks to ensure that they comply with their stated objectives and modes of operations on the one hand, and to increase understanding and cooperation between conventional and Islamic supervisory and regulatory authorities on the other.

Development of a money market

Most Islamic banks exist as a single entity. The strength of commercial banking is derived not from individual institutions but by taking all banks together. Inter-bank transactions among Islamic banks are minimal because in most countries the number of Islamic banks is very small. The evolution of short-term financial assets that Islamic banks may hold and transact among them would go a long way towards making an Islamic money market a reality.

The application of modern means of telecommunication has made it possible to transfer billions of dollars from one continent to the other in a few hours. Thus, the opportunity cost of holding short-term funds has increased tremendously. Islamic banks lack such short-term instruments in which they can profitably invest for short periods. Modern commercial banks can lend each other millions of dollars even for a day. They can also calculate interest on a per day basis. An Islamic alternative to very short-term placement of funds has yet to evolve. The establishment of an IIFM is an important development, but the market will not be effective if appropriate money market instruments are not developed.

Corporate governance

In recent years, especially after the collapse of some major US and European firms due to corporate fraud, the issue of corporate governance has been receiving a lot of attention in conventional economic literature and public policy debates. Serious concerns have been expressed that the contemporary monitoring and control mechanisms for public corporations are seriously defective, leading to suboptimal economic and social development. There is a shift from the traditional 'shareholder value centred' view of corporate governance in favour of a corporate governance structure that looks after the interest of a wider circle of stakeholders. The traditional approach of corporate governance among economists and legal scholars was based on an agent–principal relationship between the investor and the manager. The basic features of this model are that the shareholders ought to have the control; managers have a fiduciary duty to serve shareholder interest alone and that the objective of the firm ought to be the maximization of the shareholders' wealth. Economists and ethicists now argue that this profit-maximization for shareholders approach is too narrow a view for an economic analysis of corporate governance because of externalities on other stakeholders. There is a strong movement towards a broader stakeholders' model of corporate governance which implies that the firm should give due importance to a broader circle of stakeholders including employees, customers, suppliers, investors and consumers. However, the stakeholder model is largely normative and is still evolving to find a sound theoretical foundation in conventional economic literature. A critical review of the evolving literature dealing with the stakeholder model reveals that various authors support this view with diverse and often contradictory evidence and arguments.[14] Writers find it difficult to draw a clear line between who really is an actual stakeholder and who is not.

Zamir Iqbal and Abbas Mirakhor (2004) argue that the governance model in the Islamic economic system is a stakeholder-oriented model whereby governance structure and process at both the system and the firm levels protect the rights of all stakeholders who are exposed to any risk as a result of the firm's activities. Whereas the conventional system is struggling to find convincing arguments to justify stakeholders' participation in governance, the foundation of the stakeholder model is firmly established in Islam's principles of property rights, commitment to explicit and implicit contractual agreements and implementation of an effective incentive system. A firm in the Islamic economic system can be viewed as a 'nexus-of-contracts' whose objective is to minimize transaction cost and to maximize profits and returns to investors, subject to constraints that these objectives do not violate the rights of any other party (whether it interacts with the firm directly or indirectly).

Zamir Iqbal and Abbas Mirakhor (2004) go on to point out that Islam's framework of contracts places equal emphasis on obligations arising from both explicit and implicit contracts. This behaviour is expected from individuals as well as from public and private entities. Therefore, just as it is incumbent upon economic agents to honour explicit contracts, it is obligatory on them to preserve sanctity of implicit contracts by recognizing and protecting the property rights of stakeholders, community, society and state. Whereas the conventional stakeholders theory is searching for sound arguments to incorporate implicit contracts in the theory of the firm, in the Islamic economic system rights of (and obligations to) stakeholders are taken for granted.

Islam's framework of property rights and contracts also establishes guidelines regarding who can qualify as a stakeholder, and if such stakeholders have the right to influence the firm's decision-making and governance. In a very broad sense, any group or individuals with whom a firm has any explicit or implicit contractual obligations qualifies as a stakeholder even though the firm may not have formal contracts with them through mutual bargaining. In Islam, a stakeholder is the one whose property rights are at stake or at risk due to voluntary or involuntary actions of the firm. In case someone's rights are encroached upon or threatened as a result of a firm's operations, that individual, group, community or society becomes a stakeholder.

Provisions seeking to protect the (informationally) weaker party are quite commonplace in the Islamic law of contracting (e.g., *khiyār-al-ʿayb* or option against defects that seeks to protect the interest of the buyers). However, the law cannot take into account all the externalities imposed by shareholder wealth maximization choices on non-shareholder stakeholders. It is here that the role of Islamic values comes in. A saying of the Prophet (Peace be upon him) states that *'a Muslim is the one from whose hand others are safe'*.[15] An interesting distinction is often made in the literature dealing with stakeholders between explicit contracts and implicit contracts. Contracts between firms and financiers (*muḍārib* and *rabb al-māl*), wage (*ijārah* and *juʿālah*) contracts, and product warranties (*khiyār-al-ʿayb*) are all examples of explicit contracts. Many such contracts discussed in the stakeholder theory literature are rooted firmly in Islamic law. Implicit contracts or 'unwritten codes of conduct' are relatively vague and informal. Examples of implicit contracts discussed in the literature are a firm's commitment to neighbouring community, fair prices and continuing services for customers, and job security to employees. As highlighted above, such contracts are rooted in Islamic ethics.[16]

In the light of the above discussion, the corporate governance structure in an Islamic framework should be comprised, amongst others, of the following key elements:

1 The corporate governance framework should protect shareholders' rights. These include property rights, the right of representation, the separation of ownership and control, and so on.
2 The corporate governance framework should ensure the equitable treatment of all shareholders, including minority and foreign shareholders.
3 The corporate governance framework should recognize the rights of other stakeholders, whether covered by explicit or implicit contracts.
4 The corporate governance framework should ensure that timely and accurate disclosure is made on all material matters regarding the corporation, including the financial situation, performance, ownership, and governance of the company.
5 The corporate governance framework should ensure the strategic guidance of the company, the effective monitoring of management by the board, and the board's accountability to the company and to shareholders.

While all these issues are as important for Islamic banks as for any other corporate entity, there are special considerations in the case of Islamic banks that may have important implications for the corporate governance structures. These include:

1 The ownership structure of Islamic banks depicts high concentration. This introduces the possibility of monopoly power and undue influence by a few major shareholders.
2 Investment deposit holders share in the risks but have no representation on the Board, while the nature of these deposits is not very different from equity. This may encourage the management of Islamic banks to take undue risks on the part of investment deposit holders.
3 Since the current deposits are in the nature of loans to the bank, they are not entitled to any return. In theory, the principal is guaranteed but, in the absence of any deposit insurance, these deposits are exposed to more risks than in the case of conventional banks. The rights of current deposit holders need special treatment.

Human capital formation

Human resource development is another major challenge. Three aspects need special attention in this regard:

1 As mentioned above, there is a serious shortage of scholars who possess even a working knowledge of both Islamic *fiqh* and modern economics and finance. Increasing the supply of such scholars is crucial for the development of Islamic banking in the right direction.
2 Most of the managers of Islamic banks are not very well trained in the use of Islamic modes of finance. The managers of Islamic banks may have been attending some short-term courses either on the job or elsewhere, but there are not many formal training programmes that fully prepare employees of Islamic banks for the needs of the system. Most Islamic bank employees, including managers and financial experts, come from traditional sources lacking the necessary expertise in and commitment for Islamic banking. An institution is what its employees make it. Therefore, it is extremely important to have the people with the right kind of skills and commitment to run Islamic banks.
3 The employees and management of Islamic banks also need to be trained in modern techniques of financial management, especially risk management, as well as information technology.

Conclusion

Despite showing tremendous success in various areas, Islamic banking remains a nascent industry. It started in a hostile environment and has struggled for more than a quarter of a century. It has scored a number of successes but it still faces several challenges. Like any financial system, it has to be seen as an evolving reality. At each stage of its development, one has to stop and analyse past experiences and learn lessons for charting the future course of action. In this perspective, there is no dearth of problems for the industry.

There are several unresolved theoretical issues. These issues have a constraining effect on the growth of the industry because by its very nature the success of the industry crucially depends on *Sharīʿah*-compatibility. Until the *Sharīʿah* issues can be resolved in each area, no practice can begin. The problem is complicated by the fact that the jurists and the financial engineers do not communicate very well with each other since each group has its own language, methodology and mentality.

There are also several operational issues which need to be tackled. In a rapidly globalizing environment, Islamic banks have to find common interface with conventional banks. With the implementation of Basel II around the corner, Islamic banks have to employ modern risk management techniques, improve internal audit systems and enhance international standards of transparency, regulation and supervision.

8
Islamic Banking in the Twenty-First Century

Thirty years ago Islamic banking was considered wishful thinking. However, serious research work since then has shown that Islamic banking is not only feasible and viable, it is an efficient and productive way of financial intermediation. A substantial number of Islamic banks have also been established during this period. The successful operation of these institutions is sufficient to show that Islamic banking offers an alternative method of commercial banking. The fact that many conventional banks, including some major multinational Western banks, have also started using Islamic banking techniques is further proof of the viability of Islamic banking. However, Islamic banking is still a nascent industry and has a long way to go before being on par with other well-developed models of financial intermediation. From a niche market it has to earn the status of a mature international industry. This requires that Islamic banks take a critical look at their activities, correct their mistakes, identify their long-run comparative advantage and exploit it to the fullest possible extent. In the long run, for its viability and survival, Islamic banking has to rely on its strengths as an alternative model of financial intermediation, rather than on the sympathies of its clients or government support.

Where Islamic banking needs to go: the way ahead

The commendable achievements during the last 30 years do not mean that all is well with Islamic banking. In the last chapter we identified some of the challenges that it is facing. While many of these are a result of the inappropriate environment in which Islamic banks are working, there are others which have arisen from the practices of Islamic banks themselves. In this chapter we examine how in our view the Islamic financial industry needs to respond to those challenges as it enters the twenty-first century.

The need to broaden the base

The ownership structure of the Islamic financial industry is highly concentrated. Three or four families own a large percentage of the industry. The leading families include those of Prince Mohamed Al-Faisal, Sheikh Saleh Kamil and Sheikh Suleiman Al-Rajhi, all from Saudi Arabia. This concentration of ownership could result in substantial financial instability and possible collapse of the industry if anything happens to those families, or the next generation of these families change their priorities. Similarly, the experience of country-wide experiments has also been mostly on the initiative of rulers not elected through popular votes. The history of these experiments shows that a change in government can lead to a sudden turnaround. The abrupt death of General Zia ul-Haq in Pakistan turned the climate of opinion in official circles against the commitment of the country for the Islamization of the financial system. A similar thing happened in Sudan after the overthrow of Jafar Al-Numeiry. In Iran the Islamization of the financial system has not witnessed a regime change yet. It remains to be seen how well the system weathers such a change. The situation would appear even more fragile when one considers the fact that Islamic banking has not gone much beyond the '*murābaḥah* regime', the closest alternative to the interest regime. So far so good; but unless the other Islamic modes of finance, especially profit-sharing modes, are given a chance and they prove to be as efficient as the theory asserts, Islamic banking will not show its real colours. There are many people, including some sympathizers, who assert that the '*murābaḥah* regime' is more of a change in name than in substance. There is no doubt that there is a definite preference among the Muslim masses for non-interest modes of financing. This popular support needs to be converted into grassroots involvement in Islamic banking, both in terms of ownership as well as beneficiaries of bank financing. Going from non-interest financing to profit-sharing financing, or a more balanced combination of the two, is the next milestone that the Islamic banking industry should head towards. This issue needs further discussion which is covered in the next section.

The need for diversification in the use of Islamic modes of finance

Islamic financial transactions are of two kinds. One is based on a fixed charge on capital, and the other is based on profit-sharing which does not guarantee any rate of return. Both kinds provide finance through the purchase and sale of real commodities. Conventional financial transactions are based on lending and borrowing of money for a guaranteed charge (interest).

Islamic banking specialists built up their hopes on Islamic banks to provide a significant amount of profit-sharing finance. This would have economic effects similar to direct investment and would be expected to produce a strong economic development impact. In practice, the alternative modes of financing being used by most Islamic banks are dominated by fixed-return modes such as *murābaḥah* and leasing. Though such modes are clearly distinguishable from interest-based modes since transactions through these modes are always undertaken using real commodities, some scholars have argued that this is one of the most serious problems facing Islamic banking as an alternative model which is distinguished by risk sharing. Siddiqi (1983) laments:

> we cannot claim, for an interest-free alternative not based on sharing, the superiority which could be claimed on the basis of profit-sharing. What is worse, if the alternative in practice is built around predetermined rates of return to investible funds, it would be exposed to the same criticism which was directed at interest as a fixed charge on capital. It so happens that the returns to finance provided in the modes of finance based on *murābaḥah, bayʿ salam,* leasing and lending with a service charge, are all predetermined as in the case of interest. Some of these modes of finance are said to contain some element of risk, but all these risks are insurable and are actually insured against. The uncertainty or risk to which the business being so financed is exposed is fully passed over to the other party. A financial system built solely around these modes of financing can hardly claim superiority over an interest-based system on grounds of equity, efficiency, stability, and growth.[1]

He considers this issue to be the main problem of contemporary Islamic banking, (so much so that it can be characterized as a crisis of identity of the Islamic financial movement).

There is no denying the fact that the predominance of fixed return modes such as *murābaḥah* and leasing on the asset side is a problem but this should not be blown out of proportion and called a crisis of identity. The '*murābaḥah* regime' may be considered a first step in a long journey; the important thing is that it is a step in the right direction. Some people would argue that the more risky modes of financing were unfairly treated in early writings on Islamic banking. There is lot of truth in this argument. Banks, under the present circumstances, cannot afford to increase their risk exposure to any large extent. The emphasis should move to a greater reliance of businesses on equity and smaller reliance on credit. For this purpose, attempts should be made to increase the number of equity institutions such as mutual funds, unit trusts, and so on. Nobody denies that *murābaḥah* and leasing are permissible modes of financing. They also have some desirable features such as simplicity, convenience and safety. It may also be noted that if these modes are used properly, then some risk sharing *is* involved. The fact that these risks are insurable and are actually insured against should not be an issue. The important thing one should ensure is that the cost of insurance is borne by the owner of the 'asset'.

There are many reasons why businessmen do not prefer PLS contracts. These include, among others: (i) the need to keep and reveal detailed records; (ii) it is difficult to expand a business financed through *muḍārabah* because of limited opportunities to re-invest retained earnings and/or raising additional funds; (iii) the entrepreneur cannot become the sole owner of the project except through diminishing *mushārakah*, which may take a long time. Similarly, there are some practical reasons for banks to prefer fixed-return modes, including the fact that due to moral hazard and adverse selection problems in all agent–principal contracts such as *muḍārabah*, there is a need for closer monitoring of the project. This requires project monitoring staff and mechanisms, which increase the costs of these contracts. Moreover, on the liabilities side, the structure of deposits of Islamic banks is not sufficiently long term, and therefore they do not want to get involved in long-term projects. Third, PLS contracts require a lot of information about the entrepreneurial abilities of the customer. This may not be easily available to the bank.

Instruments such as *murābaḥah*, by providing investors high liquidity with low risks, are serving a useful purpose. However, an overwhelming use of these modes by Islamic banks in the absence of other Islamic financial institutions which can offer profit-sharing finance has led to some undesirable results for Islamic finance scene. These are examined below.

Confidence of clients

Since the use of risk-sharing modes, considered to be the hallmark of Islamic banking, is rather limited, clients do not notice any significant operational departure from the previous practices based on fixed rate financing. Moreover, several problems have been noted in the way *murābaḥah* is being used in practice, and consequently many have started doubting the benefits of the new model. Opponents of Islamic banking have been encouraged to even question the existence of a unique model. Even many sympathizers, especially those with strong religious sentiments, are feeling uncomfortable. In 1991, The Federal *Sharīʿah* Court of Pakistan issued a judgment obliging the Government of Pakistan to make several changes in the way Islamic banking was being practised to make it consistent with Islamic *Sharīʿah*. Banking crucially depends on the confidence of the clients. Therefore, serious attempts should be made to 'cleanse' the 'quasi' *murābaḥah* being practised by many Islamic banks at present of their undesirable features, so as to make it 'genuine' *murābaḥah*. Islamic banks must ensure that the conditions specified by jurists for the use of these modes are strictly observed.

Defaulters and the issue of compensation and penalties

By using fixed rate modes of financing, the Islamic banks are able to sidestep various problems of moral hazard and adverse selection. But precisely because of the same reason (i.e., use of debt as compared to equity), they land themselves in a serious problem. *Murābaḥah* deals create debt obligations against buyer firms. Now, while it is permissible to charge a higher price in credit sales as compared to cash sales, the wherewithal of the *murābaḥah* mode of financing, once the deal has been entered into, a fixed liability is created. If the buyer defaults on his payment, banks cannot charge anything extra because that would mean taking *ribā*. Thus, there is a built-in incentive for immoral buyers to default.

Islamic jurists have been discussing this problem. It is generally agreed that penalties, both physical and financial, can be imposed against defaulters but the bank must not benefit from these penalties. Many contemporary scholars have argued that the banks can be compensated because damage has been caused by the defaulter and Islam permits, and even encourages, compensation for damages. The issue remains unresolved.

Illiquidity of assets

Another problem caused by the predominance of debt-based modes of financing is that it is difficult to transform these financial modes into negotiable financial instruments. Once a debt has been created, it cannot be transferred to anyone else except at par value. This renders the whole structure of the Islamic financial market highly illiquid. This is one of the major obstacles in the development of secondary markets in Islamic financial instruments. Unless equity-based modes become more popular or other negotiable instruments are developed, the Islamic financial markets will remain undeveloped. Some attempts are being made to develop negotiable instruments based on *ijārah, salam* and *istiṣnāʿ*. However, these have not been used to any significant extent so far. The major hope for developing Islamic secondary markets lies in a wider application of equity-based financial instruments and securitization of some of the existing instruments.

Short-term asset structure

Banks everywhere prefer short-term investments. This is so because they work on the basis of small reserves. They have to have the ability to liquidate their assets fairly quickly, if the need arises. In the case of Islamic banks, the short-term structure of their assets is even more pronounced. This also has to do with the predominance of *murābaḥah* among the modes of finance. *Murābaḥah*, a trading practice, by its very nature is a short-term contract. Even though it is conceivable to design an instalment sale *murābaḥah* contract spreading over many years, the needs for which the *murābaḥah* contract can genuinely be used are, by and large, short term. Therefore, *murābaḥah* deals entered into by the Islamic banks have been, and are going to be, largely short term. Since *murābaḥah* comprises a very large percentage of Islamic banks' investments, the structure of their assets has also become short-term.[2]

Is it a problem? There are needs for financial resources on a long-term basis: for example, venture capital, project finance, and mortgage finance.

In the conventional framework, these needs are typically met by other financial instruments, such as bonds and securities. There can be no interest-based bonds. Islamic financial systems have to provide an alternative for them. For this purpose equities need to be a major activity in the Islamic financial market. The problem assumes a more critical dimension in view of the fact that in most of the Muslim countries, the major domain of Islamic banks, well-developed securities markets do not exist. Unless the use of profit-sharing modes is increased, Islamic finance cannot fulfil its promise of eliminating interest from the financial markets.

Another direction that Islamic finance needs to consider is to extend the application of the principle, *al-muḍārib udārib*, on which the original model of Islamic banking was developed. That principle essentially allows for subcontracting. If the principle is acceptable, there is no reason to restrict it only to *muḍārabah*. Contracts can also be designed on the basis of other classical contracts, such as *ijārah* or *istiṣnāʿ*. In other words, the original contractee may arrange to fulfil the obligations under the contract through third parties. That the principle is acceptable from an Islamic point of view is not questionable.

Moreover, *murābaḥah* as a classical Islamic contract does not involve financial intermediation. It was a contract involving only two parties, a seller and a buyer, with no financier in between. The seller sells on credit, charging a price higher than the cash price, and the buyer pays at a later date. Banks came into this business by buying at the lower cash price and selling to the ultimate buyer at the higher credit price. But since buying and selling is not the core business of banks, and they do not want to be exposed to all the risks involved, they have had to resort some intervening arrangements, which sometimes even violated the *Sharīʿah* requirements. As mentioned above, that has given rise to criticisms as well as causing uneasiness among clients. To remedy this situation, it has been proposed[3] that since financial intermediation does not involve selling goods and services directly, financial intermediaries may get involved in *murābaḥah* business indirectly. The same applies to other forms of business such as *salam, istiṣnāʿ*, leasing, and so on. A financial institution is not fully equipped to handle these businesses directly. It is often reluctant to fully expose its capital to the risks involved in direct businesses. As a result it tries to make the transactions as risk-free as possible. It does not care if this means, on the average and in the long run, obtaining a lower rate of return.

Now imagine a whole range of businesses doing *murābaḥah, salam, istiṣnāʿ* and leasing. These businesses would know the risks they are taking. They would also be able to diversify their activities as a means of reducing risk. Perhaps they are already specializing in handling different market segments in terms of the commodities involved. These businesses would need financing, which could come from Islamic financial institutions. In this way there would be a buffer between the changing circumstances of real businesses and those handling only finance. It would thus relieve the Islamic financial institutions from the need to reduce risk by making their contracts look like payment of less money now in exchange for more money to be received in future. The fact that their stake will not be in individual deals based on one of the contracts mentioned above but in a large basket of deals will make a crucial difference. In its own interest, the business being financed will have reduced the risk of loss by diversification and other methods. The financial institution will have the added opportunity of diversification by offering its funds to a variety of businesses.

Islamic financial institutions therefore would finance *murābaḥah* companies on a *muḍārabah* or profit-sharing basis. Islamic banks accepting people's savings in their investment accounts on the basis of *muḍārabah* would be giving that money out on the basis of *muḍārabah*. This would conform to the earliest form of financial intermediation discussed in Islamic jurisprudence, *al-muḍārib udārib*. The risks involved will be financial risks which financial intermediaries have learnt, and continue learning, how to handle. Business risks will become the concerns of business houses closer to those who buy and sell, even produce and import/export, or build and lease, hire and sublet, and so on. There will be no need to twist and turn a trade deal to make it serve the purposes of a financial intermediary.

The proposal, which involves separating purely financial transactions from business transactions, would have two advantages in comparison to what we actually observe today in the Islamic financial markets. First, it would comprise a mixture of sharing-based modes with trade-based modes of financing that result in creating fixed payment obligations or debts, unlike the current situation dominated by trade-based modes. Second, it would enable Islamic financial institutions to offer much-needed long-term financing, a field from which they are presently shying away. With the exception of *istiṣnāʿ* which can be a basis of long-term financing, all other trade-based modes of financing, such as, *murābaḥah*, leasing and *salam*, are suitable only for short-term financing. Given this change they could rightfully demonstrate how their activities avoid contributing to the instability of the system, something interest-based institutions are said to be prone to. By doing this the system will enjoy the unique feature of sharing-based intermediation, synchronization between revenues and payment obligations, and will still retain the flexibility which the presence of very low-risk modes of financing impart to a system. A strong presence of sharing-based modes of financing will give credibility to the claim of the Islamic financial system to be more just than the conventional system. If this vision is to be accepted, one would need to encourage the establishment of a whole range of companies: *murābaḥah* companies, *salam* and *istiṣnāʿ* companies, leasing companies, and so on, in order to channel finance from Islamic banks to those actually engaged in production of wealth. There are indications that Islamic financial industry is going in this direction.

Preparing for increased competition

So far, Islamic banks have had a fairly large degree of 'monopoly' over the financial resources of the Islamically-motivated public. This situation is changing fast and Islamic banks had better prepare for a global market. Capturing a big chunk in its home base, the Arabian Gulf, is one thing; operating in the international market place is another. Islamic banks are now facing ever-increasing competition. An important development in Islamic banking in the last few years has been the entry of some mega-international banks into the Islamic financial industry. This development is a clear recognition of the viability of Islamic banking as an alternative model but, at the same time, it has increased competition. Does it augur well for the future of Islamic banking?

The answer will depend on how the Islamic banks react to this development. In general, competition is supposed to be good for the growth of any industry: it forces inefficient firms to either shape up or ship out; it reduces the costs and improves services to consumers; it promotes innovation and brings improvements in product quality. However, there is one exception to this rule, which is the well-known infant-industry argument which states that small firms in their infancy may be protected from harsh, ruthless competition until they can stand on their feet and are able to face competition from their bigger counterparts. One may argue that Islamic banks may well deserve that treatment. The conventional banks, particularly the Western banks, have a large advantage over Islamic banks in terms of their size, experience, market coverage and long standing in the industry. This exposes the Islamic banks to possible unequal competition.

While it may be difficult to settle the point on theoretical grounds, the stark reality is that even if one could invoke infant-industry entitlements for Islamic banks, in practice there is no institutional arrangement to put those into operation. Infant-industry benefits are usually offered by governments in terms of tax concessions or provision of subsidies. No such possibility exists at present, so the survival of Islamic banks essentially depends on their own efficiency and performance.

The competition from conventional banks is expected to increase further in the near future due to globalization. Due to liberalization, the world markets are rapidly converging into a single market place. To benefit from the opportunities offered by globalization, the Islamic banks need to improve the quality of their services and develop suitable products. Technological innovations are also playing an important part in financial integration and globalization. Electronic banking and widespread use of computers in banking has transformed the way banking business is being done. The communication revolution through electronic correspondence has reduced the cost of international communication. Globalization of financial markets has led to more and more integration of capital markets. Liberalization of foreign exchange markets has further reinforced this trend. Paper currency is being replaced with plastic cards and electronic ledgers are replacing accounts books. Now, the savings of one country can be invested in other countries by the click of a mouse. Customers can 'navigate' on the Internet between competing banks, unit trusts, mutual funds and even business firms.

Islamic banks cannot remain aloof from these developments. They must carefully watch these developments and adjust their strategies accordingly. In order to operate in global markets, they have to form strategic alliances with other banks. It will also be useful to build bridges between existing Islamic banks and those conventional banks that are interested in banking according to Islamic principles. Such strategic alliances will benefit both sides. Islamic banks will benefit as the Western banks will bring their efficiency, market research, innovative capabilities, sophisticated banking and results-oriented approach to Islamic banking, which may lead to the development of new products and provision of better services to consumers. On the other hand, the conventional banks will benefit from the indigenous infrastructure, closer consumer contacts and Islamic credentials of Islamic banks.

It may be worth pointing out here that there are some genuine concerns about the operations of large multinational banks in Islamic banking practices. Naturally, their motives are purely commercial. They view it as a lucrative business opportunity, which is fair enough. However, doubts have been expressed as to whether they are following the rules of the game. It is noted that conventional banks may not be able to follow correctly the precepts of Islamic banking. In all major Islamic banks, there is a *Sharīʿah* board which regularly reviews the operations and contracts of the bank to determine their compliance with the requirements of the *Sharīʿah*. Such elaborate arrangements do not exist in conventional Western banks in most cases. Though most of them may have *Sharīʿah* advisers, the credibility gap would still remain. Alliances with well established Islamic banks might help remove that gap. Irrespective of whether these doubts are in fact true or not, common perceptions have important implications for business. Conventional banks stand to benefit greatly in this respect by working together with Islamic banks.

The need to increase the size of Islamic banks

In the wake of technological change and globalization, Islamic banks must prepare themselves to handle a much larger size of operations and to deal with internationally-minded and financially sophisticated customers. The required infrastructure and the larger and geographically wider scope of operations calls for larger bank size. There is a world-wide trend towards mergers. In the last couple of years alone, more than 20 banks and financial companies, which were already very big, have merged to form mega-banks. As against this, the available data show that Islamic banks and financial institutions are relatively small and below the optimum size, as is clear from the following facts:

1 If the assets of *all* Islamic banks were pooled, they would still be less than those of any *single* bank in the top 50 banks in the world.
2 The assets of the largest Islamic bank are equal to only 1 per cent of the assets of the largest bank in the world.

Considering that Islamic banks and financial institutions are generally very small in size, serious consideration should be given to mergers, syndicated finance, and the creation and management of joint financial services companies. Islamic banks also have to form strategic alliances with Western banks to cope with the implications of globalization in the field of finance. Financial markets can no longer be restricted to national boundaries. Furthermore, there are large Muslim communities in several Western countries. Cooperation with Western banks is also needed to provide financial services to these communities in accordance with their faith.

The emerging shape of financial firms

Until a few years ago, there was a sharp distinction between bank and non-bank financial intermediaries. On the one hand, banks were not allowed to invest in stock markets; on the other hand, non-bank financial institutions were not allowed to have current accounts. This Anglo-American model of 'banking separation' whereby commercial banking and investment banking were not allowed to be managed by a single 'bank holding company' has lost a lot of ground in the last few years. The distinction between bank and non-bank financial intermediaries has been blurred. Even the most famous law in this regard, the Glass–Steagall Act in the USA, has been repealed. A free-market approach to integrated financial service provision which will allow affiliation among all financial and non-financial companies has become popular in Europe, the USA and Japan, and may soon be enacted in many other countries.

Removal of barriers in the areas of their operations is bringing banks and security firms into direct competition. This is bound to change the profile of a financial firm in the twenty-first century. Islamic banks are in a distinctly advantageous position in this regard, because they are supposed, by construction, to take part in direct investment and trade. However, by restricting their financial operations to debt or debt-like instruments, they are behaving more like old-fashioned conventional banks which, as mentioned above, are fast becoming obsolete. In order to take advantage of new opportunities and to face competition they have to find ways and means to overcome their inhibitions and move towards a universal banking model.

Areas of potential growth

During most of the period under study, Islamic banking mostly operated in the commercial banking field. During the 1990s, 'fund management' came on the scene and showed remarkable growth. However, it is far from reaching its maximum potential. Commercial banks were the ideal financial intermediaries in the past, but things are changing. In advanced economies the role of typical commercial banks in transferring funds from fund owners to fund users is declining. Banks are losing ground to other financial institutions which are marketing innovative 'financial products'. Banks have responded, where the law permits, by entering the securities business. Structured securitized credit is fast replacing simple bank loans in Western banking systems and elsewhere.

The establishment of equity institutions

There is now a world-wide trend for establishing equity institutions such as mutual funds. Savers are now increasingly recognizing the benefits of profit-based instruments. The appeal of rate-based investment is waning. Although stock market investments have not become any less risky over the years, savers are beginning to accept the historical evidence that in any five-year period since the Second World War, with one exception, stocks have produced higher returns than bank accounts, bonds or bullion. Throughout the 1990s savers all over the world have deserted traditional bank accounts and low-yielding government bonds by the thousands. As a result, stock markets witnessed high rates of growth as well as substantial increases in stock prices. A massive reallocation of wealth took place. Institutions such as mutual funds and pension plans became increasing popular. In the USA, the relative share of pension funds in the total assets of financial intermediaries increased from 17.4 per cent in 1980 to 25.2 per cent in 1995. Similarly, the share of mutual funds has gone up from 3.6 per cent in 1980 to 15 per cent in 1995. The share of depository institutions decreased from 60 per cent to 37 per cent in the same period. In UK 10 per cent of all new savings are finding their way into stock funds. British savers held US$65 billion in personal equity plans in 1997, as compared with US$3.8 billion in 1990. The net assets of Italian mutual funds soared from US$123 billion to US$206 billion in 1997 alone. French stock funds increased by 48 per cent, while Spanish equity funds tripled. German investments in mutual funds have been growing by 20 per cent a year since 1990. Virtually all of this money was diverted from bank accounts. Stocks, which represented only 18 per cent of European household savings in 1992, accounted for more than 26 per cent in 1998.[4] The decline of stock markets during 2000–3 slowed down this trend, but only temporarily. The higher role of direct finance as compared to indirect finance seems to be irreversible. Islamic banks must prepare themselves quickly to be involved in increasingly active and growing equity markets.

Giving more importance to 'fund management' and building more stock companies, mutual funds, and offering equity-based instruments are some of the most important potential areas of growth for the Islamic financial industry.

Islamic *ṣukūk*

The Islamic financial industry has emerged as a viable alternative to the traditional interest-based financial system. However, despite the urgent need for financial instruments for public sector resource mobilization, little progress has been made. It is only recently that some initiatives have been taken to issue *Sharīʿah*-compatible instruments for mobilizing resources for public sector projects. These involve issuance of *ṣukūk*, an instrument for pooled securitizations. *Ṣukūk* are secondary instruments based on returns from real assets or their usufruct. The trend, once it gathers momentum, will lead to the development of secondary markets, a step that is absolutely necessary for the industry. Therefore in the following paragraphs we present key elements of this potentially attractive area of growth.[5]

Islamic scholars offer the following general guidelines for issuing securitized Islamic financial instruments:

1 Instruments should represent share in equity, real assets, usufruct, money or debt or a combination of some or all of these:
   (a) instruments representing real physical assets and usufructs are negotiable at market prices;
   (b) instruments representing debts in their negotiability are subject to the rules of *ḥawālah*;
   (c) instruments representing money are subject to the rules of *ṣarf* in their negotiability;
   (d) instruments representing a combination of different categories: are subject to the rules relating to the dominant category: that is, if debts are relatively larger, the portfolio's negotiability will be subject to *ḥawālah al-dayn*; if the currency component is larger, to *ṣarf*; and if physical assets and usufructs are overwhelming, to selling at market prices.

2 The issuance of securitized Islamic financial instruments based on *muḍārabah* or *mushārakah* is subject to the following conditions:
   (a) the principal and expected return on investment cannot be guaranteed;
   (b) if the financial instruments were issued for specific purposes or projects, the prospectus should include full disclosure of the nature of the activities, contractual relationships and obligations between the parties involved and the ratio of profit sharing;
   (c) the issuers of financial instruments should keep separate accounts for each project and must declare its profit and loss accounts at the date mentioned in the prospectus and balance sheets.

3 Holders of Islamic financial instruments are the owners of whatever rights these instruments represent and bearers of all related risks.
4 An instrument the object of which is debt should not be allowed to earn any return and its negotiability must be in accordance with the *Sharīʿah* rules.

In recent years, Islamic financial engineers have developed a number of certificates complying with these principles. Some of these are described in Table 8.1 (below).

Ṣukūk are a new addition to the Islamic products kit. Judged from the success they have achieved over the last few years, they offer a very promising area of growth for the Islamic financial industry. Some examples of the application of *ṣukūk* in recent years are given below.

1 The Bahrain Monetary Agency (BMA) has been issuing *ijārah ṣukūk* since 2001. These *ṣukūk* are of medium-term maturity. The government uses the proceeds for financing government infrastructure projects. The government of Bahraiṇ has so far issued *ijārah ṣukūk* worth US$730 million: $100 million in 2001, $200 million in 2002 and $430 million in 2003.

2 In July 2002, the government of Malaysia issued US$600 million Trust Certificates (TCs), due 2007. The TCs are based on the concept of *ijārah.* Each certificate-holder holds ownership of *beneficiary right* of land parcels for the July 2002–July 2007 period. These *beneficiary right* of land parcels have been sold by the government of Malaysia to the special purpose vehicle (SPV) Malaysia Global Ṣukūk Inc. (incorporated in Labuan, Malaysia, with limited liability) and then the SPV is sold to the investors for five years. The SPV kept the *beneficiary right* of the properties in trust and issued floating rate trust certificates (*ṣukūk*) to investors with pricing referenced against the government of Malaysia's sovereign credit curve rather than the value of the property assets. The receipts of the sale of trust certificates are paid to the government of Malaysia as (rent) price for the *beneficiary right* of properties for five years.

Table 8.1 Some Islamic negotiable instruments

Instrument	**Description of the instrument**
1 Certificates of ownership in leased assets	These are certificates that carry equal value and are issued either by the owner of a leased asset or an asset to be leased by promise, or by his financial agent, the aim of which is to sell the asset and recover its value from sub scription, in which case the holders of the certificates become owners of the assets jointly with its benefits and risks.

Table 8.1 (Continued)

Instrument	Description of the instrument
2(a) Certificates of ownership of usufructs of existing assets	These are documents of equal value that are issued either by the owner of usufruct of an existing asset or a financial intermediary acting on the owner's behalf, with the aim of leasing or subleasing this asset and receiving rental from the revenue of subscription. The certificate holders become the owners of the usufructs jointly with its benefits and risks.
2(b) Certificates of ownership of usufructs to be made available in the future as per description	These are documents of equal value issued for the sake of leasing assets that the lessor is liable to provide in the future whereby the rental is recovered from the subscription income, in which case the holders of the certificates become owners of the usufruct of these future assets jointly with its benefits and risks.
3 Certificates of ownership of services of a specified supplier	These are documents of equal value issued for the sake of providing or selling services through a specified supplier (such as educational programmes in a nominated university) and obtaining the value in the form of subscription income, in which case the holders of the certificates become owners of the services.
4 Certificates of ownership of services to be made available in the future as per description	These are documents of equal value issued for the sake of providing or selling services through non-existing suppliers with the description of the subject matter (such as educational programmes of a specific quality, schedule, duration, etc., without mentioning the educational institution) and obtaining the value in the form of subscription income, in which case the holders of the certificates become owners of the services.
5 *Salam* certificates	These are documents of equal value issued for the sake of mobilizing *salam* capital and the items to be delivered on *salam* basis are owned by the certificate holders.
6 *Istiṣnāʿ* certificates	These are documents that carry equal value and are issued with the aim of mobilizing the funds required for producing a certain item and the items to be produced on *istiṣnāʿ* basis are owned by the certificate holders. The certificate holders are entitled to the item or the selling price of the manufactured item.

7 *Murābaḥah* certificates	These are documents of equal value issued for the purpose of financing the *murābaḥah* commodity and the certificate holders become the owners of the *murābaḥah* commodity.
8(a) Participation certificates managed on the basis of *mushārakah* contract	These are documents that represent projects or activities that are managed on the basis of *mushārakah* by appointing either one of the parties or any other party to manage the operation. The issuer of the certificates is the inviter to a partnership in a specific project or activity. The subscribers are the partners in the *mushārakah* contract. The realized funds are the share contribution of the subscribers in the *mushārakah* capital. The certificate holders own the assets of partnership and are entitled to the profit, if any.
8(b) Participation certificates managed on the basis of *muḍārabah* contract	These are documents that represent projects or activities that are managed on the basis of *muḍārabah* by appointing *muḍārib* for management. The issuer of the certificates is the *muḍārib*, the subscribers are the capital owners, and the realized funds are the *muḍārabah* capital. The certificate holders own the assets of *muḍārabah* operation and profit-share as per agreement. The certificate holders, being the capital providers, bear the loss, if any,
8(c) Participation certificates managed on the basis of investment agency	These are documents that represent projects or activities that are managed on the basis of investment agency by appointing an agent to manage the operation on behalf of the certificate holders. The issuer of the certificates is an investment agent. The subscribers are the principals and the realized funds are the subject matter of investment. The certificate holders own the assets represented by the certificates with its benefits and risks.
9 Concession certificates	These are documents of equal value that are issued for the sake of using the mobilized funds to finance execution of a concession offer, in which case the certificate holders become entitled to rights associated with the concession.

Source: AAOIFI Exposure Draft on *Sharīʿah* Standards concerning Investment *Ṣukūk* (November, 2002).

3 During 2003 the government of Qatar needed to raise funds for the construction of Hamad Medical City (HMC), Doha Qatar. The government of Qatar, Qatar International Islamic Bank and the HSBC established a joint venture SPV, the Qatar Global *Ṣukūk* QSC (incorporated in Qatar with limited liability). The SPV acquired the ownership of Land Parcel which was registered in ownership for the HMC. The SPV kept this Land Parcel in trust and issued *ijārah*-based TCs worth US$700 million due by October 2010 at an annual floating rate of return of LIBOR plus 0.45 per cent. The proceeds are used in acquiring the ownership title to Land Parcels. Under a Master *Ijārah* Agreement, the Land Parcels are leased to the government until October 2010 at a rent of LIBOR plus 0.45 per cent.

4 *Ijārah ṣukūk* were applied in the case of constructing Zam Zam Towers in Makkah, Saudi Arabia. King Abdul Aziz Waqf, Makkah Al Mukaramah decided to develop its property located in the vicinity of the Holy Haram as residential facilities. The project named Zam Zam Towers (ZZT), was allotted to the Bin-Ladin Group of Companies (BGC) on the basis of a BOT concession contract for 24 years. The BGC, in turn, leased the ZZT project to Manshaat Real Estates for the lifetime of the BOT contract. The Manshaat sold its usufruct rights for the 24 years by dividing them into weekly time shares to investors as negotiable instruments. The mobilized funds will be paid to BGC as rents for the 24 years. The Manshaat will cover its transaction costs and profit from the rent differentials between what it receives from *ṣukūk* holders and what it pays to BGC. After completion of the lease period and the BOT period, the BGC will transfer the ZZT to the King Abdul Aziz Waqf in accordance with the BOT agreement.

5 During 1993 the Ministry of Education of the Kingdom of Saudi Arabia needed to finance buildings construction for 400 public schools. For financing these schools *istiṣnāʿ ṣukūk* were utilized. Al-Rajhi Banking and Investment Corporation constructed the schools at a cost of 3.2 billion Saudi Riyal and sold to the Government at 5.54 billion Saudi Riyal.

6 During 2003 the IDB undertook a major initiative by securitizing US$400 million worth of its prime *ijārah, murābaḥah* and *istiṣnāʿ* portfolio through Solidarity Trust Services Limited, a special purpose company established for the purpose. Citibank was the lead arranger for the issue. An important feature of the arrangement was that 51 per cent of the pool of assets securitized comprised *ijārah* assets. The certificates issued were rated AAA by Standard & Poor's credit rating agency.

7 The Government of Sudan has issued several securitized instruments. This, being the first official experience of using Islamic modes of finance for financing government budget deficits, needs more detailed description which is given below.

Government of Sudan pooled securitization

The Sudanese government has experimented with the issuance of three types of financial instruments through pooled securitization: Government

Investment *Ṣukūk* (GIS), Central (Bank) *Mushārakah* Certificates (CMCs), and Government *Mushārakah* Certificates (GMCs). CMCs have been discontinued while the other two are continuing. Here we briefly discuss the two instruments.

Government Investment Ṣukuk

The government of Sudan authorized the first issuance of its investment *ṣukūk* to the tune of 6 billion Sudanese Dinār in April 2003. GIS is a fixed face-value paper sold to individuals, companies and financial institutions with the objective of raising funds for the finance of government assets/projects through *ijārah, murābaḥah* or *istiṣnā*ʿ modes of Islamic finance. GISs are sold and bought on the Khartoum Stock Exchange and the Sudan Financial Services Company (SFSC) manages them, as a *muḍārib* or fund manager, on behalf of the Ministry of Finance (MoF). *Ṣukūk* represent shares in specific government projects, and hence the value of GIS may vary depending on the performance of the projects financed.

There are three parties to *ṣukūk* activity: the investor or fund provider, the Ministry of Finance or fund demander, and the SFSC as a *muḍārib*. *Sharīʿah*-compliant *muḍārabah* contracts underpin the relationship between investors and the company, whereas the relationship between the latter and the Ministry of Finance is based on specific contracts involving *ijārah, murābaḥah* or *istiṣnā*ʿ. The company invites investors to subscribe to an investment fund of a certain size and maturity. Investors receive *ṣukūk* according to the value of their contributions. The funds are used to finance government investment according to conditions set by a restricted *muḍārabah* agreement. The company manages the fund and investors are not allowed to withdraw their contributions in part or in full before the maturity date. However, the *ṣukūk* may be traded in the stock market or under any other legal arrangement. *Ṣukūk* proceeds are lodged in hybrid *ijārah, murābaḥah* and *istiṣnā*ʿ arrangements, with the former being preferred and given a dominant role. Profits from all operations will be distributed in a ratio of 95 per cent to investors and 5 per cent to the *muḍārib*.

The government of Sudan/MoF is obliged to refund *ṣukūk* on maturity. This obligation is to be discharged by the Bank of Sudan and is not subject to negotiation or amendment. In the case of *ijārah*, the MoF is obliged to honour the agreement until maturity unless there is a legal reason for terminating the *ijārah*. The subscription price equals 100 per cent of the face value of *ṣukūk*, which is fixed at SD10,000 for the current issue of *ṣukūk*, with a 2-year maturity. Profits are to be distributed to investors 2 weeks after maturity. In the case of oversubscription, the company may, in consultation with the MoF, increase the value of *ṣukūk* or proportionately distribute existing *ṣukūk*. In the case of undersubscription, the company has to cover the difference for the projects to be undertaken. *Ṣukūk* are to be refunded according to their market value. *Ṣukūk* are traded in the stock market only when the project/assets are in kind (i.e., the project takes off).

Government Mushārakah Certificates

The MoF and the Central Bank of Sudan introduced GMCs and CMCs by temporary privatization of public sector shares in corporations in 1998. GMCs and CMCs are issued by the Government of Sudan and Bank of Sudan respectively by establishing a special purpose vehicle: namely, the SFSC. In the case of GMCs the SFSC acts as an agent of the Government and in the case of CMCs the SFSC acts as a *muḍārib*. GMCs are issued to mobilize resources to finance the budget deficit, whereas CMCs are issued primarily as an instrument of monetary policy. The working is similar to GISs as given above.

Conclusion

So far, Islamic banks have had a fairly large degree of monopoly over the financial resources of the Islamically-motivated public. That is no longer the case. Islamic banks are now facing ever-increasing competition. World markets are rapidly converging into a single market place. The optimum size of a financial firm is increasing due to this development. From this perspective, the relatively small size of most Islamic banks could be a major hindrance to their future growth. There is a world-wide trend towards mergers and acquisitions. In view of the small size of Islamic banks, this may be a strategic option for many of them.

The very nature of the financial firm is also undergoing a rapid change. The traditional distinction between bank and non-bank financial intermediaries has lost its meaning. Islamic banks are well placed in this regard since, by their very nature, they are allowed to enter into trading and other profit-sharing activities. They should benefit from this comparative advantage. In the past, Islamic banks have not used profit-sharing modes to any considerable degree. This is unfortunate because this is where their distinction and comparative advantage lies. It was understandable as a transitional phase. Since interest was deeply entrenched in the financial dealings in the countries where the Islamic banks operate, they had to move to the closest Islamic mode in the beginning. However, in future, we believe that the most promising area of growth for the Islamic financial industry lies in a wider use of equity and profit-sharing modes of finance. In the past few years, some progress towards this end has been made via the establishment of investment trusts. This is a welcome trend, and we expect this to continue. *Ṣukūk* are a new addition to the Islamic products kit. Judged from the success they have achieved over the last few years, they offer a very promising area of growth for the Islamic financial industry.

9

Some Areas for Further Research in Islamic Banking and Finance

The Islamic financial industry as well as the Islamic theory of finance has made significant progress. Having noted the challenges facing the industry in Chapter 7 and identified the potential areas of growth in Chapter 8, in this chapter we turn our attention to some theoretical issues that need to be further researched in order to provide continued support to the practice of Islamic banking.

Banking functions can be performed in several ways. Traditionally, in Anglo-Saxon countries, otherwise known as market-based systems, capital markets have been more important in financing industry. This contrasts with bank-based systems, common in continental Europe and Japan, where the banking system is the main financier of industry. In bank-based systems the universal banking model is the 'norm' where banks can undertake a broad array of financial services business as well as hold equity stakes in non-financial firms. The German banking system is usually cited as the best example of a universal banking system. In contrast, market-based systems like those in the USA and UK have traditionally separated banking systems where commercial banks could not do investment banking and ownership of non-financial firms is severely limited. The dichotomy between universal and separated banking systems, however, is rapidly being eroded and banks in all major developed systems now operate under some form of universal banking environment, although one must remember that capital markets still remain more important in the USA and UK compared with the traditional bank-based systems of Germany and Japan.

In a bank-based system, commercial banking predominates. Commercial banking is based on a pure financial intermediation model, whereby banks mainly borrow from savers and then lend to enterprises or individuals. They make their profit from the margin between the borrowing and lending rates of interest. They also provide banking services, such as letters of credit and guarantees. A proportion of their profit comes from the low-cost funds that they obtain through demand deposits.

As a result of the fractional reserve system they produce derivative deposits, which allow them to multiply their low-cost resources. The process of bank lending is, however, subject to some problems that can make it inefficient. Borrowers usually know more about their own operations than lenders. Acting as lenders, banks face this information asymmetry. Because borrowers are in a position to hold back information from banks, they can use the loans they obtain for purposes other than those specified in the loan agreement, exposing banks to unknown risks. They can also misreport their cash flows or declare bankruptcy fraudulently. Such problems are known as moral hazard. The ability of banks to secure repayment depends a great deal on whether the loan is effectively used for its purpose to produce enough returns for debt servicing. Even at the government level, several countries have borrowed billions of dollars, used them unproductively for other purposes and ended up with serious debt problems. Banks can ascertain the proper use of loans through extensive monitoring but this may be too costly or discouraged by clients, so it is very difficult for commercial banks to know precisely all the risks involved, especially as they do not have insider knowledge of the companies they lend to. As a result, the purpose for which the loan is granted is of less importance in commercial banking than the estimated credit risk of the borrower.

In contrast, in systems where universal banking prevails, banks are allowed to hold equity and also carry out operations such as trading and insurance, which usually lie beyond the sphere of commercial banking. Universal banks are better equipped to deal with information asymmetry than their commercial counterparts. They finance their business customers through a combination of shareholding and lending. Shareholding allows universal banks to sit on the boards of directors of their business customers, which enables them to monitor the use of their funds at a low cost. The reduction of the monitoring costs, in theory at least, reduces business failures and adds efficiency to the banking system.

Islamic banking is just another way of performing the financial intermediation function. The role and basic functions of financial systems are similar, and so too are the problems that are encountered in performing these functions. Systems distinguish themselves from one another by the ways in which they address these problems. It is instructive to outline the nature of at least the most important of the common concerns. A brief consideration is given to four areas: (i) the problem of asymmetric information and the costs involved in reducing it; (ii) problems of moral hazard; (iii) the problem of verifying *ex ante* the promises and intentions that are frequently involved in financial transactions (adverse selection problem); (iv) agency costs and the need for monitoring of counterparties' behaviour.

Asymmetric information

Information is at the centre of all financial transactions and contracts. Three problems are pertinent: not everyone has the same information, everyone has less than perfect information, and some transactors have 'inside' information which is not made available to counterparties to transactions. Decisions are therefore made *ex ante* on the basis of less than complete information and sometimes with counterparties who have superior information with the potential for exploitation. In any financial system, information is not symmetrically distributed across all agents, which implies that different agents have different information sets. Put another way, full and complete information is not uniformly available to all interested parties. In addition, not all parties have the same ability to utilize the information that is available to them. In particular, some parties have more information about themselves (including their intentions and abilities) than do others. The problem arises because information is not a free good and the acquisition of information is not a costless activity. If either were the case, there would never be a problem of asymmetric information. Asymmetric information, and the problems this gives rise to, are central to financial arrangements and the way financial institutions behave to limit and manage risk.

One general solution to information problems, of course, is for transactors to invest in information. However, this is not a costless activity and free-rider problems may emerge as, in some cases, no one transactor can appropriate the full value of the costly information acquired. In some areas public policy can assist by requiring disclosure of relevant information. The Islamic financial industry needs to improve in this field. Ahmed (2002) emphasizes the role that governments can play in alleviating asymmetric information problems in Islamic finance by requiring additional information disclosure. He also observes that information disclosure, along with other measures that governments can adopt, are required not only to bolster profit-sharing modes of finance but also in the interests of efficiency in the financial system in general. There are also international standards of information disclosure set by Basel Accords. These need to be given serious attention. The establishment of AAOIFI and the IFSB are steps to fill that gap, but a lot more needs to be done.

Moral hazard problems

One problem that often arises from asymmetric information is moral hazard. Superior information may enable one party to work against the interest of another. In general, moral hazard arises when a contract or financial arrangement creates incentives for parties to behave against the interest of others. It is generally believed that moral hazard problems are much more serious in profit-sharing contracts than in interest-based contracts, which is one of the reasons for their lack of popularity in Islamic banks. One problem, for example, is the incentive the borrower may have in concealing the true level of profits, or absorbing some of the profits through unauthorized perquisites. While there may be a grain of truth in this argument, we believe the matter has been exaggerated. For one thing, these problems are not unique to profit-sharing contracts; they are similar to those that arise in any equity contract in conventional systems. For another, the problem of moral hazard also exists in interest-based contracts. After obtaining the loan, the borrower may engage in highly risky or unproductive activities which will increase the probability of default and hence greatly harm the interest of the lender. Whether the problem of moral hazard is relatively more serious in PLS or loan contracts is hard to determine *a priori*. The relative severity depends on a number of factors and not only the type of contract. The problem could be much more serious in a loan contract as compared to profit-sharing contracts. To quote only one example, the recurrent international debt crises resulted from moral hazard problems in the loan contracts used for providing financing to underdeveloped countries. The countries which borrowed huge funds from multinational banks and governments used these in unproductive investments, or their rulers simply embezzled a good part of them, which led to serious default problems. The situation would have been much better if the funds had been given on a profit-sharing basis. A more careful comparison of the relative advantages of debt and equity contracts with special reference to Islamic profit-sharing contracts is needed.

Enforcement mechanisms need also to be embedded in contracts. If ever a moral hazard arises which creates an incentive for one party not to deliver on a contract, such mechanisms assume critical importance. One solution in conventional banking, which may have only limited use in Islamic banking, is the pledging of collateral against loans whereby the borrower loses the collateral in the event of default.[1] This is a mechanism for aligning the incentives of the borrower with the interests of the lender. Islamic scholars have, however, pointed out that collateral is a poor substitute for sound assessment of the project which is a necessary feature of profit sharing contracts. Chapra (2002) argues that:

> interest-based lending makes the banks rely on the crutches of the collateral to extend financing for practically any purpose, including speculation. The collateral cannot, however, be a substitute for a more careful evaluation of the project financed. This is because the value of the collateral can itself be impaired by the same factors that diminish the ability of the borrower to repay the loan. The ability of the market to impose the required discipline thus gets impaired and leads to an unhealthy expansion in the overall volume of credit, to excessive leverage, and to living beyond means.

The experience of bank failures despite the presence of collateral in their possession lends support to that line of argument. How moral hazard problems can be minimized in Islamic banking is an area deserving further academic investigation.

Adverse selection problems

Financial transactions often involve a set of promises or undertakings from one party to another. The problem is that intentions cannot be observed and there may be incentives to lie to or mislead a counterparty. This becomes critical in profit-sharing contracts. As the profit is shared between the firm and the bank at an agreed ratio, there may be an incentive on the part of an amoral entrepreneur to report lower profit in order to keep a larger share of it for himself. In the Islamic system a particular consideration is the extent to which reliance can be placed on good behaviour dictated by the norms of Islam itself. Presumably, there is a higher level of trust between Islamic banks and their clients than is the case with conventional banks, and hence the moral hazard risks are less. This is because there is a greater degree of shared values, including ethical values related to honesty. Higher levels of trust reduce risk and uncertainty, which in turn results in lower monitoring costs for Islamic banks. However, things cannot be left only to morals; contracts must be so designed as to reduce the inducement to cheat through a reward/punishment mechanism. The fact that intentions cannot be observed in essence means that financial contracts are necessarily incomplete contracts. This implies that investors may be unable to predict future events in order to write complete contracts that specify each party's obligations in all situations.

The central problem is how one party can ensure that the counterparty delivers on promises or intentions. This may involve sanctions or creating incentive structures that align the interests of the counterparties. Constructing incentive-compatible contracts is as important for Islamic finance as for conventional finance. Obvious mechanisms include profit- or reward-sharing arrangements, imposing costs and penalties on bad behaviour, and ensuring that contracts are enforced and that all parties know that contracts will be enforced. Karim (2002) emphasizes four conditions for incentive compatibility in contracts: the entrepreneur or recipients of funds having a higher stake in net worth and/or collateral; low operating costs; having a low degree of unobservable cash flow; and having a low proportion of non-controllable costs. Using the case of *muḍārabah* contracts of Bank Muamalat Indonesia, he shows how the proportion of profit-sharing financing increased significantly after 1998 when the bank introduced its pilot project based on incentive compatible contracts for profit-sharing modes of finance. Similar further research in this area would be very helpful in designing incentive-compatible contracts for Islamic banks.

Principal agent problems and the need for monitoring

Another important ingredient, in the presence of asymmetric information, is deterministic monitoring, where the financier monitors in some states but not others. Combining a fixed-payment arrangement with deterministic monitoring, it trivially follows that debt becomes the optimal form of financing. Gale and Hellwig (1985) point to this result clearly: 'It is worth noting that the proof of the optimality of the standard debt contract follows from the definition of the problem. To prove the converse requires a number of non-trivial assumptions.' The problem arises because the agent often has superior information and expertise (which may be the reason the principal employs him). The agent can choose his behaviour after the contract has been established, and because of this the agent is often able to conceal the outcome of a contract. Agency problems arise because the agent cannot be efficiently or costlessly monitored. Unless these problems can be solved, the agency costs involved can act as a serious deterrent to financial contracting with resultant welfare losses. The challenge is to create contracts or arrangements that align the interests of the principal and the agent.

Profit-sharing contracts are one way of solving this because the agent shares the profits with the principal and so has an incentive also to behave in the interest of the principal. Still, because of the asymmetric information problems, the behaviour of counterparties needs to be monitored after a contract has been agreed to ensure that information asymmetries are not exploited by one party against the interest of the other, and also because frequently a fiduciary relationship is created by a financial contract. In both cases, agents need to be monitored to ensure that their behaviour is consistent with the interests of principals. A special characteristic of many financial contracts is that the value cannot be observed or verified at the point of purchase, and that the post-contract behaviour of a counterparty determines the ultimate value of the contract. This also creates a need for monitoring.

Monitoring is needed because many financial contracts are long term in nature and information acquired before a contract is agreed may become irrelevant during the course of the contract as circumstances and conditions change. Above all, the value of a contract or financial product cannot be ascertained with certainty at the point the contract is made or the product is purchased. This often distinguishes financial contracts from other economic contracts, such as purchases of goods. While the need for monitoring is accepted, it is an expensive activity and transactors need to balance the marginal costs and benefits of incremental monitoring.

It is sometimes argued that a loan contract minimizes the need for monitoring the project, and hence the monitoring costs. Therefore, it is better than profit-sharing contracts on this score. This again is not always true: monitoring is needed whenever there is problem of moral hazard. As shown above, loan contracts are also subject to moral hazard. Therefore, there is need for monitoring in their case also. The most obvious example is the monitoring teams being regularly sent by the IMF to debtor countries, but there are several other examples. A moral hazard problem arises because of asymmetric information. To overcome that problem, lenders regularly monitor the performance of the borrowers through obtaining additional information. They are required to submit periodic reports. In addition, there are 'rating' agencies which provide information on performance and credit ratings. Banks also send inspectors to financed projects. Therefore, on the basis of monitoring costs, a profit-sharing contract is not necessarily inferior to a loan contract. As a matter of fact, it could be the other way round. There can be no better way to overcome the problem of asymmetric information than by placing members on the Board of Directors, something that Islamic modes based on profit-sharing would permit. These relative costs and benefits of debt versus profit-sharing contracts are another area that deserves further academic attention.

Implications of the sharing features of PLS contracts

A widely held perception among economists is that sharing arrangements are less efficient compared to first-choice solutions. Stiglitz and Weiss (1981), for example, write:

> In general, revenue sharing arrangements such as equity financing, or sharecropping are inefficient. Under those schemes the managers of a firm or the tenant will equate their marginal disutility of effort with their share of their marginal product rather than with their total marginal product. Therefore, too little effort will be forthcoming from agents.

The same problem arises in corporate management. Harris and Raviv (1991) write: 'Conflicts between shareholders and managers arise because managers hold less than 100 % of the residual claim. Consequently, they do not capture the entire gain from their profit enhancement activities, but they do bear the entire cost of these activities.'

Despite the inefficiency argument, sharing is widely practised. Venture capital is a prominent form of equity financing. Sharecropping is applied in developing as well as developed economies. Explanations for existence of sharing arrangements suggest a kind of trade-off or balance of one form or another to compensate for reduction in efficiency. These include:

(a) risk-sharing properties (Stiglitz, 1974; Lang and Gordon, 1995);
(b) transaction costs (Murrell, 1983; Allen and Lueck, 1993);
(c) bargaining powers (Bell and Zusman, 1976; Reiersen, 2001);
(d) double-sided moral hazard (Reid, 1973; Eswaran and Kotwal, 1985; Bhattacharyya and Lafontaine, 1995);
(e) moral hazard over choice of project with limited liability (Jensen and Meckling, 1976; Basu, 1992; Sengupta, 1997);
(f) strategic interaction among principals (Ray, 1999);
(g) intertemporal discounting (Roy and Serfes, 2001).

Suwailem (2003) shows that under a widely observed form of uncertainty, sharing can be no less efficient than the first-choice solution, and thus there is no need for a form of trade-off to account for its usefulness. With positive bankruptcy costs and sufficiently high probability of success, sharing Pareto-dominates debt in terms of expected profits, with and without informational asymmetry. He finds that when bankruptcy costs are positive, and expected marginal gain is not less than marginal loss, aggregate expected profits from sharing exceed those of debt, under both symmetric and asymmetric information. This result holds despite the fact that effort level is the same in both contracts. Moreover, for a certain range of the opportunity cost, both the financier and the entrepreneur are better off signing a sharing contract instead of debt. Moving from sharing to debt, in contrast, cannot make both parties better off; only one party may be better off while the other must be worse off. Sharing therefore Pareto-dominates debt for the relevant range of the opportunity cost, while debt cannot dominate sharing. Under more general conditions, debt even ceases to attain efficient level of effort, while sharing preserves its first-choice solution.

It is sometimes argued that PLS financing is too risky for banks to adopt. For better risk management, contracts based on fixed returns are better for banks, whether conventional or Islamic. There are two fallacies in this line of argument. First, variability in the rate of return is not the only risk involved in financial contracts. Second, the so-called 'fixed' return contracts, like interest-based contracts, may not in fact yield a fixed return!

Variability in the rate of return is only one of the risks faced by the financier. The other risks include non-performing debts and the risk of outright default. In the case of conventional banks, non-performing debts (debts not being 'serviced' for a certain period of time) create only temporary liquidity problems and increase the costs of monitoring. If they are ultimately paid, banks can charge additional interest for the delay. In the case of Islamic banks, the non-performing debts lead to loss of revenue. Therefore, the problem of non-performing debts is more serious in the case of Islamic banks. However, the problem of outright default in many cases is a more serious risk than the risk of lower or negative rates of return in PLS contracts. Anyone who has studied the anatomy of major financial crises, such as the saving and loans crisis in the USA during the 1980s or major bank failures, is well aware that equity interests were a small percentage of the assets of these institutions. Loans were their major assets and that is what led to their failure.

That certain instruments pay 'fixed' rates of return is also not always true. One reason for that not being the case is inflation, and the difference between nominal and real rates of return. In PLS contracts rates of return automatically take care of inflation, but there is also a more subtle reason. Consider the example of fixed interest bonds. The rate of return on fixed interest bonds has two components: the fixed 'coupon' rate, and the change in the value of the bond (i.e., capital gain or loss). While the first component is fixed, the second is not. It can move in such a way that the capital loss outweighs the coupon receipts and hence the rate of return on a 'fixed' interest bond turns out to be negative! If there are no really fixed-return instruments, then what are the factors that limit the use of variable profit-sharing modes in Islamic banking? Recently, some research has appeared on this matter but the issue is far from being settled.

In view of the fact that Islamic banking theory assigns a great deal of importance to profit-sharing contracts, the issue of their lack of popularity in practice needs further investigation. In this respect the implications, both positive and negative, of using profit-sharing finance need to be carefully studied.

The need for further empirical investigations

In addition to various theoretical arguments deserving of further research there is also a host of empirical issues worthy of greater study. Many of the issues that are currently being applied to developed systems can also be investigated in the context of Islamic banking systems. One such topical area relates to the study of financial stability. With the growing concerns about market volatility, economic downturns and the soundness of banking systems there is a burgeoning body of work that investigates these issues, but almost solely from a conventional banking system standpoint. While there is an established, albeit limited, literature that investigates the pros and cons of bank-based versus market-based systems in the context of economic growth and development, as far as we are aware there have been no rigorous empirical studies that compare whether Islamic financial systems are more effective in promoting growth than conventional interest-based systems. It is also by no means certain, at least from an empirical standpoint, whether Islamic systems are more competitive than conventional banking systems. Are those markets that permit conventional and Islamic banks to work side-by-side more competitive than those that have other forms of Islamic banking practices? Are Islamic banks more competitive than other types of banks? Do the structure and ownership features of Islamic banks influence their performance differently compared to similar interest-based banks operating in the same countries (or other countries)? All these types of question can be addressed by investigating bank performance features, some of which have been covered in this book, but also by looking at specific product markets.

Research on specific product markets in Islamic banking systems remains underdeveloped. As a customer of an Islamic bank you are much more likely to be concerned about the pricing of specific products from different competitor banks rather than the overall performance of the banks per se. As such, both retail and corporate clients are likely to be more interested in specific features of different product segments: for instance, comparison of the returns generated by Islamic funds, returns generated on deposits, loan charges and so on. It may well be a fruitful area of research to conduct product-specific analysis both within and across Islamic financial systems to see the best and worst cost providers. This may also help regulators gain a stronger understanding of the price and non-price features of financial services and products available in their respective markets, as well as the structural features of these markets. Such information, although often difficult to obtain, could also help inform researchers and policy makers concerning competition and other issues related to specific market segments, such as lending to small business, mortgage finance and so on.

An important theme discussed throughout the book has been the relatively small size of Islamic banks compared with their conventional competitors. This begs the question as to the impact of possible mergers on the performance of banks through Islamic systems. There has been a glut of such literature over the last decade tackling these issues for US and European systems, but little on systems where Islamic banking is practised. While we recognize that there have not been many bank mergers in these countries, there is always the possibility of undertaking simulation exercises to investigate what may happen if mergers occur. Such simulation exercises are useful for drawing policy conclusions.

In addition to these areas, there are still substantial gaps in the literature tackling aspects of Islamic finance that are not directly linked to banks. Areas such as insurance, leasing and other sorts of Islamic financial activity are rarely covered (perhaps due to the lack of available market information). However, more rigorous work relating to these areas should be encouraged.

While the above areas for suggested empirical research are by no means exhaustive, at least they provide a flavour of the sort of subjects that require further study. In addition, it would be remiss of us not to discuss possible policy research. One obvious area relates to the monetary transmission mechanism. How has policy action influenced bank behaviour, and has this impacted on macroeconomic performance? Do banks or the real sector act as the main transmitters of monetary policy? And so on. Overall, we suggest that these types of arguments need to be further investigated, along with other broader issues relating to such matters as the policy implications of the integration of financial markets, the impact on banking systems of the proposed single market in the Gulf, and how the creation of a Islamic money market may influence bank behaviour.

Conclusion

The Islamic financial industry as well as the Islamic theory of finance has made significant progress. However, there are still several unresolved issues. This chapter discusses some theoretical and empirical issues that need to be further researched in order to provide continued support to the practice of Islamic banking. The role and basic functions of financial systems are similar; so too are the problems that are encountered in performing these functions. Systems distinguish themselves from one another by the ways in which they address these problems. Islamic banking is just another way of performing the financial intermediation function. The chapter looked at how some common concerns are addressed in this model. A brief consideration was given to four areas: (i) the problem of asymmetric information and the costs involved in reducing it; (ii) problems of moral hazard; (iii) the problem of verifying *ex ante* the promises and intentions that are frequently involved in financial transactions (adverse selection problem); (iv) agency costs and the need for monitoring of counterparties' behaviour.

The chapter then goes on to study some specific features of profit-sharing contracts as compared to debt contracts. It summarizes the controversy as to why sharing contracts exist despite the widely held perception that sharing arrangements are less efficient than debt contracts. Several explanations have been given in terms of compensating advantages of sharing contracts, such as risk-sharing features, benefiting from mutual strengths of the parties and lower transactions costs. Another line of argument is that under certain reasonable assumptions, it can be shown that sharing arrangements are not inefficient to begin with. For example, with positive bankruptcy costs and sufficiently high probability of success, sharing contracts have been shown to be Pareto-optimal.

The chapter also examines the argument that PLS financing is too risky for banks to adopt. Two fallacies are found in this line of argument. First, variability in the rate of return is not the only risk involved in financial contracts; non-return risks in debt contracts may be higher than profit-sharing contracts. Second, the so called 'fixed' return contracts, like interest-based contracts, may not in fact yield a fixed return! Therefore, the argument that PLS contracts are too risky for Islamic banks to adopt is not found to be convincing.

10
Summary and Conclusions

Islamic banks emerged on to the financial scene in early 1970s. During the last 30 years the Islamic financial industry has shown remarkable progress both from a theoretical and practical perspective. Even though Islamic banks emerged in response to market needs of Muslim clients, they are not religious institutions. Like other banks, they are profit-seeking institutions. However, they follow a different model of financial intermediation. The most important distinguishing feature of the Islamic banking model is the use of risk-sharing modes of finance. Islamic scholars working with practical bankers have developed a number of such modes, including *muḍārabah, mushārakah, murābaḥah, salam, istiṣnāʿ*, leasing and *ṣukūk*. Salient features of all of these modes have been discussed in this book. In the Islamic theory of contracts of exchange, the general rule is that of permission. Every contractual arrangement is permissible unless expressly prohibited by *Sharīʿah*. There are very few prohibitions. Basically, these are covered under two categories: *ribā* and *gharar*. These terms have been described in detail. Based on the Islamic theory of financial contracts, guidelines for Islamic financial engineering have been derived. These can be summarized in what we have called the four Cs of Islamic financial engineering: consciousness, clarity, capability and commitment:

Consciousness: the parties should consciously and willingly agree on the conditions of contract without compulsion or duress. An implication of this is that any agreement made in a state of unconsciousness (such as under the influence of intoxicants or imposed by force is not valid).

Clarity: the parties are fully aware of all the implications of the conditions laid down in a contract. Any ambiguity (with the exception of *gharar yasīr*) will make the agreement invalid.

Capability: the parties are reasonably certain that they are capable of complying with all conditions of the contract. An implication of this is that sale of any goods (or services) which are not owned and possessed by the seller at the time of the contract is not valid.

Commitment: the parties intend and are committed to respect the terms of a contract both in letter and spirit. An implication of this is that any subterfuge to evade any *Sharīʿah* condition through linguistic or legal tricks is not allowed.

Several potential benefits can arise from the emergence of Islamic banking, including the following:

1. The range of contracts available to customers is widened.
2. It creates a financial system populated by financial institutions with different *modus operandi* that has the effect of widening choice for consumers.
3. The widening of the range of financial contracts available, and differences in the *modus operandi* of conventional and Islamic banks have the effect of enhancing competition between alternative banking models which is expected, in turn, to increase efficiency of the financial system.
4. It enables Islamic religious beliefs to be reflected in financial arrangements and transactions, thereby fulfilling the financial needs of Muslims in accordance with their faith.
5. Allocation of financial resources on the basis of PLS gives maximum weight to the profitability of investment, whereas an interest-based allocation gives it to credit-worthiness. We may expect the allocation made on the basis of profitability to be more efficient than that made on the basis of interest.
6. Due to the nature of the contracts on the liabilities side of the balance sheet, Islamic banks are often less vulnerable to external shocks and are less susceptible to insolvency. This is because a wider range of liability holders share in the risks of the bank as compared with conventional banks.
7. As holders of investment deposits share in the risks of an Islamic bank (e.g., through PLS contracts) and are not offered guarantees, incentives are created for a wider range of stakeholders in the bank to monitor its behaviour and risk-taking.
8. By creating more systemic diversity, the stability of the financial system may be enhanced because the behavioural characteristics of different types of banks are likely to vary.
9. In case of both the PLS and *murābaḥah* contracts, since bank assets are created in response to investment opportunities in the real sector of the

economy, and all financing is linked to commodities or assets, the real factors related to the production of goods and services (in contrast with the financial factors) become the prime movers of the rates of return to the financial sector.

Despite these theoretical advantages, the use of profit-sharing has been limited in the operations of Islamic banks. This has raised concerns in several quarters and has even put the legitimacy and uniqueness of the Islamic banking system into question. While Islamic scholars have conclusively shown that even the present Islamic banking practice (which is largely based on fixed return modes) is unique and garners several benefits, it is desirable that the use of profit-sharing modes is enhanced. This may not be done necessarily by the Islamic banks. Other institutions, such as Islamic funds or specialized subsidiaries of Islamic banks, can also undertake this type of activity. Increasing the use of profit-sharing modes will have economic effects similar to direct investment and is likely to produce a strong economic development impact. It will also increase the confidence of clients in the genuine nature of Islamic banking business. At the same time, a decrease in fixed return modes will reduce the problem of default and the problem of compensation arising there from. Going from non-interest financing to profit-sharing financing or a more balanced combination of the two is the next milestone that the Islamic banking industry should head towards.

The practice of Islamic banking during the last 30 years has spread to all corners of the globe. This practice has proved beyond any doubt that it is a viable and efficient way of financial intermediation. While a complete Islamic financial system is still in its early stages of development, various elements of the system and institutions are fast coming into existence. These include full Islamic commercial and investment banks, Islamic banking windows in conventional banks (including some prominent international banks), Islamic investment funds, Islamic insurance (*takāful*) companies, infrastructure support institutions, and research and development institutions. Islamic banking is now well recognized as an efficient and viable system of financial intermediation. There is also strong empirical evidence to suggest that, in terms of performance, Islamic banks are by no means inferior to their conventional counterparts. As a matter of fact, most studies conclude that they usually show better results than conventional banks. Empirical analysis provided in this book confirms these findings.

The Islamic banking industry is one of the fastest growing industries, posting double-digit annual growth rates for almost 30 years. This is an achievement which can hardly be matched by any other industry. The growth of the industry was kick-started by an enthusiastic response from Muslim clients, but its continuation can be put down to economic and financial fundamentals. The research conclusively shows that the lack of an interest rate mechanism does not in any way constrain the effective use of resources placed at the disposal of Islamic financial institutions. Analysis of key performance ratios measuring soundness, effective use of resources, prudence, cost efficiency and profitability shows that Islamic banks meet, and in several cases surpass, international standards. The benchmarking exercise reported in this book, along with a more formal efficiency analysis that covers various performance indicators, strongly suggests that Islamic banks outperform their conventional peers.

Despite tremendous growth and strong performance, Islamic banking is still a nascent industry and has a long way to go before being on par with the other well developed models of financial intermediation. From a niche market, it has to move towards integration into international financial markets. It has made considerable progress towards that end but there are still several challenges that it has to confront. On the one hand, there are several theoretical issues which remain unresolved, and which may constrain further growth of the industry. On the other hand, there are several operational problems that can limit the effectiveness of the industry. The Islamic banking system, like any other system, has to be seen as an evolving reality. While various components of the system are available in different depths and quality, a complete system is still a long way off. Islamic banking started in a hostile environment and has struggled for more than quarter of a century. It has scored a number of successes, but a lot more needs to be done.

World financial markets are rapidly converging into a single market place. In an increasingly globalized environment, Islamic banks will face a lot more competition than before. Capturing a big chunk in its home base, the Arabian Gulf, is one thing, but operating in an international market place with intense competition from several quarters is another. Islamic banks need to find a common interface with conventional banks and build strategic alliances across borders in order to be able to operate in international markets effectively.

Concerns have also been expressed about accounting standards and transparency in the financial statements of Islamic banks. While it is true that Islamic banks are not using uniform standards and there is a need to increase transparency, it is unfair to use this argument for creating doubts about the credibility of Islamic banking operation. There is no reason for the international financial community to have any fears with respect to its possible use for some illegal activities. Like traditional banks, Islamic financial institutions are simply profit-seeking businesses. They are subject to essentially the same regulations as traditional banks. Compliance therewith is monitored by central banks and other financial regulatory authorities. These regulations are set in accordance with international best practice, and assign prime importance to the 'know thy customer' rule. Like other countries, Muslim countries are also updating their laws so as to be in full compliance with the recommendations of the FATF on money laundering and terrorist financing. While on these types of issues Islamic financial institutions have the same legal and regulatory obligations as traditional banks, their overall law and compliance environment is more stringent, insofar as Islamic financial institutions are also subject to the additional self-regulation needed to comply with the Islamic rules.

Of course, without the knowledge of the management or owners, and despite the best efforts of management in applying the 'know thy customer' rule, any financial institution, whether traditional or Islamic, might be misused as a transaction channel by terrorists or other criminals. But we should always bear in mind that Islamic finance has noble objectives and principles, and Islamic banks should be treated accordingly.

All the international financial community has a common cause in fighting money laundering and other financial crimes. This requires developing uniform, non-discriminatory standards and procedures to monitor the working of all financial institutions. There is a need to improve the supervisory and regulatory environment for both conventional and Islamic banks to ensure that they comply with their stated objectives and modes of operations on the one hand, and to increase understanding and cooperation between conventional and Islamic supervisory and regulatory authorities on the other. These issues are under constant review in the framework of Basel II and the recommendations of the FATF.

Corporate governance is also an important area which needs serious thought. In addition to the transparency issues mentioned above, the ownership structure of Islamic banks is also an area of concern. At present, three or four families own a large percentage of the Islamic banking industry. Such a high level of ownership concentration may lead to concerns about financial instability, especially if anything happens to those families or the next generation of these families changes their priorities. Similarly, the experience of country-wide experiments introducing Islamic financing systems and practices has not always been smooth due to the fact that these experiments were implemented on a top-down basis. Having said all this, however, we have no doubt that there is a definite preference among the Muslim masses for non-interest modes of financing. This popular support needs to be converted into grassroots involvement in Islamic banking, both in terms of ownership as well as the beneficiaries of bank financing.

Notes

2 Theoretical Foundations of Islamic Banking

1 Thus any excess given by the debtor out of his own accord, and without the existence of a custom or habit that obliges him to give such excess, is not considered as *ribā.*

2 For some other definitions of *ribā* and discussions thereupon, see Islamic Research and Training Institute (1995), pp. 77–84.

3 For the implications of this, see Chapra (1985).

4 Islamic Fiqh Academy (2000).

5 Deuteronomy 23:19, 20; quoted from the *New International Version.*

6 *Codex iuris canonici,* c.1735.

7 In some continental countries such as France, Belgium, Italy and Portugal, usury laws still exist to prohibit excessive rates of interest being charged.

8 Ṣaḥiḥ Muslim, (undated) and Sunan Ibn Majah (1996).

3 Development of the Islamic Banking Model

1 There could be more than two parties. The contract is explained using a two-party example only for simplicity.

2 However, in case of travelling outside the place of business, the *muḍārib* is entitled to travel and living expenses during the trip.

3 See Chapter 2 (section 2.2) for an explanation of the principle.

4 The new buyer has to agree to continue the lease on the conditions previously agreed unless the lessee willingly agrees to new conditions.

5 Some of these can be insured against, but this has to be done by the lessor at his own cost.

6 Except in the extreme case of bankruptcy.

4 History and Growth of Islamic Banking and Finance

1 Goitein (1971).

2 The central bank of the country laid down that the maximum rate of service charge which a bank could recover on such loans during an accounting year was to be calculated by dividing the total of its expenses, excluding cost of funds and provisions relating to bad assets and income taxation, by the mean of its total assets at the beginning and the end of the year and rounding off the result to the nearest decimal for a percentage point.

3 Participation Term Certificates were negotiable instruments designed to replace debentures for meeting medium- and long-term financing requirements of business concerns. Instead of receiving interest, as in the case of debentures, the holders of these certificates shared in the profit or loss of concerns raising finance through this device.

4 The law stipulates that rules and regulations relating to grant of *qarḍ al-ḥasanah* will be drawn up by the central bank of the country and approved by the Council of Ministers.

5 In one of the studies (Iqbal, Zubair and Abbas Mirakhor (1987), p. 24.) it is stated:

> In the case of the Islamic Republic of Iran, it has been decreed that financial transactions between and among the elements of the public sector, including Bank Markazi and commercial banks that are wholly nationalised, can take place on the basis of a fixed rate of return; such a fixed rate is not viewed as interest. Therefore, the Government can borrow from the nationalised banking system without violating the injunction of the Law.

6 A case in point is the treatment of investment deposits. In Iran, the law allows the nominal value of such deposits to be guaranteed while such a guarantee is not considered compatible with Islamic teachings in other countries.
7 See Mirakhor (1988), p. 55.
8 Osman Ahmed in Rodney Wilson (1990), p. 77.
9 This number does not include Islamic windows in conventional banks.
10 There were a few gaps in the data, which were filled through forecasting techniques.
11 See Wilson (1990).
12 For example, see Iqbal *et al.* (1998).
13 In a *muḍārabah* contract both parties share in the risk. The *muḍārib* risks his labour and the *rabb al-māl* (financier) risks his capital.
14 In practice most funds apply more stringent conditions than this.
15 Failaka.com.
16 Rodney Wilson, 'Islamic Financial Market' Seminar on Financial Institutions According to *Sharīʿah,* jointly sponsored by the Ministry of Finance, Government of Indonesia and the Islamic Research and Training Institute, held in Jakarta, Indonesia, September 1990.
17 'The West Embraces Islamic Banking', *The Financial Times,* 7 October 1994.
18 The Islamic Dinar is considered as the IDB accounting unit; it is equivalent in value to one Special Drawing Right (SDR) of the IMF.
19 For example: *Journal of King Abdulaziz University: Islamic Economics,* PO Box 16711, Jeddah 21474, Saudi Arabia; *Islamic Economic Studies,* PO Box 9201, Jeddah 21413, Saudi Arabia; *Review of Islamic Economics,* Leicestershire LE67 9RN, UK; *American Journal of Islamic Finance,* USA; *The Islamic Banker,* London, UK.

5 The Performance of Islamic Banks

1 Subordinated debt is debt that is paid off only after depositors and other creditors have been paid.
2 For the whole period the average comes out to be 8.2 per cent.
3 Other corporations need a small percentage of their resources for transaction purposes.
4 Current ratio = current assets/current liabilities.
5 Legal reserve requirements are usually different for current and time deposits, with current deposits having a higher requirement. This ratio is a rough average.
6 This applies not only in the case of Islamic banks, but also to countries where no deposit insurance is available.
7 Some Islamic banks bear some of those losses voluntarily in years when profitability is low, to protect their market share.

6 Efficiency in Islamic Banking

1 Limam (2001) uses data envelopment analysis to investigate the efficiency of 52 GCC banks for 1999, although no distinction is made between Islamic and conventional banks.

7 Challenges Facing Islamic Banking

1 *The Islamic Fiqh Academy Magazine*, Vol. VIII (1992).
2 The current standard is less than 10 per cent.
3 The standard being used at present is 50 per cent.
4 Article (4), paragraph 1-A.
5 Sunan Abū Dawood (1981).
6 For details see Khan and Ahmed (2001).
7 However, the Fiqh Academy considers the defaulting party fully responsible for compensating the aggrieved party for all the losses incurred.
8 This was done in the cases of establishment of Islamic banks in Jordan and Egypt.
9 As in Malaysia, Bahrain, Turkey, UAE and now in Pakistan.
10 Adopted from Exhibit 1 in Chapra and Khan (2000).
11 Council of Islamic Ideology Pakistan (1981).
12 Chapra (1985).
13 For further arguments in favour of this proposal, see Chapra (1985) p. 161.
14 Donaldson and Preston (1995).
15 Ṣaḥiḥ Bukhari, Volume 1, Book 2, Number 10.
16 Obaidullah (2004).

8 Islamic Banking in the Twenty-First Century

1 Siddiqi (1983), p. 52.
2 Mirakhor (1987).
3 The proposal comes from Siddiqi (2004). What follows is a summary of his proposal.
4 *Time*, 27 April 1998.
5 The following discussion is adapted from Iqbal and Khan (2004).

9 Some Areas for Further Research in Islamic Banking and Finance

1 In the Islamic system, such recourse is possible only in case of default or loss caused by negligence or wilful misconduct.

Bibliography

Abu Guddah, Abdul Sattar (1992), 'Juridical Aspects of Profit Sharing Contract in Contemporary Society', in Al-Albait Foundation (ed.), *Investment Strategy in Islamic Banking Applications, Issues and Problems*, Amman: Al-Albait Foundation.

Aggarwal, R. and Yousef, T. (2000), 'Islamic Banks and Investment Financing', *Journal of Money, Credit and Banking*, 32 (1) (February), 93–120.

Ahmad, Ausaf and Khan, Tariqullah (eds) (1997), *Islamic Financial Instruments for Public Sector Resource Mobilization*, Jeddah: Islamic Research and Training Institute.

Ahmad, Ziauddin, Khan, M. Fahim and Iqbal, Munawar (eds) (1983), *Money and Banking in Islam*, Islamabad: Institute of Policy Studies.

Ahmed, Habib (2002), 'Incentive-compatible profit-sharing contracts: a theoretical treatment', in Munawar Iqbal and David T. Llewellyn (eds), *Islamic Banking and Finance: New Perspectives in Profit Sharing and Risk*, Cheltenham: Edward Elgar.

Aigner, D., Lovell, C. and Schmidt, P. (1977), 'Formulation and Estimation of Stochastic Frontier Production Function Models', *Journal of Econometrics*, 6 (May), 21–37.

Al Gari, M. Ali (1993), 'Towards An Islamic Stock-Market', *Islamic Economic Studies*, 1 (1), 1–20

Al-Jarrah, I. M. and Molyneux, P. (2003), 'Efficiency in Arabian Banking', University of Wales, Bangor, Working Paper.

Allais, Maurice (1993), *The Monetary Conditions of an Economy of Markets*, Jeddah: Islamic Research and Training Institute.

Allen, D. and Lueck, D. (1993), 'Transaction Costs and the Design of Cropshare Contracts,' *RAND Journal of Economics*, 24, 78–100.

Allen, F. and Santomero, A. (1998), 'The Theory of Financial Intermediation', *Journal of Banking and Finance*, 21, 1,461–85.

Al-Shammari, S. (2003), 'Structure-Conduct-Performance and the Efficiency of the GCC Banking Markets', PhD, University of Wales, Bangor.

Ariff, Mohammad and Mannan, M. A. (ed.) (1990), *Developing a System of Islamic Financial Instruments*, Jeddah: Islamic Research and Training Institute.

Babikir, Osman Ahmed (2001), *Islamic Financial Instruments to Manage Short-term Excess Liquidity*, Research Paper No. 41, 2nd edn, Jeddah: Islamic Research and Training Institute.

Banker, R., Charnes, A. and Cooper, W. (1984), 'Some Models for Estimating Technical and Scale Inefficiencies in Data Envelopment Analysis', *Management Science*, 30 (9), 1,078–92.

Bashir, A. (1999), 'Risk and profitability measures in Islamic banks: The case of two Sudanese banks', *Islamic Economic Studies*, 6 (2), (May), 1–24.

Bashir, A. (2000), 'Determinants of profitability and rates of return margins in Islamic banks: some evidence from the Middle East', Grambling State University, Lousiana, mimeo.

Basu, K. (1992), 'Limited Liability and the Existence of Share Tenancy,' *Journal of Development Economics*, 38, 203–20.

Bauer, P., Berger, A., Ferrier, G. and Humphrey, D. (1998), 'Consistency Conditions for Regulatory Analysis of Financial Institutions: A Comparison of Frontier Efficiency Methods', *Journal of Economics and Business*, 50 (2), 85–114.

Bell, C. and Zusman, P. (1976), 'A Bargaining Theoretic Approach to Cropsharing Contracts', *American Economic Review*, 66, 578–88.

Benston, G., Hanweck, G. and Humphrey, D. (1982), 'Scale Economies in Banking: A Restructuring and Reassessment', *Journal of Money, Credit and Banking*, 14, 435–56.

Berger, A. and Humphrey, D. (1992), 'Measurement and Efficiency Issues in Commercial Banking', in Zvi Griliches (ed.), *Output Measurement in the Service Sectors*, National Bureau of Economic Research Studies in Income and Wealth, 56, University of Chicago Press, Chicago.

Berger, A. and Humphrey, D. (1997), 'Efficiency of Financial Institutions: International Survey and Directions for Future Research', *European Journal of Operational Research*, 98, 175–212.

Berger, A., Hunter, W. and Timme, S. (1993), 'The Efficiency of Financial Institutions: A Review and Preview of Research Past, Present, and Future', *Journal of Banking & Finance*, 17, 221–49.

Bhattacharya, S. and Thakor, A. (1993), 'Contemporary Banking Theory', *Journal of Financial Intermediation*, 3 (October), 2–50.

Bhattacharya, S. and Lafontaine, F. (1995), 'Double-sided Moral Hazard and the Nature of Share Contracts', *RAND Journal of Economics*, 26, 761–81.

Casu, B. and Molyneux, P. (2001), 'Efficiency in European Banking', in J. Goddard, P. Molyneux and J. Wilson (2001), *European Banking: Efficiency, Technology and Growth*, London: John Wiley, 121–79.

Chapra, M. Umer (1985), *Towards a Just Monetary System*, Leicester: The Islamic Foundation, UK.

Chapra, M. Umer (1992), 'Islam and the International Debt Problem', *Journal of Islamic Studies*, July, 214–32.

Chapra, M. Umer (2000), 'Why Has Islam Prohibited Interest? Rationale Behind the Prohibition of Interest in Islam', *Review of Islamic Economics*, 9, 5–20.

Chapra, M. Umer (2002), 'Alternative Visions of International Monetary Reform', in Munawar Iqbal and David T. Llewellyn (eds), *Islamic Banking and Finance: New Perspectives in Profit Sharing and Risk*, Cheltenham: Edward Elgar.

Chapra, M. Umer and Khan, Tariqullah (2000), *Regulation and Supervision of Islamic Banks*, Jeddah: Islamic Research and Training Institute.

Cole, Harold L. and Kocherlakota, Narayana (1998), 'Zero Nominal Interest Rates: Why they're good and how to get them', *Federal Reserve Bank of Minneapolis Quarterly Review*, 22 (Spring), 2–10.

Council of Islamic Ideology, Pakistan (1981), *The Elimination of Interest from the Economy of Pakistan*, Islamabad: Council of Islamic Ideology.

Deprins, D., Simar, L. and Tulkens, H. (1984), 'Measuring Labour-Efficiency in Post Offices', in M. Marchand, P. Pestieau and H. Tulkens (eds), *The Performance of Public Enterprises: Concepts and Measurements*, Amsterdam: North-Holland.

Dhareer, Siddiq al- (1997), *Al-Gharar in Contracts and its Effects on Contemporary Transactions*, Jeddah: Islamic Research and Training Institute.

Donaldson, T. and Preston, L. E. (1995), 'The Stakeholder Theory of the Corporation: Concepts, Evidence, and Implications', *Academy of Management Review*, 20(1), 65–91.

El-Gamal, M. and Inanoglu, H. (2002), 'Efficiencies and Unobserved Heterogeneity in Turkish Banking: 1990–2000', Rice University Economics working paper, October.

El-Gamal, M. and Inanoglu, H. (2003), 'Islamic Banking in Turkey (1990–2000): Boon or Bane for the Turkish financial sector?', *Proceedings of the Fifth Harvard University Forum on Islamic Finance*, Cambridge, MA: Center for Middle Eastern Studies, Harvard University, forthcoming.

El-Gamal, M. and Inanoglu, H. (2004), 'Inefficiency and Heterogeneity in Turkish Banking: 1990–2000', Rice University Economics, mimeo.

Errico, Luca and Farahbaksh, Mitra (1998), 'Issues in Prudential Regulations and Supervision of Islamic Banks', Washington, DC: IMF, WP/98/30.

Eswaran, M. and Kotwal, A. (1985), 'A Theory of Contractual Structure in Agriculture', *American Economic Review*, 75, 352–67.

Fare, R., Grosskopf, S. and Lovell, C. (1985), *The Measurement of Efficiency of Production*, Boston, MA: Kluwer Academic.

Friedman, Milton (1969), 'The optimum quantity of money', in *The Optimum Quantity of Money and Other Essays*, Chicago, IL: Aldine, 1–50.

Gale, D. and Hellwig, M. (1985), 'Incentive-Compatible Debt Contracts: The One-Period Problem', *Review of Economic Studies*, 52, 647–63.

Goddard, J., Molyneux, P. and Wilson, J. (2001), *European Banking: Efficiency, Technology and Growth*, London: John Wiley.

Goitein, S. D. (1971), *A Mediterranean Society*, Vol. 2, Berkley and Los Angeles: University of California Press.

Greenbaum, S. (1967) 'A Study of Bank Cost', *National Banking Review*, June, 415–34.

Greene, W. (1990), 'A Gamma-distributed Stochastic Frontier Model', *Journal of Econometrics*, 46, 141–64.

Greene, W. (1993), 'The Econometric Approach to Efficiency Analysis', in H. Fried, C. Lovell and S. Schmidt (eds), *The Measurement of Productive Efficiency: Techniques and Applications*, New York: Oxford University Press, 68–119.

Harris, M. and Raviv, A. (1991), 'The Theory of Capital Structure', *Journal of Finance*, 46, 297–355.

Hassan, M. K. and Bashir, A. (2003), 'Determinants of Islamic banking profitability', paper presented at the ERF Tenth Annual Conference, Marrakesh, Morocco, 16–18 December.

Homoud, Sami Hassan (1985), *Islamic Banking*, London: Arabian Information.

Hussein, K. A. (2003), 'Operational Efficiency in Islamic Banking: The Sudanese Experience', *Islamic Development Bank Working Paper*, Islamic Development Bank, Jeddah.

Ibrahim, Tag El-Din S. (1991) 'Risk Aversion, Moral Hazard and Financial Islamization Policy', *Review of Islamic Economics*, 1 (1) 49–66.

Institute of Islamic Banking and Insurance (1995), *Encyclopaedia of Islamic Banking and Insurance*, London: Institute of Islamic Banking and Insurance.

Iqbal, Munawar (ed.) (2001a), *Islamic Banking and Finance: Current Developments in Theory and Practice*, Leicester: The Islamic Foundation, UK.

Iqbal, Munawar (2001b), 'Islamic and Conventional Banking in the Nineties: A Comparative Study', *Islamic Economic Studies*, 8 (2), 1–27.

Iqbal, Munawar, Ahmad, Ausaf and Khan, Tariqullah (1998), *Challenges Facing Islamic Banking*, Occasional Paper No. 2, Jeddah: Islamic Research and Training Institute.

Iqbal, Munawar and Llewellyn, David T. (eds) (2002), *Islamic Banking and Finance: New Perspectives in Profit Sharing and Risk*, Cheltenham: Edward Elgar.

Iqbal, Munawar and Khan, Tariqullah (2004), 'Financing Public Expenditure: An Islamic Perspective', Occasional Paper No.7, Jeddah: Islamic Research and Training Institute.

Iqbal, Zamir and Mirakhor, Abbas (2004), 'Stakeholders Model of Governance in Islamic Economic System', *Islamic Economic Studies*, 11 (2), 43–60.

Iqbal, Zubair and Mirakhor, Abbas (1987), *Islamic Banking*, IMF Occasional Paper No. 49, Washington, DC: IMF.

Islamic Banker (2003), 90 (July).

Islamic Fiqh Academy (2000), *Resolutions and Recommendations of the Council of the Islamic Fiqh Academy, 1985–2000*, Jeddah: Islamic Research and Training Institute.

Islamic Research and Training Institute (1995), *Pakistan Federal Sharīʿah Court's Judgment on Interest (Ribā)*, Islamic Economics Translation Series No. 8, Jeddah: Islamic Research and Training Institute.

Jarhi, Mabid Ali al- (1981), 'The Relative Efficiency of Interest-Free Monetary Economics: The Fiat Money Case', in Khurshid Ahmad (ed.), *Studies in Islamic Economics*, Leicester: The Islamic Foundation, UK.

Jarhi, Mabid Ali al- (1983), 'A Monetary and Financial Structure for an Interest Free Islamic Economy: Institutions, Mechanism and Policy', in Ziauddin Ahmed *et al.* (eds), *Money and Banking in Islam*, Islamabad: IPS and Jeddah: King Abdulaziz University.

Jarhi, Mabid Ali al- (2001a), 'Enhancing Corporate Governance in Islamic Financial Institutions', paper presented to the Islamic Research and Training Institute–AAOIFI Conference on Transparency, Governance and Risk Management in Islamic Financial Institutions, held in Beirut Lebanon, March 2001.

Jarhi, Mabid Ali al- (2001b), 'Globalization and Islamic Banking and Finance: Challenges and Opportunities', International Seminar on the Impact of Globalization on the Islamic World: Issues and Challenges in the 21st Century, Institute of Diplomacy and Foreign Relations, Kuala Lumpur, 11–13 June, 2001.

Jarhi, Mabid Ali al- and Iqbal, Munawar (2001), *Islamic Banking: FAQs*, Jeddah: Islamic Research and Training Institute, Occasional Paper No. 4.

Jensen, M. and Meckling, W. (1976), 'Theory of the Firm: Managerial Behavior, Agency Costs, and Capital Structure', *Journal of Financial Economics*, 3, 305–60.

Jondrow, J., Lovell, C., Materov, I. and Schmidt, P. (1982), 'The Estimation of Technical Inefficiency in the Stochastic Frontier Production Function Model', *Journal of Econometrics*, 19, 233–8.

Kahf, Monzer and Khan, Tariqullah (1992), *Principles of Islamic Financing*, Jeddah: Islamic Research and Training Institute.

Kamel, Saleh (1998), *Development of Islamic Banking*, IDB Prize Lecture, Jeddah: Islamic Research and Training Institute.

Karim, Adiwarman A. (2002), 'Incentive–compatible constraints for Islamic banking: some lessons from Bank Muʿāmalāt', in Munawar Iqbal and David T. Llewellyn (eds), *Islamic Banking and Finance: New Perspectives in Profit Sharing and Risk*, Edward Elgar.

Khan, Mohsin S. (1986), 'Islamic Interest-Free Banking', *IMF Staff Papers*, 1–27.

Khan, Tariqullah (1995), 'Demand for and Supply of PLS and Mark-up Funds of Islamic Banks – Some Alternative Explanations', *Islamic Economic Studies*, 3 (1), 39–77.

Khan, Tariqullah and Ahmad, Habib (2001), *Risk Management: An Analysis of Issues in the Islamic Financial Industry*, Occasional Paper No. 5, Jeddah: Islamic Research and Training Institute.

Khan, Waqar Masood (1983), *Towards an Interest Free Islamic Economic System: A Theoretical Analysis of Prohibiting Debt Financing*, Leicester: The Islamic Foundation.

Lang, K. and Gordon, P. J. (1995), 'Partnerships as Insurance Devices: Theory and Evidence', *RAND Journal of Economics*, 26, 614–29.

Leightner, E. and Lovell, C. (1998), 'The Impact of Financial Liberalisation on the Performance of Thai Banks', *Journal of Economics and Business*, 50, 115–31.

Limam, I. (2001), 'A Comparative Study of GCC Banks Technical Efficiency', ERF Working Paper Series, WP 0119, Economic Research Forum, Cairo, Egypt.

Majid, A. Mariani, Nor Ghani Md. Nor and Said Fathin Faizah (2003), 'Efficiency of Islamic Banks in Malaysia', Paper presented to the Fifth International Conference on Islamic Economics and Banking, Bahrain, 7–9 October, 2003.

Mallat, Chibli (ed.) (1988), *Islamic Law and Finance*, London: Graham & Trotman.

Meeusen, W. and Van den Broeck, J. (1977), 'Efficiency Estimation from Cobb–Douglas Production Functions with Composed Error', *International Economic Review*, 18, 435–44.

Mills, Paul S. and Presley, John R. (1999), *Islamic Finance: Theory and Practice*, London: Macmillan.

Mirakhor, Abbas (1988), 'The Progress of Islamic Banking: The case of Iran and Pakistan', in Chibli Mallat (ed.), *Islamic Law and Finance*, London: Graham & Trotman.

Mirakhor, Abbas (1997), 'Progress and Challenges of Islamic Banking', *Review of Islamic Economics*, 4 (2), 1–11.

Mirakhor, Abbas and Khan, Mohsin (eds) (1987), *Theoretical Studies in Islamic Banking and Finance*, Texas: The Institute for Research and Islamic Studies.

Mirakhor, Abbas, (1987), 'Short-term Assets Concentration in Islamic Banking' in Abbas Mirakhor and Mohsin Khan (eds), *Theoretical Studies in Islamic Banking and Finance*, Texas: The Institute for Research and Islamic Studies.

Murrell, P. (1983), 'The Economics of Sharing: A Transaction Cost Analysis of Contractual Choice in Farming', *Bell Journal of Economics*, 14, 283–93.

Nienhaus, Volker (1988), 'The Performance of Islamic Banks: Trends and Cases', in Chibli Mallat (ed.), *Islamic Law and Finance*, London: Graham & Trotman.

Obaidullah, Mohammed (2004), 'A comment on "Stakeholders Model of Governance in Islamic Economic System"', *Islamic Economic Studies*, 11 (2): 71–4.

Obstfeld, Maurice (1998), 'The Global Capital Market: Benefactor or Menace?', *Journal of Economic Perspectives*, 12 (4), 9–30.

Omar, Fouad al- and Haq, Mohammed Abdel (1996), *Islamic Banking, Theory, Practice and Challenges*, London: Zed Books.

Osman, Ahmed (1990), 'Sudan: The Role of Faisal Islamic Bank', in Rodney Wilson (ed.), *Islamic Financial Markets*, London: Routledge.

Presley, John R. (1988), *Directory of Islamic Financial Institutions*, London: Croom Helm.

Presley, John R. and Sessions, John G. (1994), 'Islamic Economics: The Emergence of a New Paradigm', *The Journal of Economic Theory*, May, 1994, 584–96.

Ray, T. (1999), 'Share Tenancy as Strategic Delegation', *Journal of Development Economics*, 58, 45–60.

Rees, R. (1985), 'The Theory of Principal and Agent: Part 1', *Bulletin of Economic Research*, 37, 3–26.

Reid, J. D. (1973), 'Sharecropping as an Understandable Market Response: The Post-Bellum South', *Journal of Economic History*, 33, 106–30.

Reiersen, J. (2001), 'Bargaining and Efficiency in Sharecropping', *Journal of Agricultural Economics*, 52, 1–17.

Rodrik, Danz (2000), 'How Far Will International Economic Integration Go?', *Journal of Economic Perspectives*, 14 (1), 177–186.

Roy, J. and Serfes, K. (2001), 'Intertemporal Discounting and Tenurial Contracts', *Journal of Development Economics*, 64, 417–36.

Ṣaḥiḥ Muslim, Edited by Fuad A. Baqi (1955), Beirut: Dār Aḥya al-Turath al-ʿArabī, 1211.

Ṣaḥih Muslim, Annotated by Al-Nawawi, Part III (undated), Riyadh: Dār 'Alam al-Kutub, 154.

Samad, A. (1999), 'Comparative efficiency of the Islamic Bank vis-à-vis Conventional Banks in Malaysia', *IIUM Journal of Economics and Management*, 7(1), 1–25.

Sarker, A. (1999), 'Islamic Banking in Bangladesh: Performance, Problems and Prospects', *International Journal of Islamic Financial Services*, 1 (3), 1–22.

Sealey, C. and Lindley, J. (1977), 'Inputs, Outputs and a Theory of Production and Cost at Depository Financial Institutions', *Journal of Finance*, 32, 1251–66.

Seiford, L. and Thrall, R. (1990), 'Recent Developments in DEA: The Mathematical Approach to Frontier Analysis', *Journal of Econometrics*, 46, 7–38.

Sengupta, K. (1997), 'Limited Liability, Moral Hazard and Share Tenancy', *Journal of Development Economics*, 52, 393–407.

Siddiqi, M. Nejatullah (1967), *Banking Without Interest* (Urdu), Lahore: Islamic Publications; rev. edn (1983) Leicester: The Islamic Foundation, UK.

Siddiqi, M. Nejatullah (1983), *Issues in Islamic Banking*, Leicester: The Islamic Foundation, UK.

Siddiqi, M. Nejatullah (1988), 'Islamic Banking: Theory and Practice', in Mohammad Ariff (ed.), *Banking in Southeast Asia*, Singapore: Institute of Southeast Asian Studies.

Siddiqi, M. Nejatullah (2004), *Ribā, Bank Interest and the Rationale of its Prohibition*, Jeddah: Islamic Research and Training Institute.

Stiglitz, J. (1974), 'Incentives and Risk Sharing in Sharecropping', *Review of Economic Studies*, 41, 219–55.

Stiglitz, J. and Weiss, A. (1981), 'Credit Rationing in Markets with Imperfect Information', *American Economic Review*, 71, 393–410.

Sunan Abū Dawood (1981), Part 10, Istanbul: Cagri Yaginlari, p. 19.

Sunun Ibn Majah Edited by Sheikh Khalil Mamoon Shaiha (1996), Beirut: Dār al Mʿarafah, 33.

Sundararajan, V., Marston, David and Shabsigh, Ghiath (1998), 'Monetary Operations and Government Debt Management under Islamic Banking', WP/98/144, Washington, DC: IMF.

Suwailem al-, Sami (2003), 'Optimal Sharing Contracts', Paper presented to the Fifth International Conference on Islamic Economics and Banking, Bahrain, 7–9 October, 2003.

The Banker Magazine, Financial Times: London, UK (various issues).

The Islamic Fiqh Academy Magazine (1992), Vol. VIII.

Udovitch, Abraham (1970), *Partnership and Profit in Early Islam*, Princeton, NJ: Princeton University Press.

Usmani, Muhammad Taqi (1998), *Introduction to Islamic Finance*, Karachi: Idaratul Ma'arif.

Uzair, Mohammad (1955), *An Outline of an Interest-less Banking*, Karachi: Raihan.

Vogal, Frank E. and Hayes, Samuel L. (1998), *Islamic Law and Finance: Religion, Risk and Return*, The Hague: Kluwer Law International.

Wilson, Rodney (ed.) (1990), *Islamic Financial Markets*, London: Routledge.

Wilson, Rodney (1992), 'Islamic Banking and Finance', in *The Middle East and North Africa*, 32nd edn, London: Europa.

Yasseri, Ali (2002), 'Islamic banking contracts as enforced in Iran', in M. Iqbal and David T. Llewellyn (eds), *Islamic Banking and Finance: New Perspectives in Profit Sharing and Risk*, Cheltenham: Edward Elgar.

Zarqa, M. A. (1983a), 'An Islamic Perspective on the Economics of Discounting in Project Evaluation', in Ziauddin Ahmad, Munawar Iqbal and M. Fahim Khan (eds), *Fiscal Policy and Resource Allocation in Islam*, Islamabad: Institute of Policy Studies.

Zarqa, M. A. (1983b), 'Stability in an Interest Free Islamic Economy: A Note', *Pakistan Journal of Applied Economics*, 22, 181–8.

Index

Notes: ch = chapter; n = note; t = table; **bold** = extended discussion or heading emphasized in main text.